Peter Norton's
Network Security Fundamentals

Peter Norton
and
Mike Stockman

SAMS

A Division of Macmillan USA
201 West 103rd Street, Indianapolis, Indiana 46290 USA

Copyright© 2000 by Peter Norton

International Standard Book Number: 0-672-31691-9

Library of Congress Catalog Card Number: 99-62303

Printed in the United States of America

First Printing: November 1999

01   00   99   4   3   2   1

Trademarks

All terms mentioned in this book that are known to be trademarks or service marks have been appropriately capitalized. Sams Publishing cannot attest to the accuracy of this information. Use of a term in this book should not be regarded as affecting the validity of any trademark or service mark.

Warning and Disclaimer

Every effort has been made to make this book as complete and as accurate as possible, but no warranty or fitness is implied. The information provided is on an "as is" basis. The authors and the publisher shall have neither liability nor responsibility to any person or entity with respect to any loss or damages arising from the information contained in this book.

Acquisitions Editor
Angela Kozlowski

Development Editor
Tiffany Taylor

Managing Editor
Charlotte Clapp

Senior Editor
Karen A. Walsh

Copy Editor
Gene Redding

Indexer
Kevin Fulcher

Proofreaders
Cynthia Fields
Tony Reitz

Technical Editor
Eric Richardson

Team Coordinator
Pamalee Nelson

Copy Writer
Eric Borgert

Production
Eric S. Miller

Cover Designer
Aren Howell

Interior Designer
Gary Adair

Contents at a Glance

Contents

About the Authors

Computer software entrepreneur and writer **Peter Norton** established his technical expertise and accessible style from the earliest days of the PC. His Norton Utilities was the first product of its kind, giving early computer owners control over their hardware and protection against myriad problems. His flagship titles, *Peter Norton's DOS Guide* and *Peter Norton's Inside the PC* (Sams Publishing) have provided the same insight and education to computer users worldwide for nearly two decades. Peter's books, like his many software products, are among the best-selling and most-respected in the history of personal computing.

Peter Norton's former column in *PC Week* was among the highest regarded in that magazine's history. His expanding series of computer books continues to bring superior education to users, always in Peter's trademark style, which is never condescending nor pedantic. From their earliest days, changing the "black box" into a "glass box," Peter's books, like his software, remain among the most powerful tools available to beginners and experienced users, alike.

In 1990, Peter sold his software development business to Symantec Corporation, allowing him to devote more time to his family, civic affairs, philanthropy, and art collecting. He lives with his wife, Eileen, and two children in Santa Monica, California.

Mike Stockman has been writing documentation and training users in the U.S. and Europe for more than 12 years. He has written about networking products for Windows 3.*x*, 95, and NT, as well as numerous other projects for Windows, MacOS, Solaris, and other operating systems. He is currently working freelance in the Baltimore area, building a NAT router for his home network, and dabbling with Linux for PowerPC in his copious spare time.

Dedication

This book is dedicated to my wife Chris and my new son Adam, both of whom waited patiently until my writing was just about done to initiate the next phase of our lives.
—Mike Stockman

Acknowledgments

I want to thank all of those who provided valuable editing assistance connected with this project, including Angela Kozlowski, Tiffany Taylor, Karen Walsh, Gene Redding, Cindy Fields, and Tony Reitz. I'm also grateful for the technical editing and reviewing of Eric Richardson and Dallas Releford. In addition, I'd like to thank my agent, Chris Van Buren, for the guidance and encouragement he offered throughout all phases of this project.

—Mike Stockman

Tell Us What You Think!

As the reader of this book, *you* are our most important critic and commentator. We value your opinion and want to know what we're doing right, what we could do better, what areas you'd like to see us publish in, and any other words of wisdom you're willing to pass our way.

You can fax, email, or write me directly to let me know what you did or didn't like about this book—as well as what we can do to make our books stronger.

Please note that I cannot help you with technical problems related to the topic of this book, and that due to the high volume of mail I receive, I might not be able to reply to every message.

When you write, please be sure to include this book's title and author as well as your name and phone or fax number. I will carefully review your comments and share them with the author and editors who worked on the book.

Fax: 317-581-4770

Email: mstephens@mcp.com

Mail: Michael Stephens
              Associate Publisher
              Sams Publishing
              201 West 103rd Street
              Indianapolis, IN 46290 USA

Introduction

This book is designed to give network administrators of any level an overview of the issues and practices involved in keeping a computer network safe from intrusion from any source, whether outside or inside the network. This area has been important since the first computers started talking to each other, but interest in this area has grown in recent years as more computers have networking cards and software built in, and as the cost of the networking infrastructure (cabling, hubs, routers, and so on) has plummeted.

An even stronger driving force behind the interest in networking security has been connectivity to the Internet, which is not only more available than ever, but is also becoming faster and more accessible. "Always On" is a big marketing point for cable modems and Digital Subscriber Lines (DSL), but the same connection that lets you and your users connect to the Internet at will also allows others to enter your network by the same path. This book shows you how to restrict access so that you have as much control as possible over who can see and change your vital systems and data.

The news has been full of reasons why you need to stay informed on networking security. Crackers (malicious computer criminals, as opposed to hackers, who explore and manipulate computers without necessarily having any malicious intent) are constantly devising new ways to enter your network through bugs in your servers, flaws in Web browsers, misconfigured access privileges, weak passwords, trojan horse programs, and numerous other methods. Even worse is that newly discovered security holes are soon picked up by "script kiddies," or people who don't have the skill or intelligence to discover these flaws themselves but who seem to have unlimited time on their hands to exploit the flaws once others make them known.

There is no perfectly secure server, router, network operating system, or any other networking component. There is no such thing as an uncrackable network, except for one that isn't connected at all. The most powerful elements you have working for you are *preparation* and *information*. This book can help you get started on both, so you can prepare your network against most intrusion and set your systems up to notify you if an attack does occur. It can also help you with information about how attacks work and where to go to find the latest updates on flaws and fixes, and what to replace with more secure alternatives.

Your allies in this fight to secure your information and systems are the security analysts such as L0pht Heavy Industries and eEye, the governmental and educational security forces such as CERT and CIAC, and the developers of the security products you can add to your network for protection, such as firewalls, routers, and intrusion detection systems. These allies are mentioned throughout this book, as well as listed (partially, but not exhaustively) in Appendix A.

This book also describes how to win the cooperation of your primary allies in the fight against network crackers: your users. Through the education of your users, you can prevent social-engineering attacks (where your users are tricked into providing illicit access to your network), password-cracking attacks (where too-simple passwords provide the hole into your network), and other attacks from inside and outside of your network. Without the education and cooperation of your users, none of the solutions in this book will keep you safe for long.

Finally, this book describes ways in which you can provide, rather than restrict, access to your network, but in a safe way that supports your users while protecting your resources.

Who Should Read This Book

The primary audience for this book is the network administrators for networks of any size who are concerned with the security of the systems on their networks and who want to make access as safe and secure as possible. You need this book if you're in charge of network configuration and access, whether for 2 computers or 2000. Using this book, you'll gain understanding of how and where you're at risk and how to go about eliminating or reducing that risk without cutting off the reason for having a network in the first place: communication among computer users and resources.

As with other books in the Peter Norton series, this book is written in a way to make it accessible to all network administrators, whether you just started the job yesterday or you've been managing enterprise networks for years. You should be comfortable with the networking concepts for the operating systems in use in your organization but, beyond that, most concepts are described thoroughly, without unnecessary or overly technical description.

This book applies to computer networking security for any kind of computer network, whether you are setting up a cable modem–based home network with two computers and a printer, or if you are administrating three sites around the world with thousands of systems connected by leased lines or Internet connections.

We'll spend time discussing networking for MacOS, Windows (all flavors), and UNIX-like operating systems, as well as Windows networking, UNIX, and Novell NetWare servers. Each of these has its own security strengths and flaws, and each of these needs to be maintained and updated to provide the strongest security possible.

If you want the best overview of networking security and solutions available, this is the book for you.

What You Will Learn

Here are some of the important topics I cover in this book:

- How the different types of networks operate and create potential security holes
- The types of attacks and threats you may encounter
- Finding the flaws in your own network, and fixing them
- The trade-off between safety and convenience, and how to balance them to your benefit
- Safeguards to place on your network, including firewalls of all kinds
- Where to place safeguards on your network for maximum protection
- How to provide access to your network without compromising security
- Dial-in access and Virtual Private Networking (VPN) and how you can use them safely
- Passwords: Why they need to be strong and how to strengthen them
- Rules for setting passwords to provide for your users
- Added authentication that can foil most password and network crackers
- Questions to ask and answer before setting up your network
- Why fewer services provide greater security and how to balance them
- Powerful networking features of desktop operating systems, such as MacOS and Windows, and how to make sure they don't compromise your security
- Powerful features of network operating systems, such as Windows NT, Novell NetWare, and UNIX, and how to make sure they don't compromise your security
- How to know when you've been cracked, and what to do about it
- Where to look for the latest products, news, and security updates

You need to understand the risks to your network before you can protect yourself from them, and you need to understand the solutions before you can implement them. Once you collect the necessary information, and once you establish a security plan for balancing safety with convenience, you can secure your network against intruders and use the network for its intended purpose of making your users' lives run more smoothly.

PART I

Identifying the Threats

Networking and Security Overview

An isolated computer is useful, but only to a point. As soon as you want to print, email, upload, download, or find information outside of your own hard drive, you need to connect. A *network*, which consists of a number of nodes connected by some kind of communication pathway, is how your computer communicates with other devices in your office, your building, and the world.

The most commonly known network is the Internet, which is actually made up of hundreds of thousands of smaller networks. Other networks, such as local area networks (LANs) and wide area networks (WANs), can also be connected to the outside world. Once your computer is hooked up to devices outside of your office walls, however, you and your data become vulnerable. People may try to steal data, use your accounts for inappropriate purposes, or simply damage your systems just because they can. Fortunately, there are many precautionary steps you can take to keep this from happening, and those steps are provided throughout this book.

Note: Although much of this book deals with security breaches coming from outside of your network, be aware of the fact that many, if not most, security attacks come from people inside the organization. Don't make the mistake of locking the wolf inside with you; good security means that systems and users are protected from attacks originating from inside the network just as well as they are from outside attacks.

This chapter deals with most of the concepts you'll need to know to discuss networking security. Along with definitions of these concepts, you'll also find examples and, most importantly, a description of why you should be concerned with them from a security point of view.

What Is Security?

I once consulted for a company that had a dial-in line for its email server. There was no dial-in password; the dial-in system depended on the same usernames and passwords people entered to log on from their desktops. To demonstrate the problem, I logged on to the president's email account with my laptop and sent some mail, with the president watching. She had no password, because her office was locked when she wasn't there, and she hadn't known about the dial-in system or her part in protecting it.

What was missing from this picture? The two elements that make up network security:

- The barriers, both physical and virtual, that you place between services on your network and those who would do it harm
- The plan you implement, together with your users, to keep outsiders from compromising your network

The barriers you create can be as simple as eliminating access to your computers altogether or as complex as connecting them to each other and to other computers all over the world. The reality will be somewhere in between.

The plans you implement with your users can be as simple as posting a sign asking people to use passwords on their file sharing or as complex as issuing reams of regulations and requiring retinal scans or fingerprinting to read email. Again, the reality will be somewhere in between.

> **Note:** There is no such thing as a completely secure computer network. The nature of a network is to allow communication. Any communication can fall into the wrong hands. The purpose of this guide is to help you secure your network without putting a halt to its use and put in place the safeguards to detect when your security is breached.

In the earlier example, the company should (at a minimum) have implemented dial-in accounts that were distinct from the users' email accounts, with regularly changing, complex passwords. Once the users were logged in, they should have had to enter a valid username and a complex, frequently changed password to read mail. The users should have had a clear set of guidelines for setting up passwords for their accounts and how to keep those passwords a secret.

Of course, the truly secure option would be to eliminate dial-in access to email. But if company operation requires email access, that isn't an option.

> **Note:** Be sure the users of your network are educated and accept your security plans. If you don't have user cooperation, they won't follow your guidelines and they'll create holes in your plan. We've all been to offices where the users had notes with their passwords hanging off of their computer monitors.

Safety Versus Convenience

The decisions you make concerning the security of your computer network involve a tradeoff between safety and convenience:

- **Safety**   The safest computer is one that's turned off. If it must be turned on, the closest you can come to pure security is to remove the network connection, keyboard, mouse, monitor, floppy drive, and printer. While doing so isn't realistic, it demonstrates the principle that the more access you provide to a computer, the more the computer's security is compromised.

- **Convenience**   The most convenient way to use your computer is to make it available to you from anywhere in the world, allowing you to read and write information without hindrance, using all possible networking protocols, and without any passwords whatsoever. The problem with this scenario is that if *you* have this kind of access to your computer, so does everybody else in the world, and there is no security in that.

This tradeoff between safety and convenience is a constant struggle for network administrators. The people using your network will ask for more access, more availability, and simpler methods, and each of these requests will appear to you to be throwing open another door to the crackers and thieves in the world.

Microsoft was responding to user needs when it implemented peer-to-peer file sharing back in Windows for Workgroups, a feature still found in all versions of Windows today. However, if you open the Network Neighborhood icon on a Windows computer in any office, you'll probably see every employee's computer listed, and a great majority of them will probably have no password or a painfully obvious one.

> **Interesting Story:** In many areas, a cable modem provides a high-speed connection to the Internet, and each subnet is often shared by a number of households. When I first received my cable modem connection and turned on my Windows 95 computer, I found computers from over a dozen other households listed in my Network Neighborhood, and most were open for browsing.

Implementing complex passwords (combinations of letters, numbers, and punctuation) can help make your network more secure by making brute-force password cracking more difficult. Forcing your users to change their passwords weekly or monthly can prevent a stolen password from being useful. Both of these precautions will almost certainly cause some user backlash, because complex passwords are more difficult to remember, and changing passwords frequently makes it even harder to keep track.

Peter's Principle: An Inverse Relationship

There's an inverse relationship between "secure" and "convenient." Absolute security means an absolute pain for users, and complete ease of use for your users means tossing security out the window. Be tough but fair, and remember to put yourself in the user's shoes as well as the cracker's.

Why Networks Are Vulnerable

Networks are vulnerable for two main reasons: connectivity and complexity.

Connectivity

The whole point of a network is to connect computers to each other. A computer in a locked room without any connections is almost perfectly secure, but once it is connected to another computer or device, it becomes vulnerable.

When Computer A is connected to Computer B, Computer A's user can try to get to the data on Computer B, and the reverse is equally true. If you connect Computer A to a large network with hundreds of users, all of those users become a risk to Computer A.

The more connections, the more risk. Many desktop systems, including Windows 98 and MacOS 8.5 and higher, can install a personal World Wide Web server on each system, which many users may enable to serve pages or files to colleagues. If the Web server is misconfigured (likely, considering that most users are not Webmasters) or contains security flaws, that opens up the system to intrusion. The same is true for peer-to-peer file sharing, FTP services, and other potential security risks.

This leads us to the first rule of networking security:

> Disable *right now* all networking features you don't absolutely need.

Although you have to provide the access your users require, the first step you should take in securing your network is to disable all the features that aren't currently in use.

For example, you should never enable more networking protocols than you need to get the job done. Novell NetWare file servers may use the IPX/SPX networking protocol, whereas many other services on your network (email, Web servers, and all Internet access) use TCP/IP. If your users need to dial in to your network to reach the NetWare file servers, *disable* all protocols other than IPX/SPX on your dial-in server. Enabling TCP/IP if your users don't need it opens an unnecessary set of security holes.

As another example, suppose your Accounting department has a computer and printer dedicated to handling paychecks (a very sensitive collection of data). Is there any reason to include that computer or printer on the network? If the hardware has a single purpose and that purpose doesn't require network access, your data will be far safer if you simply keep the hardware off the network entirely. You should still password-protect the accounting data and restrict physical access to that computer, but simply eliminating the network connection makes a huge difference.

> **Note:** Incidentally, this example demonstrates why your internal security must be as strong as your external. If you were to remove the passwords in the morning from an internal accounting server because the firewall keeps away crackers from outside your network, you would find that every user in your organization knew your salary by nightfall. There are crackers on both sides of the firewall, and you should take precautions accordingly.

When it comes to networking security, keep it as simple as possible.

Complexity

There are always more ways to break into a network or into devices on that network than anybody knows about. A computer in a locked room without any connections is *almost* perfectly secure, until you think about

- How many keys to that room are floating around
- Whether you can really trust the janitorial staff
- Where that air vent leads
- Whether the CIA can *really* read what's on a computer screen by scanning for the electromagnetic patterns from a hundred yards away through the walls of the building

And that's the simplest network security situation that exists.

Once you hook up your computer to a network, you have to consider not only who has physical access to the computer, but also

- Who has network access to the computer
- Which networking protocols are in use
- Which desktop operating system is in use and what *known* security holes exist in that system
- Which network operating system is in use and what *known* security holes exist in that system
- Which networking applications are being used and what security holes they provide

All these questions—and many more—point to an infinite number of ways in which your network can be compromised.

The situation isn't hopeless, however. For each person out there who's trying to crack your network for fun or profit, there are smarter people working to find and close the security holes. In much the same way that virus creators and anti-virus software makers are locked in a constant struggle for supremacy, so too are the crackers and their security industry counterparts working to counter each other's actions. Each vulnerablility that is discovered by crackers is most often quickly publicized and patched by security analysts and computer software manufacturers.

Also remember that many of the people outside of your network trying to crack your network will be unsupervised teenagers with too much time on their hands who are cracking for fun, rather than determined professionals who are cracking for revenge or profit. This may or may not be reassuring to you, considering that an unskilled cracker or aspiring cracker may cause more thoughtless damage than the expert.

A Quick Note on User Education

Although connections and complexity are the primary factors in putting a network at risk, another factor is often overlooked: the process of getting the users on your side.

Users can be passive causes of security breaches, such as when they select simplistic passwords, or when they stick notes on their computers with their password written on it because it's too hard to remember. I once encountered a cubicle-dwelling colleague who was very careful to password-protect his computer's network access but had a blank login password when he turned on his computer because, as he put it, "Anybody with physical access to my computer must work here, right?"

Users can also be active participants in security violations, often without realizing it. Any caller pretending to be from the company's network administration group can pry a password out of a user, and users will often run programs attached to email messages, not realizing that they can contain remote control applications (such as Back Orifice and the like) or password-collecting software.

While you could strip all attachments from incoming email, force users to choose a new complex password every day, and require a network administrator to be present whenever a computer is turned on, you can avoid these extreme measures and make your job much easier (and your network more secure) if you follow some of these steps:

- Post your security plan where all users can see it.
- Let your users know that *nobody* will ever ask for their passwords, no matter what, and that the passwords should exist nowhere but in their heads. People do forget passwords, however, so make sure your department is easy to work with when a password needs to be reset (after properly verifying that the authorized user is actually the person requesting it, of course).
- Solicit user feedback whenever you modify the network security plan, and test any new measure with a small group of users before rolling it out for the whole organization.
- Use the network operating system features and other security tools to notify you when passwords aren't being changed enough, or when passwords are too simple, and so on.

> **Looking Ahead**
>
> You should be sure to inform people of what you're doing, be clear about what's expected of them, and always remember that you're working with real people who need to get the job done *without* security getting in the way. For more information on user education, see the "Fix the Education Deficit" section of Chapter 3, "Identifying Risks to Your Network."

Also note that many network intrusions are inside jobs, meaning that users in your own organization attempt unauthorized access far more often than outside crackers. Posting your security plan and educating your users have the side benefit of indicating just how serious about security you really are, possibly discouraging internal users from trying anything questionable.

About LANs

The basic unit of computer networking is the local area network (LAN). It's a collection of computers connected together in a small space, such as a single floor, an office building, or a close collection of buildings. The connection is most often made using cables connecting the network interface cards (NIC) in each computer, although wireless networking connections are becoming available as well that use the infrared (IR) or broadcast spectrum.

For example, the simplest LAN is two computers connected by an ethernet cable. Many home offices have LANs made up of one or more computers and a printer to simplify the process of sharing files and other resources. In a commercial office, the LAN may consist of hundreds of computers, file servers, printers, and so on.

The fundamental component of the LAN is the network operating system (NOS) you are using. This NOS determines the network protocols you will use, the user account setup and authentication methods, access and configuration controls, and so on. Common network operating systems include

- Microsoft Windows NT
- Novell NetWare
- UNIX and UNIX variants, such as BSD and Linux
- AppleShare

The NOS you are using determines a great deal of your security options. This book provides specific examples where appropriate; however, most of the concepts described here apply to any NOS.

Security Issues for LANs

The most essential part of the LAN is that it's limited in scope. A simple LAN doesn't have security risks from the outside, as long as no actions are taken that connect it to the outside world. If a LAN stops at the walls of the building and has no access by modem or other public network connection, then the only risks are those from inside the office.

Should the operator of a LAN worry about security, then? The answer is yes, if any situations similar to the following exist:

- You open a connection between the LAN and an Internet provider. Unless precautions are taken, anybody with Internet access can reach your network through your link with the Internet provider.

- You provide dial-in access to allow employees to connect from home or on the road. The same connection that provides access to your employees can provide access to others, unless safeguards are in place.

- You want to place restrictions on what employees within your office can see, change, or delete. Should your employees all have unrestricted access to your payroll data? What about departmental budgets or closely held research plans? If not, you need internal security blocks to keep unauthorized users out.

  This also applies to protecting the integrity of systems inside your network. Unauthorized internal users can delete the wrong files, crash systems, and generally wreak havoc if you have inadequate internal security in place.

Each of these examples provides a reason to examine your network security and make sure it is sufficient to protect your information.

About WANs

A wide area network (WAN) is similar to a LAN, but it's created when you connect computers or networks of computers that are geographically separated, such as two offices on opposite ends of town or in different countries or continents. Note that, although you can create a WAN using privately owned or leased networks, you can also create a WAN using publicly available connections, such as standard telephone lines or existing networks such as the Internet. This option is becoming more and more popular as high-speed connections to the Internet become more readily available.

For example, a company in New York may have satellite offices in California and Idaho, with a permanent leased-line connection between them. Each office building in the company may have a LAN set up, but the leased-line connection between them creates the company's WAN.

Security Issues for WANs

The security issues for a WAN are similar to those of a LAN: Is there dial-in access? Is there a connection to the Internet? Other questions depend on how the WAN has been set up.

For example, if you are using a private dial-up connection, the only additional security concerns would be whether an unauthorized person can tap that line or dial in pretending to be an authorized user.

> **Looking Ahead**
>
> If your WAN uses the Internet, you can use secure options such as virtual private networking (VPN) to connect the separate LANs together. See the section "About Virtual Private Networking" later in this chapter and Chapter 2, "Risks and Planning Security," for more information.

About Firewalls

A *firewall* is software running on the gateway server (or the *access point* for your network) that protects the resources inside your network against intrusion from outside the network.

A firewall is usually set up to block all incoming and often outgoing traffic, with a list of known exceptions. For example, you might set up your firewall to block everything and then turn on selected incoming email traffic, incoming Web traffic (usually on port 80), and so on.

One company I worked with used a very restrictive firewall, and most new technology that came out wouldn't work unless the IS department first modified the firewall to allow it. For example, I was unable to use QuickTime's streaming audio feature because the ports it used to transmit data were blocked. Because I was the first to want this feature, I had to contact the IS department to have that set of ports opened on the firewall—after I justified the need for it, of course.

The firewall is another example of the tradeoff between convenience and safety. While it may be safer to block the ports used for World Wide Web traffic, many users need Web access today to do their jobs, and blocking those ports would be too inconvenient to be implemented.

Security Issues for Firewalls

Firewalls provide additional security, and therefore the security issues involved in using them center around determining how best to use the firewall to protect yourself.

> **Looking Ahead**
>
> One question you should ask is what resources, if any, you want to place *outside* the firewall. For example, some companies place their public Web and FTP servers outside the firewall. There are benefits and risks associated with this, many of which are discussed in Chapter 4, "About Firewalls."

About the World Wide Web and HTTP

A World Wide Web server provides a way to place documents (text, pictures, forms, and data of all kinds) on a network for users to view and download, using a Web Browser such as Netscape Navigator, Microsoft Internet Explorer, Opera, iCab, HotJava, Lynx, and others.

You can place a Web server on an *intranet* (an internal network, not connected to the outside world) or on the Internet, where it is accessible to anybody with a computer and a Web browser.

For example, you might set up a customer database and order entry system on your intranet with a front-end running from a Web server. Your sales representatives would then use their Web browsers to connect to all the customer information they need.

Security Issues for Web Servers

Security issues for your Web server include protecting the server's contents from being seen, preventing the contents from being changed or damaged, and protecting the server itself from damage, as shown in the following situations:

- **Sensitive data on the server**   Many Web servers either contain or have access to sensitive data. A server used for electronic commerce may contain customer records and credit card information, all of which must be kept from prying eyes. If your server has different access levels, you might display some information to the general public, with other information available only to paying subscribers.
- **Protecting the Web server content**   Some Web servers are attacked by crackers who want to change the content (as a prank, to display a political message, and so on) or crash the server altogether.

In addition to these situations, the Web server can provide a gateway to the rest of your network if it is not set up carefully. Web servers are capable of running programs, executing commands, and so on. If these programs have access to your network, unauthorized users can take advantage of these features to gain similar access. Depending on the program and the level of access, a cracker may be able to roam freely throughout your network.

About Virtual Private Networking

Virtual Private Networking (VPN) is a private network connection established over a public networking infrastructure. VPN can involve a single computer connecting to a remote network or connecting one network with another network.

The process of setting up a private network connection using VPN involves encrypting the data at one end of the connection and decrypting it at the other end. Doing so creates a virtual tunnel between the two sites through which they communicate and which is not visible or accessible at any point in between.

For example, a person working at home (or *telecommuting*) might need to connect to the network at the office for access to file servers, the email system, a customer database, and so on. Rather than use the telephone lines to set up a dial-in connection (see "About Remote Access and Remote Control," below), which might require a long-distance call or be inconvenient for other reasons, the telecommuter might simply make a regular Internet connection and then use a VPN connection over the Internet to reach the office.

Once the telecommuter sets up the VPN connection, it's the same as being physically connected to the network at the office. All network services are available in a way that's reasonably secure from outside intervention.

Given the global reach of the Internet, VPN technology allows any authorized user anywhere in the world to connect to your office LAN.

Security Issues for VPN Connections

Security issues for your VPN connection are similar to the issues for any networking issue. Your office VPN server and the user's VPN client software must use a robust method of encrypting data, a requirement that has been handled for you by most of the manufacturers. In addition, you need to make sure that your users are following standard security precautions (discussed in the "Fix the Education Deficit" section of Chapter 3) to prevent unauthorized logins and compromised accounts.

About Remote Access and Remote Control

One of the most popular ways to provide users with access to an office LAN is dial-up remote access software or remote control software. Here's how they work:

- **Remote Access** The user runs a program on her computer, using a modem, ISDN terminal adapter, or other communication device to call directly to a similar device on a remote access server connected to the remote network. The remote access server answers, authorizes the user's access privileges, and establishes the network connection. After that, the user is connected to the network as a *remote node*; that is, the remote computer is connected to the network the same as any computer at the site.

- **Remote Control** The user runs a package on her computer (such as Timbuktu, PCAnywhere, or LapLink) using a modem, ISDN terminal adapter, or other communication device to dial in to another computer running the same package. Once the user is authorized and a connection is established, the user can control every aspect of the remote computer as if she sat at its keyboard and moved its mouse.

These methods of dialing in to a remote site have advantages and disadvantages that are outside the scope of this book. However, their security risks and requirements are nearly identical.

Security Issues for Remote Access and Remote Control

The security issues for these methods of dialing in are the same, regardless of which you choose. The issues are how you determine whether a dial-in user is authorized and how much access to give that user once the connection is made:

- **Authentication**   Accepting a username and password is the simplest form of authenticating the incoming call, and it can be a good form of defense if the user has set up a complex password that can't be guessed or cracked easily. However, more robust forms of authentication that change often over time (such as SecureID) can make your remote access or remote control system more secure.

- **Access to the network**   Once the user has connected, the amount of access he has to the network should be limited to the minimum necessary to get the job done. That's easy to do with a remote access connection, since most remote access servers let you determine which protocols and which parts of the network the dial-in user can see. However, when the user connects to a remote control system, he has the same access as if he were sitting at a desk in the office, and that can be dangerous if the user's dial-in account is somehow compromised.

Summary

This chapter described the basic concepts of networking security and delved into what makes a network insecure. Now that you know what a complex subject network security really is, you can proceed to the chapters that address your situation to simplify the subject and make your network—and all services running on it—as secure as possible.

Before you continue, however, be sure to do the following:

- Make a list of all network operating systems (AppleShare, Windows NT, UNIX, and so on) that are running on your network.

- Make a list of all network services running on your network, such as Web serving and browsing, email, file serving, and so on.

- Begin to weigh your network's security needs against your users' needs so you can make the appropriate decisions as you read.

Risks and Planning Security

Networking security is becoming more and more complex with each passing month. Most computers either have built-in networking or can have it added for under $20.00, and the Internet explosion makes sure that almost any computer can have a permanent or on-demand connection to millions of other computers.

With increasing connectivity comes increasing complexity. Software that never before needed to be aware of network services is suddenly reaching out over a LAN or the Internet. For example, the applications in the Microsoft Office 2000 suite can open and save documents over any TCP/IP connection. Numerous applications that otherwise have no need for networking nevertheless use the network for upgrading (Symantec's Norton Utilities, for example) and for copy protection (Quark's QuarkXPress, among others). More and more programs are using the network connection to send in the user's registration information.

With all of this traffic bouncing around your LAN, WAN, or the Internet, it has become very difficult to keep track of exactly *where* you are at the most risk for network security holes, as well as how to close those holes before somebody else finds them.

For this reason, it has become more important than ever to be methodical about identifying and repairing security holes on your network. Simply running around solving security threats as they appear leaves you open to the likelihood that while you are closing one security hole, crackers have found others to exploit more quietly.

This chapter focuses on the main types and categories of security threats, such as password cracking, denial of service attacks, buffer overflows, and so on. It also discusses some types of attacks that are less technological but just as effective, most of which fall into the category of *social engineering* (manipulating people inside the network to help the outside threat).

Many of these threats, in concept, are not operating system dependent, but can be adapted in some way to any network operating system (NOS). Threats that apply mainly to a particular NOS are described as such in the text.

Note: Identifying risks and planning security is an ongoing process, not a single event. The first time you put these processes into place may be the most time consuming, but the process will never be complete. New risks are identified every day, and new solutions need to be implemented just as quickly.

Several vigilant organizations track security threats and post known information about them, and many software manufacturers post patches and updates to their software as they become aware of security holes. See Appendix A for a list of Web sites where you can find this information.

Major Types and Categories of Security Threats

A security threat can be as simple as interfering with your network's normal operation (usually called *Denial of Service*, or DoS, attacks) or as complex as actively cracking your security and changing or taking control of network resources. This chapter specifically discusses the following types of threat:

- Denial of Service (DoS) attacks
- Buffer overflow
- Trojan horses
- Intruders and physical security
- Intercepted transmissions
- Social engineering
- Lack of user support

Often these attacks are combined to suit the cracker's goals. For example, a buffer overflow attack (described later in this chapter) crashes the service that is running (as a DoS attack might), but the crash serves the larger purpose of executing unwanted and dangerous code that can give the cracker control over something on your network.

Peter's Principle: Why Hackers Are Your Friends

Hackers are not bad people. *Hacker* is computer industry slang for a clever programmer, or somebody who is particularly adept in an area of computing, as in calling someone who raises UNIX programming to an art form a "UNIX hacker." The general public, led by the mass media, has corrupted the term "hacker" to refer to the criminals of the computing world. However, those in the computing industry (and this book) refer to computer criminals and those otherwise up to no good as *crackers*. This usage is similar to a type of security attack, *password cracking*, where somebody is trying to determine the password to an account. Another similar word outside the computer world is *safecracker*.

For the purposes of this book, and networking security in general, *crackers* are the enemy. *Hackers*, on the other hand, are the kinds of people who act quickly to develop software patches and updates to close security holes before your data is damaged.

Many of the attacks described here exploit bugs in the network operating system. For example, the Ping of Death attack (described later in this chapter) can crash a server due to a widespread bug that affects many different operating systems. Fortunately, most software manufacturers whose products suffer from this bug have released patches or updates to solve the problem, but the problem was unforeseeable without a great deal of software testing.

As with the Ping of Death attack, most of the known attacks and security holes have been addressed by the leading software developers of the vulnerable products. If a fix for a particular attack has been released, this book will indicate where to look for an update, but if a fix isn't mentioned here, contact the manufacturer of your software product for more information. The company's Web site is usually a good place to look first.

Denial of Service Attacks

In a Denial of Service (DoS) attack, a malicious person performs some action on your network or server designed to interfere with normal operation.

For example, a Web server can handle only a certain amount of traffic before it slows to a crawl. A ping utility (a program that can send packets of data to a host machine to verify that it's active and to see how long the echo takes to return) can be configured to send repeated packets very quickly to a single host (called *flooding*). The host, dealing with the huge number of ping requests that are arriving, might be too busy to respond to any legitimate requests for data.

In another case, a cracker might configure a utility to send packets in unexpected sizes or containing unexpected data, causing the server to crash, hang, or slow down.

DoS attacks are not particularly useful for the cracker, because all they do is prevent others from using a system—they don't provide the cracker with a way to break in, but they prevent legitimate users from connecting to the server. Such an attack can cause embarrassment, customer service issues, or loss of income for the victims, whose network service is being interrupted. Imagine if an e-commerce site were shut down by DoS attacks, when the site is the company's sole source of revenue. Every hour the server is down could cost the company huge amounts of money.

However, in reality, most DoS attacks are petty attempts by the cracker (or, more likely, aspiring cracker) to exercise some power and gain attention or recognition but without any particular further goal.

The following sections describe some of the more common DoS attacks and how to handle them.

SYN Flooding

During a normal network connection between a client and a server, the client sends a SYN message, the server responds with a SYN-ACK (for "acknowledge"), and finally the client responds with the ACK message. At this point, the connection is open, and data can flow between the client and server.

The SYN Flood attack, first identified in 1996, consists of sending a server many SYN messages that appear to come from an address that is, in reality, unavailable. As the server tries to deal with these incoming SYN requests by allocating connection records as if a genuine connection is being created, it no longer has the resources to deal with legitimate SYN requests from genuine users.

Many operating systems have been patched to handle SYN floods, and settings adjustments have been posted that can help your servers handle them.

Some of the technologies being built into operating systems now to handle SYN floods are called "SYN cookies," or an alternative called "RST cookies." Upon receiving a SYN request, the server doesn't allocate a connection record and instead requests additional information from the source of the connection to verify that a genuine connection (and not a bogus attempt to flood) is being requested.

In the case of a SYN cookie, the server sends back a carefully calculated connection sequence number; if a response containing that sequence number comes back, then a genuine connection exists, and the server allocates a connection record. With RST cookies, which aren't used as widely because of conflicts with Windows networking, among other reasons, the server sends an erroneous SYN-ACK back to the requester. If the requester responds indicating that something is wrong, then a genuine connection request exists, and the server allocates a genuine connection record.

For complete information on SYN attacks, see the document posted by the CERT Coordination Center at

```
ftp://info.cert.org//pub/cert_advisories/CA-96.21.tcp_syn_flooding
```

Land Attacks

A Land attack, like other DoS attacks, crashes the host by taking advantage of a bug in the way TCP/IP is implemented on some operating systems. Essentially, a SYN packet (the packet sent to a host to initiate a connection) is sent that contains a false, or *spoofed*, source address and port number. These spoofed packets can cause the host to crash or hang.

Land attacks can be addressed by updating or patching your system and modifying your firewall to drop any outgoing packets that have an address other than one of your internal addresses. You can read more about this in Chapter 4, "About Firewalls," or Chapter 10, "When You've Been Cracked."

Smurf Attacks

The Smurf attack has been around for some time. It is similar to a ping flood, except that the header and addresses in the ping packet have been modified so that they appear to come from the intended target of the attack. The result is that large numbers of spoofed ping packets are broadcast. Since each packet may be picked up by hundreds of hosts, a multiplied number of responses come in to the target's system, tying up all resources or crashing or hanging the system.

Both the intended target (which ultimately receives huge quantities of return packets) and the intermediaries (who must echo back to numerous ping requests) are the victims of this attack. The packets are forwarded from the attacker to the victims mainly by intermediate networks with misconfigured routers that allow directed broadcasts. You can make sure you're not supporting attacks such as this by making sure your network's routers are configured correctly. A number of organizations appeared when Smurf attacks were first recognized to scan networks for this vulnerability and notify their administrators, and as a result the incidence of this attack has dropped significantly.

IP Spoofing

IP Spoofing refers to sending a packet to a host that appears to come from someplace other than its actual source. The attacking client sends a SYN message (the packet sent to a host to initiate a connection) that contains a false source address and port. The host then replies with the SYN-ACK message and waits with a half-open connection for the expected final reply.

Eventually, this half-open connection expires (that is, the host gives up and closes it down). But in an IP Spoofing attack, the requests for new, false connections are coming in faster than the host lets them expire. Eventually, the host is too busy handling these false connections to handle any genuine ones, and denial of service occurs.

Although it's difficult if not impossible to prevent being the recipient of IP Spoofing attacks, there are ways to alleviate their effects, such as shortening the time it takes a connection attempt to expire. Also, you can prevent your own network from being the source of such attacks by configuring your routers to filter out any outgoing packets that don't have a valid source address *for your network*.

Teardrop (and Bonk/Boink/Nestea/Others)

Teardrop is a DoS attack that can crash or hang the target host, although most operating systems have been upgraded or patched to fix the vulnerability that this attack uses.

IP packets can be as large as 64 kilobytes, but most network hardware cannot handle packets that large. For this reason, the packets are fragmented into manageable pieces along the way and then reassembled at their destination. The IP packet header contains the necessary information to reassemble the whole packet, including whether the information is a fragment of a packet, what size the whole packet is, and where in the packet this fragment belongs.

The Teardrop attack and other similar attacks send TCP or UDP packets that misrepresent this header information, so that the host attempts to reassemble a complete packet based on false information. The result can be crashes, hangs, or extremely slow performance.

Ping of Death

The now-infamous Ping of Death attack exploited a bug in network operating systems—including many variations on UNIX, Windows, and MacOS—that caused the host to hang or crash when it received an illegally large ICMP Echo Request packet (greater than 64 kilobytes).

The Ping of Death has been fixed or patched in most recent versions of operating systems. However, to avoid ICMP-based attacks of all kinds, you can configure your firewall to drop all incoming ICMP requests, but not incoming ICMP replies or echoes. The result of this is that nobody outside your network can ping your internal hosts at all, which is usually safer, but those inside your network can make ping requests, and the ping replies will return successfully. You may need to experiment with the firewall rules to make this work optimally.

Other DoS Attacks

Most Denial of Service attacks are variations on the examples provided. But new attacks, usually based on previously undiscovered bugs in network operating systems, are sure to be discovered by persistent crackers. Be sure to follow the advice in Appendix A, "Keeping Track of Security Developments," to find out about new cracks and solutions and how to be notified quickly when new attacks are found.

Buffer Overflow

A buffer overflow occurs when some function on a server is carried out with more data than the function knows how to handle. Let's first discuss how a buffer works, and then see how an overflow can attack your system.

Description of a Buffer

A *buffer* is a temporary holding area in the computer's memory, and it is usually created at a specific size by the program that needs to use it. For example, a program might create a 32K buffer to hold the data a user enters, after which that data might be verified, changed, or written to a file on disk.

A robust program either creates a buffer large enough to hold the data it might be given or it keeps track of the data it is receiving and refuses to accept more than it can hold in the buffer.

For example, suppose you were running a program that let you enter information onto a form. If the program has a buffer for the form data that is 16K in size and you attempt to enter 18K of data, one of two things can happen:

- The program can check the data as you enter it on the form and beep or refuse to accept data once the maximum of 16K is reached.

- The program can allow you to enter data without interference, regardless of size.

In the second case, if you enter more than 16K of data, the information has to go somewhere in memory. If the buffer isn't large enough to hold it, the "extra" data is written beyond the end of the buffer into other memory. If there is already something important in that section of memory—such as part of the computer's operating system or, more likely, other data or the application's own code—it is overwritten (lost).

When an Overflow Becomes an Attack

A buffer overflow on a network server can cause data loss or corruption, or it can cause the program or server to crash. Many programs are vulnerable to this kind of bug, but software developers usually fix them as soon as they are identified. However, that's not the worst result possible.

The biggest risk occurs if the buffer overflow causes data to overwrite an adjoining section of memory, and the adjoining memory is part of the computer's instruction stack. If crackers know the buffer overflow bug on a server, they can create a piece of data so that the part that overflows into the instruction stack actually contains *new* instructions for the computer. Those instructions will be executed with the same security privileges as the program currently running (that contains the buffer overflow bug), and in this way crackers can provide themselves with complete access to the computer.

Exploiting the CGI

Another attack is often included with buffer overflows that, technically, isn't a buffer overflow at all. Many Web servers run CGI (common gateway interface) programs, which are often used to perform some action based on input from Web pages that are beyond HTML's abilities to display or manipulate. Some CGI programs call a shell to execute other programs on the server. If these programs blindly accept input from the Web page (entered by the Web site user) and pass that input along to the shell, they can provide access to any cracker who tries to get in.

The following fictional example shows how a CGI would be exploited to list the contents of the UNIX password file:

```
http://fake.name.com/cgi-bin/name.cgi?fqdn=%0Acat%20/etc/passwd
```

This URL connects to the Web server fake.name.com, asks for the CGI called name.cgi, and passes it an argument that is a UNIX shell command (cat) to list the contents of the file /etc/passwd.

Note: When a CGI is tricked into executing a shell command, that shell command executes with the same access privileges as the CGI program itself. Be sure to run your CGI programs (and your Web server) using the most limited access privileges possible.

The solution to the CGI security hole is to be sure your CGI programs filter out all characters (such as ! and ;) that aren't necessary for the CGI program's operation. Without those more risky metacharacters, the chances of the CGI executing an additional or unexpected command is lower. Another solution is to include in the CGI program a short list of the valid information that *can* follow metacharacters and strip out anything else.

Trojan Horses

A *trojan horse* is a program that appears to have a useful function but also contains a hidden and unintended function that presents a security risk.

The simplest example is a program that pretends to be the login program for a computer or terminal. Suppose the last person to use the computer didn't actually log off, but instead left a program running that *appears* to be the login prompt or dialog box. The next user to come along enters a name and password, which the trojan horse records (or sends to a predefined email drop). The trojan horse then passes the information along to the legitimate login program, at which point the user is authenticated without knowing anything unusual is happening.

As another example, a user might download a program from a newsgroup or private Web site that claims to be an update for Microsoft Internet Explorer. When he runs the program, a message appears indicating that the update has been applied—but in reality, running the program installed a utility that runs in the background and deletes files, collects passwords and mails them to the cracker's account, or carries out other malicious behavior.

More recently, crackers have started attaching executable programs to email messages with subject headings such as "Here's the information you requested," or "Check out this cool game." When the unsuspecting user runs it (and this is the reason you should not allow your users to be unsuspecting), a trojan horse is installed on the system. This is different from an email- or document-based macro virus (such as Melissa), which runs when the email or document is opened in an environment that allows macros to execute, but the results are almost the same.

A trojan horse has the same access privileges on the computer as the user who runs it. It can therefore perform any action that user is authorized to perform, including moving directories, duplicating or deleting files, and so on. A trojan horse can be an obvious, blundering event that causes huge amounts of damage, or it can be a subtle, quiet spy, watching user activity and collecting files to deliver elsewhere.

Tip: One of the more insidious trojan horses available today is called Back Orifice, which runs on Microsoft Windows and UNIX. Although the developers of Back Orifice—the Cult of the Dead Cow (true name!)—claim that this program is "a self-contained, self-installing utility which allows the user to control and monitor computers running the Windows operating system over a network," it is in reality a "stealth" program that can install itself without the user's knowledge and remain hidden while it provides remote control to anybody who notices it's there.

Back Orifice and similar cracker tools, such as NetBus, provide a serious security risk because they can masquerade as legitimate programs, and thus users can often be tricked easily into installing them. They can be "piggybacked" onto seemingly legitimate utilities, such as games or self-running animations. However, they are a security risk only if your users are in the habit of downloading and installing programs from unknown sources.

Users install these programs for a variety of reasons, usually as a result of being tricked or seduced in some way. A trojan horse can masquerade as a new or amusing game or appear to be the only fix for a devastating bug in some common software. Perhaps the most insidious example would be a program that claims to detect and remove viruses and trojan horses.

Once a trojan horse is identified, the only real solution is to remove it and wipe the system on which it was found, rebuilding it from the original (and presumably reliable) source, with new and different security measures (usernames, passwords, and so on) in place. However, for many trojan horses, you may be able to find a virus scanning program that can recognize and remove trojans as well, in which case you may be safe in allowing that utility to do its work. This involves some additional risk over simply erasing and rebuilding the infected system, but the time and energy required are lower.

Some anti-virus software can detect trojan horses, but for the most part you'll have to put safeguards into place to prevent them from ever being installed on your systems. This process is discussed in more detail in the "Fixing the Security Holes" section of Chapter 3.

Intruders and Physical Security

The danger posed by people physically entering your offices and tampering with computers on your network is often overlooked. Many companies go to great lengths to make sure their networks are completely secure, only to leave their primary Windows NT domain server in the first cubicle by the side entrance to the building.

Interesting Story: While consulting for one company, I was given a "spare" office to use as my base while onsite. That office also contained the department's file and mail server, which was usually left logged in to the administrator's account.

Even if you trust your employees implicitly, strangers enter your company on a regular basis. Outside vendors, consultants, janitorial staff, vending machine delivery personnel—all of these visitors pose a risk to your network, both during and after hours.

Once an unauthorized person has physical access to a computer, she may be able to install a trojan horse on it, reboot it from a floppy disk or some other volume that could bypass normal security, or steal sensitive files (such as the password file) to be cracked at a more leisurely pace somewhere else.

To be safe, place your most sensitive servers in offices that can be locked, and then make sure to lock them. To discourage the casual snooper, use screen savers that require a password to restore the screen. If your operating system supports it, set up all computers to log out of the network after a certain amount of inactivity.

More precautions you can take for this security risk are described throughout this book.

Intercepted Transmissions

The standard way to log on to a service over a network is still to enter a user ID and a password and have that information sent to the service to be accepted or rejected. Some of the more robust products on the market today have encryption built in, so that the ID and password you enter are encrypted before being sent and are decrypted at the other end by the service you are connecting to. However, many services continue to handle your authentication without any encryption, so that your ID and password are sent as clear text across the network connection.

When you log on to a service, your authentication sequence may be open to observation by anybody else on the network who may be trying to intercept the data. The most basic way to intercept network traffic is by running a *network sniffer*.

Normally, your computer's network card ignores the constant stream of network traffic flowing past unless it sees a packet addressed to it. A network sniffer running on the cracker's computer places the network card into *promiscuous* mode, which is a way of saying that the network card is watching each and every network packet that goes by, whether it's addressed to the network card or not. The network sniffer records the network traffic in a log file, in a window, or some similar way to make it available for analysis and browsing for useful information. For example, if the network sniffer is running on your network as you log on to an email server, your user ID and password might be recorded, because many email programs send their authentication information as clear text.

Network sniffers are readily available for most computing platforms and operating systems. On UNIX-based computers, the most common sniffer is tcpdump, but there are many other utilities as well.

Social Engineering

Social engineering is a low-tech method of cracking network security by manipulating people inside the network into providing the necessary information to gain access.

For example, I once contracted for a company over a period of months. One morning when I tried to start up my computer, I found that my password was not accepted. After repeated attempts to log in, I contacted the IT department for help. The support rep who answered was surprised at my call, since he recalled talking to "Dan" from another department from my cubicle the night before. Dan had said he was standing there with me and we were unable to log in for a demonstration I was giving, and could the support rep please reset the password on my account? The support rep had helpfully filled the request, telling Dan the new password to use. I, of course, had spoken to Dan only once weeks before, and never did find out why he needed to use my account to log on to the network. Of course, I had the support rep change my password immediately.

Dan's actions in this example constitute a fairly clumsy method of social engineering. It was clumsy because he was not trying to hide his identity in any way. It was, however, good social engineering, because he convinced the support rep that I was standing right there and had authorized the entire process. Other examples of social engineering might include any of the following, plus an infinite number of other possibilities:

- Contacting a user, claiming to be the network administrator, and asking the user to verify some account information (such as the user ID and password).
- Claiming to have forgotten a keycard needed to enter the server room, and asking an authorized employee to let you in.
- Logging on to a chat room using an "official" sounding name (such as sysadmin or root) and telling the other participants that they must provide their passwords to verify who they are or be removed from the room.
- Sending email to a user about a great contest with valuable prizes and providing a Web address to enter. The Web site, of course, looks completely authentic and requires a user's account name and password to enter. This tactic has become a favorite way to lure America Online users lately, and the target Web site looks the same as a genuine AOL Web page.

The solution to this security risk, of course, is education and planning, including telling your users that *nobody* in the organization will ever ask for their passwords for any reason.

Lack of User Support

One of the big problems with setting up a secure network is receiving the cooperation of your users. It's not enough to set up firewalls, patch risky software, and scan your network for vulnerabilities if your users have passwords such as "password," their last names, their four-digit ATM numbers, and so on.

If your network is going to be as secure as possible, your users must help with the following:

- Password security, including using complex passwords, not writing down the passwords (especially near their computers), and changing their passwords regularly
- Logging off the network when they leave their computers
- Avoiding giving away information to outsiders, such as the operating systems your network uses, version numbers of server software, and so on
- Refraining from downloading software from sites outside the company unless they've been notified that the organization posting the software is trustworthy

All of this can be accomplished by educating your users thoroughly and updating them regularly, as new risks become apparent.

Summary

The risks to your network security are many and they are extremely varied and inventive. However, the precautions you can take not only protect you from the existing attacks, but against future attacks as well. The trick is to put safeguards into place and maintain them carefully, even when there is no apparent danger.

If you haven't set up your network access yet, plan for security before doing so, by using the latest operating system versions and patches, setting up a strong firewall, and implementing email virus and trojan horse scanning. Also, educate your users as much as possible so they aren't seduced by tempting offers or seemingly reasonable requests for their account names and passwords from anyone.

If your network is already running and connected to the outside world, put the essential protections described in this book into place first, then fine-tune them to suit your needs as you go.

Identifying Risks to Your Network

This chapter describes not only how to identify the security risks on your network but also how to go about finding the means to fix them.

Essentially, there are several steps you should take toward identifying and fixing security holes in your network:

- Disable all unnecessary network access (a general rule, discussed in more detail in Chapters 8, "Security Overview for the Major Network Operating Systems," and 9, "Security on the Desktop")

- Scan your network for known security holes, using available software tools

- Set up ways to be notified if security is breached (through the use of intrusion detection tools, discussed in Chapter 10, "When You've Been Cracked")

- Fix the education deficit (include your users in the solution)

- Contact software manufacturers and security watchdog groups for information about holes and fixes

Each of these steps is described in the following sections.

Finding the Holes in Your Network

Of course, your network needs to be safely behind a firewall, as described in Chapter 4 of this book, "About Firewalls." However, by itself the firewall is not enough protection. The firewall has to be configured to allow "legitimate" traffic to reach your internal network, but even legitimate traffic can carry a threat.

For example, as we saw in the previous chapter, a publicly accessible server can be tricked, through buffer overflows or poorly written CGI programs, into providing more access to your network than you intended. Your firewall may be configured to allow Web traffic through, but if that Web traffic can be dangerous (and it can), you need a second line of defense.

This section describes the process of tracking down the holes before the crackers do.

Keeping Up with the News

Not surprisingly, many networking product manufacturers are not particularly forthcoming with information about security holes in their products. Often, they admit to failings in their products only under the glare of publicity.

For example, a security team recently discovered a security hole in a major company's Web server software. This security hole was a buffer overflow that, if properly exploited, could give the cracker complete command-line access to the Web server, including the ability to run programs, send email, transfer files, and so on. In theory, if the Web server had access to any other resources on your network, those would be at risk as well.

Upon discovering the security hole, the security team notified the software company of the risks and received some vague replies. They persisted, and the company continued to apparently ignore the problem. Finally, after more than a week of waiting for a response, the security team made an announcement about the security hole and provided a simple tool for people to use to test for it on their own servers.

If this sounds familiar, it should, since this story (or variations) has happened repeatedly over the years. From some points of view, the software company is being cautious and the security team impatient; but from the security team's point of view, ignoring the problem and hoping nobody else finds it is an approach that's doomed to failure.

The security industry opinion generally seems to be that the more information that is released, examined, and disseminated further, the better off and safer we'll all be. Some of the commercial software and hardware developers feel this way as well, although not all do.

For this reason, a number of organizations, both commercial and nonprofit (often associated with various governments or universities), work hard to discover security holes, bugs, and weaknesses and report their findings as they are confirmed. Many of these groups have regular mailings, Web sites, and FTP sites that contain the details of their work.

> **Looking Ahead**
>
> For a list of the most well-known organizations that track security holes and how to see their reports, see Appendix A of this book, "Keeping Track of Security Developments."

Using Port Scanners

A *port scanner* is a program designed to find which services are running on a network host. For a cracker to gain access to a host, she first has to know where the host is vulnerable. Running a port scan on the host to see where it's "listening" eliminates a lot of time-consuming, frustrating hunting around to see which services are running. Once the cracker knows, for example, that an FTP server is running, she can start hitting the host with known FTP weaknesses. Port scanning can provide a big advantage in cracking a system.

Peter's Principle: About Ports

Different network services run on different *ports*. Any network service runs on a particular address (such as 192.168.1.1) and is listening on one or more of the port numbers between 0 and 65535 (such as 80, for a Web server or 23 for a Telnet daemon). Together, the address and the port make up a *socket address*, which is enough to uniquely identify the service on a network.

The first 1024 port numbers (0 through 1023) are reserved under the category of *Well-Known Numbers*, as a UNIX convention and as described in RFC 1700 and assigned by the Internet Assigned Numbers Authority (IANA). The next range of port numbers, 1024 through 49151, are referred to as *Registered Ports*, which are recorded and tracked by the IANA. Ports 49152 through 65535 are referred to as *Dynamic* or *Private Ports* and are used for private applications or assigned for use as needed by networking applications.

Table 3.1 shows the results from a sample port scan, looking only at the TCP ports 0–1023 to see if anything useful is running.

Table 3.1   Sample Port Scan Results

Port	Service
21	File Transfer Protocol (FTP)
23	Telnet
25	Simple Mail Transfer Protocol (SMTP)
37	Time
70	Gopher
79	Finger
80	World Wide Web (HTTP)
109	Post Office Protocol 2 (POP2)
110	Post Office Protocol 3 (POP3)
111	Sun Remote Procedure Call (RPC)
113	Authentication Service
139	NetBIOS Session Service (Windows networking)
143	Internet Message Access Protocol (IMAP)
513	rlogin (remote login)
514	rsh (remote shell)
515	lpd spooler (printer)
901	SAMBA 2.*x* configuration server

This list shows a number of services running on this host, many of which may not be necessary. For example, if this server isn't routing electronic mail, ports 109, 110, and 143 should not be listening for connections. A quick search of the security advisories shows that certain older versions of IMAP and POP servers carried a buffer overflow vulnerability, so if these services are running for no reason, there's a potential security hole.

> **Tip:** Any unnecessary service is an unnecessary risk.

There are utilities you can run on a host (depending on the host's operating system) that can notify you when a port scan occurs. Considerable debate exists as to whether port scanning represents an attack or simply a warning of impending attack. (In fact, there are those who argue that it's neither and that a port scan may just be simple curiosity.) Regardless, if one of your systems has its ports scanned, you should immediately assume you're at risk and act accordingly. This might include closing down unneeded services and avoiding known security holes (by upgrading versions, reading security bulletins for configuration advice, and so on).

Using Network Scanning Programs

In April 1995, a free UNIX utility was released called Security Administrator's Tool for Analyzing Networks (SATAN). This utility's sole purpose in life was to scan and gather information about any hosts on a network, regardless of which operating systems or services the hosts were running. The scan that SATAN performed involved looking for all of the services running (such as mail, FTP, Telnet, Web, and others) and checking for known vulnerabilities. These vulnerabilities could include known bugs or security weaknesses in a product, inadequate password protection on accounts, and so on.

SATAN, as with most other network scanning utilities prior to and since its release, could scan any host it could reach on the network, whether the person running SATAN had permission to scan the host or not. The release of SATAN as a freely available product, whose source code was made public and which could be compiled for virtually any UNIX environment, meant that anybody with a computer could find and, theoretically, exploit the weaknesses in any network.

There was a great deal of outcry at the time SATAN was released, suggesting that it was a cracking tool too dangerous to simply give away to anybody who wanted it. However, the result of SATAN's release seems to have been an increase in network administrators' vigilance. The network administrators who had already secured their networks double-checked their work using tools like SATAN, and the administrators who hadn't properly secured their networks saw SATAN as a reason to start.

Since SATAN's release, other similar products have been released. Some are freely available and some are commercial products, including

- HackerShield, from BindView Corporation (www.bindview.com), to scan Windows NT and UNIX

- NOSadmin from BindView Corporation (www.bindview.com) for Windows NT or Novell NetWare 4 and 5

- Kane Security Analyst (http://www.securitydynamics.com/products/intrusion.html), to scan Windows NT or Novell NetWare servers
- STAT (Security Test and Analysis Tool, www.statonline.com), to scan Windows NT
- Nmap (www.insecure.org, a free UNIX-based port-scanning utility from a hacker, not a cracker, who goes by the handle "Fyodor")
- Internet Scanner, from Internet Security Systems (www.iss.com)
- Network Associates' CyberCop Scanner and other products (www.nai.com)
- Axent Technologies Inc.'s NetRecon (www.axent.com)

> **Note:** A very early product called COPS (Computer Oracle and Password System) was a precursor to these tools. It scanned for poor passwords, dangerous file permissions, dates of key files compared to the dates of CERT security advisories, and so on.

These tools can scan the hosts you specify on a network for a variety of known vulnerabilities, including the following:

- Weak passwords
- Missing or weak security, such as anonymous FTP access you may not have intended, or services that have no passwords assigned
- Specific buffer overflows
- Accessible UDP or TCP ports that may pose a risk, or that belong to known trojan horses. For example, Back Orifice is widely known to listen to port 31337 or 12345 (although it can be configured for any port), so if a program finds that scanning your server on port 31337 yields a response, it will warn you that Back Orifice may be present.

Generally, you'll want to use one or more of these tools regularly to probe your network for weaknesses. The commercial network scanning utilities are upgraded regularly as new security holes are discovered, as are some of the freeware products.

You'll also want to be sure to scan your network from inside your firewall as well as from outside. The firewall (discussed in Chapter 4) should keep out all network traffic except what you authorize, but even authorized traffic can carry a threat. For example, valid Web traffic can carry a buffer overflow attack, a denial of service attack, or other dangers. Weak passwords are even more of an opportunity to those inside your organization than they are to those outside, because those inside your organization know where the valuable information is.

Typical Security Holes

This section describes the most common security holes that exist on a computer network. You can identify many of these vulnerabilities using the network scanning tools, but

many of them will take some careful, regular examination of your network and the
resources available on it.

Passwords and Authentication

The most basic form of security on any computing resource consists of asking who
exactly is being given access, usually through the use of some identification name (generally called a user ID or username) and a secret way to verify that the name is authentic
(generally in the form of a password).

The user ID is usually fairly simple and easy to remember, such as the user's last name
or a first initial plus the last name (as in *PNorton* or *MStockman*). For systems with large
numbers of users, you might see combinations of numbers and names, as in *Rawlins002*
or *Mpatel211*.

The form the password takes depends on how well you plan your network security and
how well your users follow your instructions, if you give them the option to choose at all.

Given a choice, a typical user would pick one easy-to-remember password (such as his
child's first name or his initials), keep it to approximately four characters, and use it to
authenticate all of his accounts.

Given the same choice, a network administrator would pick a password for a given user
that is a random string of letters, numbers, and punctuation, perhaps 16 characters long.
The user would have a different password for each account, and a new password each
time she logged on.

As usual, the best option lies somewhere between these two extremes. While the user's
password cannot be permitted to be too easy and provide a security risk, the password
cannot be so difficult to remember and use that it renders the user's account unusable,
as secure as that might be.

The ideal password should be complex enough to be relatively secure and difficult to guess,
but simple and memorable enough for the user to log in without too much difficulty.

Selecting a Good Password

If the user must memorize a password, here are a few suggestions that can help you and
the user select one that will work:

- Use seven characters or more, depending on the system where you're setting up
  the account. For example, some older systems may permit only 8-character passwords, while newer systems may allow 16 or more.

- Include letters, numbers, and punctuation as much as possible, while keeping the
  password memorable. One technique is to join multiple random words with punctuation (as in *door%wet* or *wander?politics*) or to combine two words with a number (as in *force206blue* or *ring12ding*).

- Use the first letters of a long phrase you can remember. For example, the phrase
  "Parking is prohibited between six and nine p.m." would yield a password of

PIPBSANPM or, even better, *PIPB6A9PM*, where the numbers appear literally instead of by their initial letters. The advantage is that you can remember the phrase, but the password is a seemingly meaningless string of characters.

- Use a familiar store name, interspersed with the number from its street address, as in *Sa2fe4way6*.

- Drop vowels and replace letters in a memorable word. For example, you might take the word *personnel* and make it *p3rsne1l* or some other mangled variation that you can still remember.

Replace Passwords Frequently

Most network operating systems and services let you set up an expiration time for passwords, forcing users to change them weekly, monthly, after a certain number of logins, and so on.

> **Tip:** Remember that throwing out passwords too often will make them more difficult to remember. If the user can't remember his password, he's more likely to choose simple, easy-to-crack passwords, such as his initials or his spouse's name. Consult your users to see what would be a comfortable interval for them, such as 30 or 90 days, and make sure they agree with the necessity before setting the policy. See Chapter 6, "About Authentication and Passwords," for more suggestions on selecting password expiration times.

Given that even you and your fellow network administrators shouldn't know a user's password, be sure to have the users change their passwords after the first time they log on to a new account. Until then, you might set a default password that is still difficult to guess, such as the user's name and birthdate combined, or you might simply assign a very robust password of random letters, numbers, and symbols, and communicate it to the user in a secure way (off the network).

As with the expiration date, some systems let you force the user to change the password right away; if not, make it a matter of policy and follow up occasionally by testing the original password to make sure it no longer works.

Use Constantly Changing Passwords

Some products on the market (usually referred to as *third-party authentication* because they are add-ons to existing services) can change the password on a user's account automatically at set intervals, virtually eliminating the possibility that a cracker could use a "brute force" method of finding the password.

This system works by giving the user a small token, a smart card, or another computing device that changes the password in the same way, at the same interval, as the security device on the host. Because the user's token always matches the host, but the password is changing regularly, the user ID and password are difficult to crack.

For example, Security Dynamics makes a product called SecurID. A device on the host is constantly changing the user's password (usually a series of numbers). The user carries a token in the form of a keychain or credit-card shaped device with an LCD that also updates to show the current numeric password. When the user wants to log on, she connects to the host, enters her user ID, and enters the current password shown on the token or card. (These features can be enhanced further by requiring the user to enter a secret number directly onto the token or card to see the current password.)

The advantage to changing the password so often is that even if a cracker is *shoulder surfing* (watching over the user's shoulder to see the password entered) or discovering the password in any other way, the information is useful only for the next minute or so. However, this can also be an expensive solution and should be weighed against the other precautions available.

Denial of Service Vulnerabilities

Some of the network scanning tools actually launch a series of known denial of service (DoS) attacks on the targets you specify, letting you find out during a deliberate test whether you are vulnerable to this kind of attack.

> **Warning:** Network scanning utilities usually let you specify whether to include DoS attacks when scanning a network or host since, if the DoS test is successful, some or all of the services running on the host will be interrupted. You should not run these tests during any hours where service is vital, for obvious reasons.

If the network scanning utility finds a known DoS vulnerability, the scan log will indicate which vulnerability was found. You can use this information to contact the manufacturer or vendor of the targeted system for an update that fixes the security hole.

Using Network Intrusion Programs

Just as it's important to identify and close existing security holes, you also need to put some watchdogs into service. Network intrusion programs, such as the following monitor-specific hosts on your network, identify suspicious activity and report it so you can take all necessary action:

- Computer Associates' (formerly AbirNet's) SessionWall-3 (`www.sessionwall.com`)
- Axent's Intruder Alert (`www.axent.com`)
- ISS' RealSecure (`www.iss.com`)
- Network Associates' CyberCop Network (`www.nai.com`)
- Security Dynamics' Kane Security Monitor (`www.securitydynamics.com`)

Using these tools is an ongoing process. They need to be operating constantly so that all unusual behavior on your network is caught immediately.

More information on this subject is available in Chapter 10.

Patching the Security Holes

Once you have identified the security holes, fixing them is an ongoing process, rather than a practice you can perform once and be done with.

Fix the Education Deficit

The first step you should take in fixing your network security problems is to educate, enlist, and enable your users. Without the support of your users, most of your other efforts will be doomed to failure. There's no point in setting up a secure FTP server if one of your users sets up FTP on his own computer with full anonymous access.

There are many examples of users undermining what would otherwise be adequate security precautions. The previously mentioned habit of attaching sticky notes with the current password to the side of the computer is the most obvious. Other examples include

- Allowing other users access to their accounts.
- Opening insecure access on their personal computers (such as the aforementioned FTP server or running a small Web server that may or may not be as secure as the "official" servers).
- Sharing information with unauthorized personnel, such as telling passwords to others, mentioning the products and versions of products used on your network, and so on.
- Selecting easily guessed passwords.
- Running email attachments from unknown people or unexpected applications that appear to be from a familiar person. These are common ways to distribute trojan horses or worms on the user's system.

The following sections describe a series of policies you can use as a starting point for your own network users. Don't just post this list blindly; some of these policies may pose an undue burden for your users, while others simply won't integrate well into the way your operation works. The best way to use this list is to distribute it as a proposal, with any modifications you think apply to your organization, and then have a meeting or set up a feedback mechanism to get user input. You can apply this input to a final list that is customized for the people affected.

Peter's Principle: Republic, Not Tyranny

If you impose harsh and restrictive measures on your organization in an attempt to secure the network, your users will rebel in ways that will actually undermine security. Not only that, but their rebellion will be in ways you may not be able to see or fix. Network security isn't a democratic process, but neither should it be a totalitarian process.

Be sure not only to ask for user input on your policies but to listen to it as well. If you find that a policy is too harsh, you can adjust it. If you find that it must be harsh, explain why to your users so they can accept it as well.

Rule 1: Choose Secure Passwords

All passwords should contain at least 7 and more than 12 characters if your network system supports it. All passwords should follow the guidelines described earlier in "Selecting a Good Password."

Note that if you teach the user to use some mnemonic devices that are meaningful *to her*, such as the example given earlier of stringing together the first letters of a memorable phrase, the user will then find it less of a burden to change her password so often.

Rule 2: Change Passwords Regularly

If you aren't going to implement a single-use password system—such as SecurID, where the user carries a small token displaying the current password at any moment—you should at least be sure to change the user's password regularly.

Most modern user management systems allow you to force passwords to expire after a certain amount of time. Find out from your users how long that interval should be, and come to a decision that works for everybody.

For example, if your users are frequently on the road for weeks at a time, don't set your dial-in passwords to expire every few days or even every week. One of the worst times to have your password expire is when you're stuck in a hotel room in a strange city after office hours, in case the process of defining a new password fails in any way. Take your users' schedules into account when you set your policy.

> **Tip:** Forcing a password change isn't very useful if the user chooses the same password every time. Many systems today (such as Windows NT) keep a record of passwords that have been used, to prevent a user from using the same password without some number of different passwords in between. For example, you can set up the system so that once a password is used, the user can't select it again until three other passwords have been used. See your system's documentation for the details on setting up this option.

Rule 3: Be Careful of Email Attachments

How strictly you apply this rule depends a lot on your users' needs and level of sophistication. Any kind of file can travel as an email attachment. This includes documents that are mostly harmless (except for macro viruses, mentioned later) as well as trojan horse applications that can wreak havoc on your network.

For example, the trojan horse application Back Orifice and other similar applications can masquerade as something harmless, such as a game or a simple utility. Once the user downloads and runs the program, however, a "server" is installed on the computer that provides hidden remote control capabilities over the network, similar to the legitimate commercial applications Timbuktu, PC Anywhere, and LapLink Professional. The main difference between Back Orifice, NetBus, and other trojan horses is that they are usually installed without the user's knowledge and provide unauthorized access to all resources on the user's computer to somebody other than the user.

Your first impulse might be to forbid your users to download any executable attachment. After all, a recent "virus" called Worm.Explore.Zip that traveled around the Internet appeared to be from somebody familiar to the user and contained an attachment called `zipped_files.exe`. The accompanying message, too, seemed innocuous:

```
Hi <name of recipient>
I received your email and I shall send you a reply ASAP.
Till then, take a look at the attached zipped docs.
Bye.
```

Any typical user would certainly open an attachment like this, infecting her computer with this virus. It would seem that users should be restricted from downloading any attachment that can be executed.

However, with some additional education and anti-virus software, users can be trained to be cautious without restricting their use of email attachments. Any or all of the following techniques can help protect your network without cutting off all attachments:

- Teach users to be suspicious of any attachment they weren't expecting, and to double-check with the sender to make sure the attachment is valid.

- Install anti-virus software on users' computers and keep it up to date. Make sure to configure it to scan all downloaded files, including email attachments. Doing so will also help protect you from macro viruses (such as *Melissa*), which have started appearing in email recently.

- Point out to all users that other file transfer methods—such as Web browsers, FTP clients, and many chat utilities such as ICQ and AOL Instant Messenger—can also transfer dangerous executables to their systems. Anti-virus software can scan these files, but users should be absolutely certain of the source before running any downloaded file.

- Install a utility such as PGP (Pretty Good Privacy, available at http://www.nai.com/) that can verify *digital signatures*, which are sometimes provided with downloaded software. These signatures help verify both the originator of the files and whether they have been tampered with in any way since being posted, both of which can help avoid dangerous downloads.

With some precautions, attachments and downloaded software can remain a convenience for your users without being a danger to your network.

Rule 4: No Network Modifications Without Permission or a Security Consultation

This rule seems fairly basic, but it needs to be emphasized strongly for your users. Enabling or disabling any network function on a desktop computer can compromise security for the whole network.

For example, suppose one of your users enables file sharing on a Windows 95 computer when you specifically disabled it during installation. If you have configured your firewall to stop TCP traffic on ports 137 through 139, all is probably well; but if for some reason those ports have been left open, that user's desktop PC is open to the world. If a cracker logs on to that user's system and places a copy of a remote-control program such as Back Orifice where it won't be noticed, your entire network can be compromised.

The same rule applies to enabling any kind of file access, servers, network games, additional network protocols (or removing existing protocols), and so on. If it changes the network configuration, it can change your carefully arranged security setup.

To prevent this danger, set up a clear policy for making networking changes, and make it easy to follow and carry out. Remember, if it's too much of a pain to request that an FTP server be set up, the users will set it up themselves, regardless of the consequences.

Rule 5: Talk to Nobody

Users, as well as unwary network administrators, can let information slip to potential crackers without realizing it. For example, telling which software package and version number you are running on your Web server can provide compromising information. If a particular version of a server package is known to have certain security holes, you're saving a cracker hours of trial-and-error when you reveal the version of a package you're using.

For this reason, users should be convinced that any questions about the software your organization uses, the hardware your network contains, which firewalls you use, and any other question about your network or its security operations should be redirected to your office. They must take this step whether those questions come from phone calls (representing a bogus telephone, gas, or electric company is a popular cracker method of "social engineering"), newsgroups, chat forums, instant messages, and so on.

> **Note:** Tell your users this simple statement: "Nobody from this organization or any other will *ever* ask your for your password, so never, ever give it out." Make sure this statement is true; if your security system doesn't give you, as administrator, full access to a user's configuration, you'll have to clear the password if you need access to the account. If you ever contact the user for the current password, you open the door for anybody convincing or charming enough to do the same thing.

Rule 6: Secure Laptops While Out of the Office

Many network access programs automatically save login IDs, passwords, dial-in numbers, and so on to make life more convenient for the user. Outside of preventing passwords from being saved, there's not much you can do to avoid this information being stored, on laptops in particular. However, you should educate your users about how valuable a treasure this information is for a cracker who has open access to that laptop for any length of time.

A cracker who finds a laptop unattended in a conference room or hotel room can write down network settings or dial-in settings, copy locally stored password files to be cracked at leisure somewhere else, install compromising software to steal data in the future, and so on—all in a matter of minutes.

To prevent this security breach, users should be sure never to leave laptops unattended, even in "safe" areas such as private hotel conference rooms or another company's office suite. Even a hotel room may not be safe, although a break-in there will more likely result in stolen hardware, along with stolen data.

One excellent way to safeguard laptop data is to implement passwords, both on the computer's BIOS (to require a password at startup) and on screen savers (to require a password when the computer is simply idle). Another method that may be useful is to encrypt the entire system with something like PGPdisk from Network Associates; but if the user is careful, that step may not be necessary.

Software Updates and Patches

No software is perfectly secure, no matter what the manufacturer may tell you. The bigger and more complex a package is, the more likely it contains undiscovered security holes, just waiting to be found by a cracker with much too much time on his hands.

If we're lucky, those security holes will be found first by the manufacturer or a benign public or commercial security group. For example, Microsoft has a mailing list dedicated to sending out security bulletins as security holes or risks are discovered (or, sometimes, acknowledged) in Microsoft products.

Other general sources of computer security alerts include groups such as the Computer Incident Advisory Capability (CIAC) group at the U.S. Department of Energy (ciac.llnl.gov) or the Computer Emergency Response Team (CERT) Coordination Center at Carnegie Mellon University (www.cert.org). Numerous commercial security organizations also identify and publicize security problems regularly, such as l0pht Heavy Industries (www.l0pht.com) and eEye Digital Security Team (www.eEye.com).

Once a new security hole is identified, the developers of the product(s) involved usually release an update, patch, or workaround to repair the problem as quickly as they can. Often, a patch will be available the same day the security hole is announced.

If you're responsible for an organization's security, it's your job to keep up with these security announcements and to make the necessary changes as quickly as possible to secure your network.

> **Warning:** Once a security hole and methods to address it are announced, you can be sure that the lazier members of the cracker community are going to start trying to exploit the "new" holes. Network administrators who *haven't* seen the security announcements are at the greatest risk immediately after the news gets out, when crackers who can't figure out their own methods take advantage of the work done by others.

Appendix A of this book has an extensive list of online resources and mailing lists for updates, patches, and workarounds for new security holes. Subscribe to the mailing lists that are relevant to products you use, and be sure to work quickly when new information arrives. Don't panic, however; there will seldom be a flood of patches all at once. I've had as many as five or six new security holes appear in one week, but often several weeks can go by without anything significant being discovered. Of course, the larger your network and the more products and services you use, the more announcements will apply to you.

Modifying Software Options

There's no rule that says you have to enable all of the services a network software package, router, firewall, or server offers. For security reasons, you can modify options in your routers, firewalls, and servers to minimize the risk you're under.

For example, many servers offer remote management, letting you attach to the server through Telnet, a Web browser, or special client software to manage users, access privileges, enable and disable services, and so on. However, if all your servers are in a convenient physical location, you may find it safer to disable the remote management feature (if possible). It's similar to walking through a dangerous part of town at night; sure, you can carry protection to ensure your safety, but if you don't have to be in that part of town, you'll be even safer if you simply avoid it.

If your Web server isn't using any CGI scripts, remove the default `cgi-bin` directory. If a server isn't using Telnet or FTP, disable those services and make sure they stay disabled.

In some cases, you may want to replace insecure software packages included with the operating system or server software with more secure equivalents, such as disabling Telnet and FTP and installing SSH (for secure shell access) and SCP (a utility for secure file transfers).

In other cases, you can add more secure software on top of existing software. For example, installing TCP wrappers on a UNIX machine can enhance security; TCP wrappers are small programs that sit between the client and the service being requested. If the TCP wrapper is running between the Telnet client and the Telnet server, then the incoming Telnet request is first handled by the TCP wrapper, which logs the request. It then checks to make sure access is allowed from that IP address, location, or other information and then passes the request to the Telnet server. This approach provides a bit of added protection over and above the Telnet server's regular authentication.

If you run network scanning software, many of these modifications may be suggested as the scanning software finds potential security holes in services you may not need, packages that may be upgraded to more secure versions, and so on.

For details on common configuration issues and strong replacements for weaker products, see Chapters 8 and 9 of this book.

Security by Obscurity

The phrase *security by obscurity* means that your network is using something so unusual, uncommon, or unpopular that no one has bothered to learn how to crack it.

For example, if you need to run a basic Web and FTP server, you could use a maces-based system. The reason for doing so is that Macintosh has a market share around 10 percent, and of the servers on the Internet, that percentage is probably much lower. This approach would provide a minor security benefit, because the maces has some very robust Web and FTP server software, but most of the common buffer overflow and denial of service attacks would not work because the architecture is so different from UNIX-like or Windows NT systems.

Of course, if a very determined cracker realized which server software you were using and took the time to discover its weaknesses, your server would still be at risk. But you'd be more protected from the unsophisticated crackers who simply use the existing tools that are available to exploit known security holes.

I encountered one network that was behind an NAT (network address translation) router, which provided a form of IP masquerading. All incoming traffic that was not specifically configured on the router was dropped, providing some firewall protection as well. The software used to operate this router was not a Windows- or UNIX-based package, but was instead a DOS-based utility called *IPRoute* (`http://www.mischler.com/iproute`). This utility provided some additional protection over other routers because it wasn't as widely used as the others, and because it was based on DOS, which isn't a net-work operating system and therefore didn't provide any additional networking holes.

> **Note:** This is *not* a reliable security method, but if you've taken all other pre-cautions mentioned here, including using a network scanning program to check for known holes and DoS attacks, it can give you an added edge against being cracked.

Summary

A large part of securing your network is not so much securing against specific attacks as it is securing whole areas of your network's operation and structure. Putting a good set of policies into place, educating your users thoroughly, and eliminating risky services go a long way to closing up holes you don't know about and may never need to know about.

Even with the best precautions, however, be sure to scan your network regularly to see how it looks from a cracker's point of view. A good port scanner or network security scanner can give you a good overview of the state of your security and, even though it doesn't catch everything, it can draw attention to some vulnerabilities you might otherwise miss.

PART II

Security Tools

About Firewalls

The term *fire wall* was originally used to describe the fireproof wall used in buildings to prevent fire from spreading if it broke out. For example, two row houses would have a fire wall between them so that if one house caught fire, the other wouldn't necessarily have to suffer. Another fire wall in the physical world is the wall between an automobile's engine and the passenger compartment, designed to protect the passengers in case the engine catches fire.

This concept was used by the computer industry to describe a *network firewall*, which is a device placed at the connection point for an internal network to control network traffic to and from the outside world. The firewall is in a position to see every packet that comes through, and it can identify whether the packet came from the internal, trusted network or the external, untrusted network.

Note: Historically, fire walls have helped prevent or slow fires from spreading, but in many cases the fire spread anyway, by going around the firewall or by finding a way through. Take this lesson to heart; a firewall is an important *part* of your network security, but it cannot save you from every danger.

In practice, a firewall provides the perfect trade-off between safety and convenience, as discussed briefly in Chapter 1, "Networking and Security Overview." A firewall could be configured to block all traffic in or out, which would be almost perfectly safe but would also defeat the purpose of having a network connection.

By the same token, the firewall could be configured to allow all traffic through from anybody, which would almost completely defeat the purpose of having a firewall. This setup would, of course, be very convenient for the users, while being no help to security whatsoever.

The ideal solution is to start with a firewall that blocks all traffic, and then configure it to allow traffic for which you have identified a clear need and for which you have developed a clear set of rules for allowing or denying it. For example, if you know your users must have unlimited access to the World Wide Web, you would open up port 80 to any internal requests on your firewall. The first user who tried, say, to run a network game such as Quake would be in for some disappointment, because the default ports that Quake uses (TCP ports 27500, 27015, and 26000) would not be open. On many business networks, the user would need to make a very compelling case before the firewall would allow network gaming traffic to pass.

The advantage to firewalls is that they can stop unauthorized network traffic from passing into or out of your network. This means, for example, that even if a trojan horse such as Netbus or Back Orifice were to be installed on a user's computer, the firewall would stand a good chance of preventing the cracker behind that incursion from taking advantage of it.

The disadvantage of firewalls is that they are not foolproof. Many trojan horses can be configured to use "friendly" ports (so that Back Orifice might attempt to pass through the hole you set up for Web traffic by using TCP port 80). Some programs, as a convenience for the user, will try a series of ports on the network to try to reach their servers. For example, in the RealPlayer software from RealNetworks, the Preferences dialog box contains an Auto-Configure button that lets it try different ports until it finds one that works.

Also, incursion to your network may come from other sources. If you provide dial-up access to your network for users who are on the road or working from home, the dial-up server that is on your internal network provides a way around the firewall. Be sure you recognize that the dial-up server is a vulnerability and therefore requires strong security, such as token authentication cards or one-time use passwords to prevent unauthorized use.

> **Note:** In general, firewalls work by placing controls between your internal network and your external network. This arrangement doesn't address the issue of unauthorized traffic within your organization. One solution to this problem may be to place *each segment* of your network (accounting, engineering, support, or whatever your needs require) behind a firewall. Doing so can keep unauthorized traffic between departments to a minimum.

There are ways to work around these disadvantages, but you may never catch *all* of the exceptions. The trick is to stay vigilant, and watch the firewall activity logs for signs of trouble.

> **Interesting Story:** One company I consulted for had a robust firewall set up on their network that allowed almost no Internet access except for the Web, Telnet, and FTP file transfers. When I needed to check my mail on an outside account, I was unable to do so (they were not allowing POP3 mail, which travels on ports 109 and 110). Fortunately, I had a shell, or command line, account on a UNIX system outside of the company. I was able to Telnet to that account and set up a mail program on that system to read and reply to my mail. A better solution would have been for the company to allow outgoing mail connections on their firewalls or to set up a mail proxy server. These concepts are discussed in more detail throughout this chapter.

0 550276

How Firewalls Work

Firewall is a generic term that refers to any number of different methods of controlling incoming and outgoing network traffic for security reasons. There are a number of different ways of controlling this traffic, and you'll be better off if you implement more than one of them. This section describes the general categories of firewalls you can set up and discusses the advantages and disadvantages of each.

Packet Filtering Firewalls

The first generation of firewalls and the most basic form of firewall checks each network packet passing through and either drops it or allows it, depending on a collection of rules you set up. This is referred to as a *packet filtering firewall*.

Essentially, a packet filtering firewall is *multihomed*, meaning it has two or more network adapters or interfaces. For example, the device acting as a firewall might have two *network interface cards* (NICs), one connected to your internal network and one connected to the public Internet. The job of the firewall, then, is to act as a traffic cop, directing packets and stopping those that are up to mischief.

The following diagram indicates where a packet filtering firewall would be installed on a basic network.

FIGURE 4.1
A firewall between the Internet and the Internal Network.

Firewall

The Internet

Peter's Principle: Use Dual-NIC Firewalls Only

Don't be tempted to set up any of the available packages that claim to provide firewall features with only one network interface card (NIC). They work on the premise that the "firewall" device is on the same network as your other computers and devices, but all traffic has to pass through the firewall before getting to or from any of the other computers. While this setup may be useful for sharing a connection among multiple computers, it doesn't provide any added security. In this setup, the connection to the public network has as much access to the rest of your computers as it does to the firewall, so any attack can simply bypass the firewall and go directly to any device on your network. The only way a firewall can be useful for security is if every packet coming into your network must pass through it.

The packet filtering firewall examines each packet coming in, looking at the basic information available in that packet (source and destination addresses, source and destination port numbers, protocol, and so on). It then compares that information to the rules you have set up. If you have blocked incoming Telnet connections and the destination port of the packet is port 23, the packet is discarded. If you have allowed incoming Web connections and the destination port is 80, the packet is forwarded.

More complex combinations of rules are also possible. If you allow Web connections, but only to a particular server, both the destination port and the destination address must match the rule before the packet is forwarded.

Finally, you can determine what will happen if a packet arrives for which no rule has been defined. Usually, for security reasons, any packet that does not match an incoming rule is discarded. If you have reasons to let the packet through, set up a rule to handle it.

Examples of rules you might set up on a packet filtering firewall include the following:

- For packets coming from the private network, allow packets only if they come from internal addresses, because any other packets contain false header information. This rule prevents anybody inside your network from launching attacks that depend on *spoofing* (computer-speak for forging or falsifying) their source address. Also, if a cracker has somehow acquired access to a machine inside your private network, this filter might prevent the cracker from launching an attack from your network.

- On the public network, allow packets only if they are intended for port 80. This rule allows incoming connections only if they are Web connections. This rule also allows any connection that uses the same port as a Web connection, so it's not foolproof.

- Eliminate IP spoofing attacks by dropping any packets coming in from the public network that have a source address inside your network.

- Eliminate source routing attacks by dropping any packets that contain source routing information. Remember that in a source routing attack, the incoming packets contain routing information that overrides the normal route the packets should take across the networks, possibly bypassing existing security methods. By ignoring source routing information (which isn't generally used for purposes other than debugging networks), the firewall eliminates that mode of attack.

Advantages and Disadvantages

The advantages of using a packet filtering firewall include the following:

- The firewall exercises low-level control over each packet coming in and out of the network.

- Each field of an IP packet is checked, such as the source address, destination address, protocol (TCP, UDP, and so on), port number, and service type (FTP, Telnet, and so on). The firewall applies filtering rules based on that information.

- The firewall can identify and discard packets with spoofed source IP addresses.

- The packet filtering firewall is the sole source of access between the two networks. Because all traffic must pass through the firewall, it's difficult to get around.
- Packet filtering is often included in router packages, so you don't have to acquire additional systems to handle this feature.

The disadvantages to using a packet filtering firewall include the following:

- It can be difficult to configure. Because packet filtering firewalls are so complicated, people often miss setting up some necessary rules, or misconfigure the existing rules, leaving holes in the firewall. However, this drawback is being addressed in many of the newer versions of firewalls on the market, as their developers implement graphical user interface (GUI)–based configurations and more straightforward rule definitions.
- A danger exists that the ports you open for particular services (such as port 80 for http/Web access, or port 21 for FTP) can be used for other transports. As mentioned in a previous example, one harmless application called RealPlayer can test the network for any port that allows it to connect to a RealAudio server, whether that port is commonly used by another protocol or not. Often, RealPlayer ends up using port 80 precisely *because* that port is left open on most firewalls for Web access.
- There may be other ways into your network that bypass the firewall, such as dial-in connections. While this isn't necessarily a drawback of the firewall itself, it's a reason not to depend solely on the firewall for security.

Sources of Packet Filtering Firewalls

Packet filtering firewalls are best used by smaller networks or those without critical security needs. However, while they're being replaced by the more sophisticated stateful packet inspection firewalls available commercially now (discussed in the next section), you can still find packet filtering firewalls in many of the following places and companies:

- **Linux, BSD, and other UNIX-like distributions**   Most UNIX-like OS distributions can be set up as routers and can include a set of rules for acting as a packet filtering firewall. To set up these rules and accounting systems, you can use packages such as ipfwadm, ipchains, and others. If your UNIX-like system has two network cards and you're willing to remove or disable all other non-essential services from the system, you can set up a simple firewall without any additional hardware. The only drawbacks to using a UNIX-like operating system for this purpose is that you'll need to do a lot of homework to be able to build the necessary software and to keep up with security updates as they are made available. However, security updates are likely to appear more quickly with open-source operating systems than with most commercial packages, so this may balance out.
- **Routing software and hardware**   Most routers from Cisco, Sonic Systems, Lucent/Ascend, and other companies can be configured to perform basic packet filtering. If the router in question is routing traffic between the Internet and your internal network, you may simply want to enable the packet filtering features and begin setting up rules.

- **Windows NT's Routing and Remote Access Services**   This service, built into Windows NT and expected to be included in Windows 2000, provides routing services as well as packet filtering, among other features. This service can be useful if you are running the Microsoft Proxy Server or other Windows-based proxy or firewall services in addition to packet filtering. The only drawback to using this service is similar to that of using a UNIX-like operating system: You'll need to disable all unnecessary networking services to close as many potential holes as possible.

Stateful (or Dynamic) Packet Inspection Firewalls

A *stateful packet inspection* firewall (also called *dynamic packet inspection*) attempts to keep track of the network connections and packets that pass through it so the firewall can apply an additional set of criteria in deciding whether to allow or deny traffic. It does this by applying technologies on top of those used by a basic packet filtering firewall.

When a packet filtering firewall sees a network packet, that packet exists in isolation. It has no past or future, as far as the firewall is concerned. The decision about whether to allow or deny the packet depends entirely on the information contained in the packet itself, such as source address, destination address, port number, and so on. The packet is considered *stateless*, in that it has no information to describe its place in the flow of information; it simply exists.

A stateful packet inspection firewall keeps track of more than just the information contained in the packets. In keeping track of the packet's state, the firewall records useful information that helps identify a packet, such as existing network connections, outgoing requests for data, and so on.

For example, if an incoming packet contains streaming video data, the firewall might have recorded information about an application at a particular IP address that sent out a request for streaming video recently to the source address sending the packet. If the incoming packet is addressed to the same system that made the request, the firewall has a match, and the packet can be allowed through.

A stateful inspection firewall, in its simplest configuration, lets you block all incoming traffic while allowing all outgoing traffic. Because the firewall is keeping track of internal requests as they go out, all *requested* incoming data is allowed through until the connection is closed. Only unsolicited incoming traffic is blocked. (This is also true of NAT routers, discussed later in this chapter.)

If you are running a server from inside the firewall, the configuration becomes slightly more complicated, but stateful packet inspection is a powerful and flexible technology. You can, for example, configure the firewall to allow traffic coming in on a particular port to be forwarded only to a particular server. If you are running a Web server, the firewall forwards incoming traffic on port 80 *only* to the Web server you specify.

> **Note:** When you are running a server that is available outside your network, you may want to place the server on a DMZ (de-militarized zone). A DMZ is neither on the external network nor on the internal network, but is actually on a third network accessible to both. See the "Where to Place Firewalls on the Network" section later in this chapter for more information on DMZs.

Other firewalls that inspect the state of the packets can provide additional services, such as

- Redirecting certain types of connections to authentication services. For example, connection to a private Web server might be sent to a SecurID server (for one-time password use) before the Web server connection is allowed.
- Denying network traffic that is carrying certain data, such as incoming mail messages with executable programs attached, or Web pages that contain ActiveX programs.

The manner in which the connection state is tracked depends on the type of packets passing through the firewall.

TCP Packets

When a TCP (Transmission Control Protocol) connection is established, the first packet through that sets up the connection is identified by the packet's SYN flag (as part of the SYN, SYN-ACK, ACK exchange that sets up a connection).

Under normal circumstances, the firewall drops all external connection attempts, unless a specific rule has been set up to handle them. (This is one way to avoid a SYN denial of service attack, which brings up multiple connections half-way and never closes them, using up all available connections on the server and freezing it. If external connection attempts are dropped by the firewall, no SYN attack ever reaches the server.)

For internal connection attempts to external hosts, the firewall notes the connection packet and allows the responses and subsequent packets between the two systems until the connection ends (indicated by a packet containing a FIN flag).

An incoming packet is allowed through only if it corresponds to an existing connection set up in this way.

UDP Packets

UDP (User Datagram Protocol) packets are much simpler than TCP packets because they don't contain any connection or sequence information. They contain only the source address, the destination, a checksum, and the data being carried.

This lack of information can make it difficult for a firewall to determine their validity, because no "connection" is opened to rely on as a test for whether incoming packets should be allowed. However, if the firewall is keeping track of the state of the packets, it can determine that, for an incoming packet, the addresses being used and the protocol the UDP packet carries match an outgoing connection request, and therefore the packet should be allowed.

As with TCP packets, no incoming UDP packet is allowed through unless it corresponds to an outgoing request or specific rules have been set up to handle it.

For other kinds of packets, the situation is similar to UDP packets. The firewall carefully tracks outgoing requests and records the addresses, protocols, and packet types used and checks incoming packets against that saved information to be sure the packets were requested.

Advantages and Disadvantages

The advantages of a stateful inspection packet firewall include

- The ability to check each field of an IP packet, such as the source address, destination address, protocol (TCP, UDP, and so on), port number, and service type (FTP, Telnet, and so on), and to follow filtering rules based on that information.
- The ability to identify packets with spoofed-source IP addresses.
- The firewall's status as the sole source of access between the two networks. Because all traffic must pass through the firewall, it's difficult to get around.
- The ability to verify the state of a packet based on previous communications, such as allowing a return FTP packet based on an FTP connection that has already been set up.
- The ability to verify the state of a packet based on application information, such as allowing a previously authenticated connection to continue communication with authorized services.
- The potential to log detailed information about each packet that passes through. Essentially, all of the information the firewall uses to determine the state of the packet can be logged, including the application requesting the packet, duration of the connection, internal and external systems making the connection request, and so on.

The only drawback to stateful packet inspection firewalls is that all of this logging, testing, and analyzing can cause some lag in the network connection, especially if you have many connections active at the same time or a large number of rules for filtering network traffic. However, faster hardware is making this problem less noticeable, and manufacturers of firewalls are working to speed up their products.

Sources of Stateful Packet Inspection Firewalls

There are many sources for stateful packet inspection firewalls, which often include other kinds of firewall protection as well (including packet filtering and application proxy services). The following list is by no means complete, but it should give you a starting point to find software or hardware packages to serve this need:

- **Major network router manufacturers**   Companies such as Cisco (with its PIX firewall), Sonic Systems, Lucent/Ascend, Nortel Networks, and others provide high-end router and switching systems that include advanced firewall technology.

- **UNIX-like operating systems**   Again, the UNIX-like operating systems have numerous solutions available, such as FWTK (Firewall Toolkit, available at www.fwtk.org). Check with the distributors of your OS for more information.

- **Commercial packages**   There are many, many companies selling software- and hardware-based firewalls, including (but certainly not limited to) CyberGuard Corporation, Check Point, Network Associates, Inc., and others.

Application Proxy Firewalls

An application proxy firewall doesn't actually allow traffic directly between networks to which it's connected. Instead, it accepts traffic from a particular client application on your internal network and then sets up a separate connection on the public network to the server. The client inside your network never communicates directly with the external server, so the server can't gain access directly to any aspect of your internal network.

Also, if you don't install the proxy code for a particular application, that service isn't supported and no connections can be made for it. This setup provides additional security and control by denying any connections that are not explicitly configured.

For example, a user's Web browser would connect to the HTTP proxy firewall on your internal network, possibly on port 80 (the standard HTTP port) but often on port 1080 (which is the default for many proxy servers). The firewall would then take that connection request and redirect it to the requested Web server.

This connection and redirection is transparent to the user because it is all handled automatically by the proxy firewall.

Some common applications that proxy firewalls can usually support include

- HTTP (Web)
- HTTPS/SSL (secure Web)
- SMTP (email)
- POP3 (email)
- IMAP (email)
- NNTP (newsreaders)
- Telnet (shell access)
- FTP (file transfer)
- IRC (chat)

> **Tip:** Another benefit to application proxy firewalls that is not directly related to networking security is that many proxy firewalls can *cache* local copies of frequently requested information, such as DNS, FTP, and HTTP (Web) pages. This caching can speed things up considerably for users, because the local copy of the data can load much faster than the remote copy. See the documentation included with your firewall to determine whether caching is an option for your system.

An application proxy firewall can be configured to allow any connection from the internal network; it can also be configured to require user authentication to make the connection. Requiring authentication can provide an additional level of security by restricting outgoing connections only to known users. If your network is compromised, this feature makes it less likely that an attack can be launched from your location.

Advantages and Disadvantages

The advantages of using an application proxy firewall include

- Specific control over connections, such as allowing or denying access to a server based on its IP address, or based on the IP address of the user requesting the connection.

- Eliminating unnecessary services from your network by restricting outgoing requests to certain protocols. For example, you might set up a firewall to allow HTTP (Web) requests but not FTP (file transfer) connections. If a service is not enabled, it can't be used or attacked.

- The capability of most proxy firewalls to log all connections, including source address, destination address, and duration. This information can be useful for tracing attacks and episodes of unauthorized access that do occur.

Disadvantages of using application proxies include

- You must customize the user's system to a certain extent, depending on the applications in use. For example, most Web browsers support several kinds of proxy servers and must be configured to "see" the proxy connection. Other applications require additional configuration.

- Some applications may not support proxy connections at all. Check the documentation or contact the software manufacturer if an application's support for proxies is unclear.

Generally, an application proxy firewall can be a useful addition to your network; but, as with most of the solutions we discuss here, this kind of firewall is not a complete security solution.

Sources of Application Proxy Firewalls

As with the other kinds of firewalls, application proxy services can be built into existing firewalls, or they can be standalone systems that are either inside the network (that is, with a firewall between the application proxy and the Internet) or on a DMZ.

Sources of application proxy firewalls include

- **Software packages to run on existing systems**   These packages include WinGate, SyberGen Software's SyGate, Network Associates' Gauntlet (proxy plus packet filtering), and others. For Windows NT or 2000 systems, Microsoft Proxy Server provides this functionality as well, as does SOCKS, a widely used package available from NEC Networking.

- **Major network router manufacturers**   Again, companies such as Cisco (with their PIX firewall), Sonic Systems, Lucent/Ascend, Nortel Networks, and others provide high-end router and switching systems that include some application proxy firewall technology.
- **UNIX-like operating systems**   As in the other firewall categories, the UNIX-like operating systems have numerous solutions available, such as FWTK (Firewall Toolkit) or SOCKS. Check with the distributors of your OS for more information.

NAT Routers

A certain kind of router deserves to be mentioned under the subject of firewalls, although it's not technically a firewall at all. A Network Address Translation (NAT) router translates multiple IP addresses on the internal network to one public address that is sent out to the Internet.

In other words, you may have a single public IP address, such as 172.16.0.25 (note that this example is in a private range, but for this example we'll pretend it's a public address). You would then assign that number to your NAT router, and all of your internal hosts would be assigned numbers in the ranges of private IP addresses, such as 10.0.0.0 through 10.255.255.255, 172.16.0.0 through 172.16.255.255, or 192.168.0.0 through 192.168.255.255. These numbers are not valid for public use, but for a private network they're the best choices to use.

NAT routers are used often on SOHO (small office, home office) networks to share a single IP address with multiple clients, as well as provide some security from the Internet connection.

When an internal client opens communication with a public host, the NAT router keeps track of which internal client made the request, modifies the outgoing packet so it appears to come from the single public IP address, and opens the connection. For example, if computer 10.19.0.2 inside your network connects to a Web server outside the network, the NAT router replaces the IP address in all of the outgoing packets (10.19.0.2) with a public address (172.16.0.25, from the previous example). Once the connection is established, all traffic flows back and forth between the internal computer and the Web site transparently.

When an unrequested incoming connection is attempted from the public network, the NAT router has a set of rules to determine how to handle it. If no rules have been defined, the NAT router simply drops all unrequested incoming connections, just as a packet filtering firewall will.

However, as with a packet filtering firewall, you can configure the NAT router to accept incoming connections on certain ports and forward them to a particular host address. For example, if you were running a Web server on 10.19.0.7 on your internal network, you might configure the NAT router to accept all traffic coming in on the public address (port 80) and forward it to 10.19.0.7, where the Web server would handle it normally.

Advantages and Disadvantages

Running a NAT router has several benefits:

- All of your internal IP addresses are concealed from outside view, hidden behind the single public address you are using. For this reason, nobody outside your network can direct an attack at any particular machine inside the network by specifying an IP address.

- If for any reason public IP addresses are scarce, whether for financial or logistical reasons, a NAT router allows you to use only one for your entire internal network.

- Basic packet filtering firewall security is enabled, because all incoming packets that aren't specifically configured on the NAT router are dropped. None of the computers on your internal network has direct access to the external network.

The disadvantages to running a NAT router are the same as the disadvantages for running a packet filtering firewall. It helps to secure your internal network, but it has similar limits. A trojan horse on the inside of your network can make an external connection through a NAT router just as easily as it can through a packet filtering firewall.

Note that many newer firewalls, especially stateful packet inspection firewalls, can provide NAT functionality on top of their other features.

Sources of NAT Routers

Many routers and firewall systems provide NAT or IP Masquerade functionality as an optional service, so check the documentation or Website for your chosen system.

Personal Firewalls

One of the newer utilities developed to protect individual desktop systems is an application level, or *personal*, firewall. A personal firewall is a software package that runs directly on the user's computer, and attempts to protect that one computer from attack using many of the same methods as a stateful packet inspection firewall. Usually, these firewalls are installed at a very low level of the computer's networking interface, which allows them to monitor all networking traffic as it comes and goes on the NIC.

Personal firewalls, once installed, can either filter traffic based on a complex series of rules, or can be placed in a "learning mode" in which, for each new kind of network traffic encountered, the personal firewall prompts the user once to ask how that kind of traffic should be handled. The personal firewall then remembers the response and applies it to future traffic of that type.

For example, if the user had a personal Web server installed, such as those installed by the Mac OS or Windows 95, the personal firewall might flag the first incoming Web connection and ask the user whether to allow it. The user could then allow all Web connections, connections from certain IP address ranges, and so on, and the personal firewall would then apply that rule to all incoming Web connections.

Essentially, you can think of a personal firewall package as setting up a *virtual* network interface on the user's computer. Instead of the computer's operating system communicating directly through the network interface card, the OS instead talks to the personal firewall software, which in turn communicates through the NIC while checking the network traffic carefully.

Advantages and Disadvantages

The advantages to personal firewall packages include:

- An added level of protection without additional hardware resources. Your network should already have a dedicated firewall protecting it, but if a cracker should somehow penetrate your network firewall, a personal firewall could provide enough added protection to foil the attack.

- Internal protection, in the event that (as is often the case) your network is attacked from a cracker operating inside your own organization. Remember that most security breaches are inside jobs; your network firewall does nothing to stop one system inside your network from reaching another system on the inside. A personal firewall could protect from internal attacks that a network firewall would not stop.

- Protection for individual systems on the public network. For users of cable modems, ISDN, DSL lines, and other always-on connections, a hardware firewall might be too costly or too cumbersome to set up. If those users are connecting to your network from home, however, you should be sure their home systems are just as secure as their systems in your offices, and a personal firewall provides a strong level of protection where otherwise none would exist.

The main disadvantage to a personal firewall package is that there is only one physical interface to the public network. Remember that a true firewall monitors and controls the network traffic between two or more network interfaces. With two network interface cards in the firewall, the firewall has complete control over the traffic that passes between the internal (local) NIC and the external (public) NIC. With a personal firewall, there is only one NIC in the system, and the firewall software is managing local and public networking traffic on the same connection. The software is more susceptible to being compromised or having a weakness exploited to allow traffic to bypass the firewall rules.

As with all single-NIC firewalls, you shouldn't depend entirely on them for protection, but if you have adequate protection on the rest of your network, a personal firewall package can provide a useful and necessary added level of protection.

Sources of Application-Level Firewalls

Numerous companies are releasing personal firewalls now, and more will certainly follow. This market is relatively new and is likely to continue expanding for some time.

For Windows computers, you may want to investigate some of the personal firewall products, including

- Black Ice Defender, from Network Ice at www.networkice.com
- atGuard, from WRQ, Inc. at www.wrq.com
- ConSeal PC Firewall from Signal9 Solutions, Inc. at www.signal9.com

- F-Secure Workstation Suite from DataFellows at www.datafellows.com
- eSafe Protect, from Aladdin Knowledge Systems, Inc. at www.esafe.com

For Mac OS computers, the following list describes some of the products available that provide personal firewall protection:

- DoorStop, from Open Door Networks, Inc. at www.opendoor.com
- NetBarrier, from Intego at www.intego.com
- IPNetRouter from Sustainable Softworks (www.sustworks.com), which provides a network router with some NAT and firewall capabilities that can control access to a single machine or for many systems

For the UNIX world, numerous firewall packages can protect the system they're running on, but most of these products are designed to act as a classic firewall, operating on the system that controls access to the outside network. However, some products do exist, such as Mediator One from Comnet Solutions (www.comnet.com.au). If you use ipchains or ipfwadmin as firewall solutions, be sure to set up the rules to protect the system on which they're running as well as the rest of the network, if necessary.

Virtual Private Networking

Another networking security feature that is often built in to firewalls is the capability to set up a virtual private network, or VPN, between your LAN and another remote LAN using the public networks.

Chapter 1, "Networking and Security Overview," described VPNs from the point of view of a telecommuting user connecting a single computer to your network over an Internet connection. The VPN feature built in to many firewall products involves connecting one LAN to another LAN, although beyond that the principles are very much the same. Figure 4.2 shows how the VPN connection is set up to connect two networks.

FIGURE 4.2
A VPN connection using the public Internet.

Essentially, the firewall on your local network contacts the matching firewall on the remote network over the Internet and sets up a secure "tunnel" between your site and the other site.

Whenever your local firewall receives data that is meant for the remote LAN (such as peer-to-peer file sharing connections, database access, email server traffic, and so on), the VPN software on your firewall encrypts that data and sends it to the remote LAN's firewall, where it is decrypted and forwarded to its intended destination.

There are numerous solutions that provide this kind of connection, and these solutions are only as secure as the encryption standard they implement to protect your data. There are several common encryption standards used for VPN connections:

- **PPTP**   Point-to-Point Tunneling Protocol, or PPTP, is used in Microsoft NT 4.0 for VPN connections. However, PPTP supports mainly single client-to-LAN connections, rather than LAN-to-LAN connections (which is difficult to do with PPTP), and is therefore not used between firewalls. In addition, Microsoft's implementation of PPTP has been reported to contain numerous security flaws and should probably be avoided for even single-user connections to your network.

- **L2TP**   Layer 2 Tunneling Protocol, or L2TP, is rapidly overtaking PPTP as the secure open standard for establishing VPN connections, for both single-user and LAN-to-LAN connections. L2TP includes IPSec, developed by the Internet Engineering Task Force (IETF) to develop a single, robust open standard for IP communications, including VPN connections. This encryption standard is the most commonly used security standard built into firewall-based VPN servers. (Note that Windows 2000 is expected to include L2TP for VPN connections in addition to PPTP.)

- **IPSec Alone**   IPSec can be used as a tunneling encryption standard by itself, but since it can tunnel only IP traffic, it's not useful in cases where other protocols (IPX, NetBEUI, AppleTalk, and so on) need to be encapsulated and passed through the tunnel. For this reason, IPSec included in L2TP is a more secure and flexible solution, unless IP is the only protocol you need to support between the two LANs.

There are other encryption standards that have been in use over the years, but the undisputed leader at this point seems to be L2TP with IPSec. Check with your firewall vendor to see if VPN connections are supported and, if so, the method of encryption that is used.

Advantages and Disadvantages

The advantage to setting up a VPN connection between physically separated networks is mainly that you can create a secure wide-area network (WAN) using the connection to the Internet you already have.

The advantage to using your firewall to set up this connection, if your firewall supports this feature, is that you already have a robust, well-protected system on each of the two networks, and you might as well use them. Otherwise, the VPN server is placed inside your network (on the inside, or trusted side, of the firewall), and you must set up rules on your firewall to permit the incoming VPN connection.

The only disadvantages to setting up a VPN connection—if you need this functionality at all—is that the overhead of encrypting data can slow down the connection significantly. If the user is dialing in using a modem, this slowdown can be too much to be worth setting up the VPN connection. Over a cable modem, DSL connection, or other high-speed connection, a VPN connection is somewhat slower than other connections, but it should be tolerable, depending on the VPN solution you use. If you need to connect two networks, VPN is a very solid way to do so using public networks. If you don't need to connect two networks, for security reasons you should not enable this (or any unneeded) network service.

Sources of VPN Servers

Many routers and firewall systems provide NAT or IP Masquerade functionality as an optional service, so check the documentation or Website for your chosen system.

Where to Place Firewalls on the Network

The strongest position in which to place a firewall of any kind is between the internal network and the external network. The firewall should be the only line of direct communication between the two.

All of the hosts on the internal network connect through a single point to the Internet; that point is the firewall. The firewall is configured with the necessary rules to eliminate all unrequested incoming access and to allow only certain kinds of outgoing access that the network administrator has deemed necessary.

DMZ Networks

An addition to the basic *protected versus public* issue, firewall configuration involves setting up a third network that is accessible to both the internal and external networks. This third network is referred to as a DMZ, or *demilitarized zone*.

Usually, you'll set up a DMZ only if you have servers that you need to make available to the outside world or the public network. For example, if you were running a Web server to provide information for the general public and an FTP server to distribute software, you would place those servers on the DMZ network.

To accomplish this arrangement, a multihomed firewall (which you'll recall supports two *or more* network interfaces) has not two but three network interface cards or connections. One connection is for your internal network, the second is for the public network, and the third is used for the DMZ network.

The advantage of the DMZ is that you can limit severely the access provided to any services on the DMZ network. For example, if your Web server is the only service connected to the DMZ, you can limit traffic in and out of the DMZ network to HTTP and HTTPS protocols (ports 80 and 443) and filter out all others.

Also, because the public servers are placed on their own network, it becomes much more difficult for them to be used, if they are compromised by crackers, as a launching point for attacks on other systems on your network.

The result is similar to having two firewalls: one between your internal network and the DMZ and one between the DMZ and the external network.

I recommend that any of your publicly accessible services be placed on a DMZ network, in addition to your other safeguards.

Reporting Attempts on Your Network

One of the features to look for in setting up any kind of firewall is the way in which the firewall reports any unusual or forbidden activity to you.

Of course, you'd like to have some evidence occasionally that the firewall is doing its job. Simply setting it up and forgetting about it is dangerous, because the absence of attacks isn't proof that you're safe from attacks. (Simply because no elephants have stampeded through your home doesn't mean your elephant repellent is working, or that your home is stampede proof. The elephants may just not have shown up yet.)

Fortunately, most firewalls provide a way to report any suspicious activity to you, along with the results indicating how (or even if) it was handled. These reporting methods can include any or all of the following:

- **Saving all activity to an internal log**   To see the log, you would have to connect to the firewall over the network, or possibly work directly at the firewall to open the file. This method would usually save all available information about the event, including the source and destination addresses, the reason it was suspicious, and so on.

- **Sending all log messages to another host on your internal network**   That could be a UNIX system running the syslog daemon, an SNMP trap host, or any other system running the required software to accept the log messages. (Syslog-compatible applications exist for the Macintosh operating system and Windows, as well as all flavors of UNIX.)

- **Sending log messages to an email address**   In this case, you configure the firewall with the address of an outgoing mail server and an account to use for sending and, when activity occurs, a mail message is sent. Usually, if a firewall provides this feature, it also provides a way to prioritize the severity of a log message, so you can configure it to send only the higher priority messages. As an additional feature, there are cellular phone and pager services available that can accept a short text message via email and send it as a pager message, for the absolute highest priority messages from your firewall.

Using the information from the log messages, you can determine how to proceed. If the event was an authorized activity, you could then modify the firewall rules to allow the connection (and handle it more gracefully) in the future. If the event was, indeed, an attack, you could configure the firewall to continue refusing that type of connection, but to log it at a lower priority in the future.

You might also notify the administrator (or root account, or possibly "abuse" account) of the apparent source of the attack with all pertinent information so he could either discipline the user or, more likely, close the hole by which the cracker was passing through the system on her way to attacking you.

Reporting Methods

The other information-gathering feature to look for in a firewall is how sophisticated the reporting method is. While many low-end or freeware firewalls may simply log activity as described earlier, some of the newer and more polished firewall systems come with reporting engines that can collect, manipulate, and organize information for analysis. Statistics such as the frequency of recognized attacks, the number of attacks from particular IP address ranges, and so on can be valuable in evaluating the adequacy of your existing security setup and your future needs.

Preventing Unauthorized Incoming Access

Once you set up a firewall, you need to determine how much incoming access to allow.

Most firewall products, whether they're software based or complete hardware solutions, come with a collection of rules already defined, usually with the most secure options configured by default. Generally, the philosophy behind a firewall's default settings is "if it's not specifically authorized, it's forbidden." That is, all traffic is stopped until you configure the firewall to allow it.

Generally speaking, the rules you set up should continue that philosophy, especially where incoming access is concerned.

Preventing Unauthorized Outgoing Access

One of the underused features of a firewall is to prevent unauthorized *outgoing* access to the Internet. A firewall can be configured with rules that prevent any outgoing activity, including

- Unauthorized browsing of Internet sites. Depending on the firewall you use and the technology you implement, a firewall can restrict users to a list of approved sites or omit sites that contain inappropriate or undesirable content.
- Use of any "non-essential" Internet services, such as Usenet newsreading, streaming audio or video, IRC or other Internet chat features, and so on.
- Authenticated use of certain features, requiring a user ID and password to make certain kinds of connections.

- Access to certain services based on IP address. If you were managing a school network, for example, you might assign a range of IP addresses to teacher and administrative workstations and allow that IP address range unlimited access to the Internet. The student range of addresses would have more limitations.

- Downloading dangerous files or attached information, such as Java or ActiveX applets from Web sites or virus-laden attachments through email or file transfers.

Different firewall vendors support different subsets of these features, although many of the commercial vendors are implementing "incoming packet inspection" to support any or all of the above features. For example, the CyberGuard firewall advertises that it can block access to "inappropriate sites." Microsoft, Raptor, and other firewall and proxy server manufacturers have created partnerships to support CyberNot, a service to filter out a large variety of Internet content.

Check with your firewall vendor to see if any filtering options are available to limit your users' access to certain services, if you find that level of control necessary.

Also, you may want to visit the ICSA web site at www.icsa.net. The ICSA is an independent computer security association that is an affiliate of the GartnerGroup. The ICSA tracks and reports on security issues, and has a program for certifying networking security solutions, including firewall products.

Summary

Security starts with having something protecting your network from the public network outside. Firewalls are the tools developed to provide this protection.

Firewalls have evolved over the years from simple packet filters to sophisticated packet inspectors, deciding which traffic to allow or block depending on what its purpose, source, and destinations may be. A stateful inspection packet firewall is the most powerful protection your network can have.

If you need protection from incoming connections and you don't have or need a full set of public IP addresses for your network, a NAT router can share a single IP address with all your computers while protecting you from any incoming traffic. This can provide a good alternative to more powerful systems.

Finally, a good firewall should provide good logging and reporting features so that you can stay informed concerning the job the firewalls are doing and any intrusions that may be attempted on your network.

Letting Users Connect Securely

One of the big concerns for any organization is how to let offsite users connect to the internal network *without* opening up the organization to every 13-year-old with a modem connection causing mischief on your servers.

It's a question that is becoming more pressing as more users are getting high-bandwidth connections—such as 56K modems, cable modems, and digital subscriber lines (DSLs)—and are asking to connect from home more often.

Clearly, the safest response would be to refuse all requests for connectivity. But because the goal is to use the network rather than close it up completely, you need to find ways your users can connect without compromising security too badly.

You can provide a number of solutions to remote users who need access to your network:

- **Dial-In Networking Services** Setting up a dial-in access server (usually a PPP server of some kind) provides modem users with a way to reach your network directly over phone lines. Once connected, their access is the same as if they were physically in your offices connected to a standard network connection, although you can customize this access to some extent.

- **Virtual Private Networking (VPN)** For users with their own Internet connections (such as cable modems or DSL users), a client-to-LAN VPN connection is as fast as the slowest connection in the link. If the user and your network both have high-bandwidth connections, this solution can provide a very fast hookup.

- **Direct Dial-In Servers** Some of your network services may have limited remote access built in. For example, users can use their Lotus Notes mail clients to dial in directly to a Notes server to retrieve mail, view data, participate in discussions, and so on without having any additional access to your network.

Each of these methods is described in this chapter, along with the security pros and cons for each.

Determining the Needs of Users

Before you can determine which method(s) you'll be implementing for your users, you need to determine what their needs are. Then, compare those needs to what the different solutions can provide. Ask yourself (or your users) the following questions.

Which Network Services Do You Need to Use When You're Not Physically on the Network?

Common network services that users might need while on the road or at home include:

- Electronic mail

- Database access

- Files from a central file server (using Windows networking, UNIX's Network File System, NFS, or other connection methods)

- Files from the user's own internal system

- Instant messaging with colleagues

- Shell access to an internal system (Telnet, for example)

- Client/server applications, in which the client resides on the user's system and uses remote procedure calls (RPC) to communicate with the server

Note that not all of these services require that you provide the user with full access to your network. For example, email can be provided by placing a POP3 or IMAP mail server in the DMZ on your network and providing authenticated access to the user from anywhere on the Internet, the same way you would if the user were onsite.

Files, if they're not too sensitive, can be provided on an SSH server for an encrypted but externally accessible connection. SSH can also be used, in addition to VPN solutions, to "tunnel" encrypted connections for almost any protocol into your network.

See the solutions below to provide access to many of the above services. But examine each individual service the users need, to determine the extent to which you really need to open your entire network.

Which Protocols Do You Need to Use?

The networking protocols the users need may determine the kind of access you're going to provide. For example, if your users need access to IPX/SPX (primarily used for Novell's network access), you can't implement an IP-only access method.

Protocols the users need may include

- TCP/IP (Internet protocol, almost always available with any connection method)

- NetBEUI (Microsoft's proprietary networking protocol)

- IPX/SPX (primarily used for Novell's network access, such as NetWare servers, although other network systems may use it as well)

- AppleTalk (the native Macintosh networking protocol for printing, file servers, peer-to-peer networking, and so on, although IP is becoming more prevalent on that platform)

- Banyan VINES networking protocol

- DECNet

Basically, you need to make sure that whichever solution you provide can handle all of the protocols your users may need. Many dial-in and VPN connections support Point-To-Point Protocol (PPP), which can carry many of the protocols in the above list; but not all solutions can handle all protocols.

What Connection Methods Will Be Available to You When You're Offsite?

A user may have access only to telephone lines, or he may have his own T1 networking connection. How he connects determines the remote access methods you can provide. Connection methods available to roaming users include

- POTS lines (Plain Old Telephone Services, a genuine acronym)
- ISDN lines
- xDSL (any of the family of high-speed Digital Subscriber Lines, including ADSL, IDSL, and so on)
- Cable modem connection
- Some other organization's Internet-accessible network

Obviously, the faster the connection available to your users, the better for them, but the method by which they connect also determines the services you must set up to accept their connections.

For example, if a user has access to a telephone line but no Internet provider at the remote site, you'll have to set up a dial-in networking server to accommodate him. Many of the other connection methods lend themselves well to VPN or secure shell access. Once you have answered the question of connection, you can decide which solutions to begin implementing.

Dial-In Networking Services

As a concept, dial-in networking is not very different from making a VPN connection, but your security needs are different for each.

Whether the user is making a VPN connection or a dial-in connection, the method of connecting is the same. The user initiates some *client software* on her computer, telling it to open a connection to a remote access server on your network. The user configures the client software to use specific networking protocols once the connection is opened—usually TCP/IP and possibly others, such as IPX/SPX (used for NetWare networking, among other services), NetBEUI (used for Microsoft networking, among other services), or AppleTalk (used for Apple Macintosh networking).

The diagram in Figure 5.1 shows the basics of making a dial-in connection.

FIGURE 5.1

A standard dial-in connection between the user's computer and a remote access server on your network.

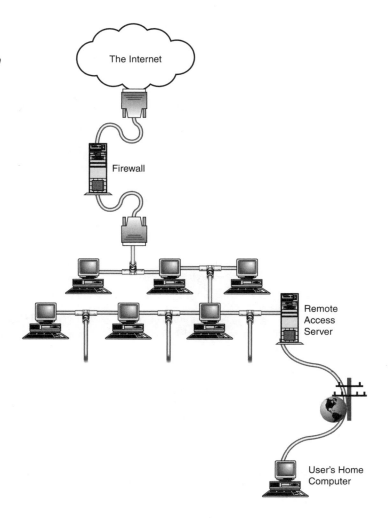

Physically, a dial-in networking connection travels from the user's computer, through a modem or terminal adapter and over telephone lines (POTS, ISDN, or a DSL line), to another modem or terminal adapter on your telephone system, into a remote access server, and through that to your network.

Advantages and Disadvantages

The main advantage to setting up a dial-in connection for your users is the convenience. Most hotels and airports have telephone lines available, and (although this situation may be changing) very few of them provide any other connections for the public. Virtually all laptops have a modem available, making a dial-in connection a readily available way to connect to your network.

Another advantage is that most modern operating systems include a dial-in client by default:

- Microsoft Windows 95, 98, NT 4, and later versions of Windows all include the Microsoft Dial-Up Networking client, which can provide remote access to all of the networking protocols that Windows supports.

- The Apple Mac OS includes the Remote Access client, which provides dial-up support for the AppleTalk and TCP/IP protocols.

- Most UNIX-like operating systems also provide optional PPP dial-up capabilities for TCP/IP access.

The only disadvantage to using dial-in networking is that the remote access server resides on your network, inside the firewall. This means that anybody who cracks the security on the dial-in lines may have virtually unrestricted access to your network.

However, you can take steps to protect your remote access server from unauthorized access. Once you have secured your remote access server as well as you can, dial-in networking provides a useful and safe solution for giving your users network access.

About the Remote Access Server

Remote access server (often using the acronym RAS) is the general term used to describe the hardware/software combination that answers and routes dial-in networking calls. Types of remote access server include

- **File Servers with Dial-In Access** The class of remote access server that is based on a network operating system server. The system providing remote access services probably provides other services as well, such as file or printer serving, network routing, and so on. For example, a Windows NT server can have Remote Access Services (RAS) enabled, allowing it to answer incoming calls to the network.

- **Dedicated Dial-In Servers** A standalone box that contains modems (or serial ports for external devices), network cards, and the software required to set up remote access connections. Physically, the box may be anywhere in your organization that has both network and telephone connections. Companies that provide remote access servers include Cisco, Lucent, Intel, and Sonic Systems.

Caution: Any Windows 95 or 98 computer with a modem and telephone line can also be configured to act as a remote access server. This poses a great security risk to your network if any Windows computers in your organization have telephone lines that can be reached from the outside. Be sure to take steps to avoid this risk, including educating your users to be sure they don't enable this feature and performing regular checks of your computer systems to make sure this feature isn't installed.

Remote access software—whether on a file server or a dedicated remote access server—provides some built-in user authentication to allow only authorized users to dial in, along with some level of access control to determine which networking services each user can use. For example, you might set up a group of users with access only to a particular sub-network, but not to the rest of your internal network. As another example, you might allow some dial-in users to have access to the Internet beyond your local network, whereas other users are restricted to local traffic only.

Remote access servers usually permit several kinds of authentication, depending on your security needs:

- **Internal User Lists**   The most basic form of authenticating dial-in users involves the remote access server maintaining its own internal list of users, passwords, and access privileges. This is the least secure method available, because the passwords are stored on the server itself. If the remote access server is compromised, the entire user list (including the passwords, which usually are not well encrypted) becomes available to the cracker. The advantage to this technique is that the list of names and passwords is generally unique, so if the remote access server is compromised, no other system is compromised at the same time.

- **External or Shared User Lists**   In this case, the remote access server looks to another system (such as a Windows NT server or a UNIX system) and uses that other system's user and password list to determine access. The advantage of this method is that you can set up your user lists once and reuse them for other devices. Also, your users need to remember only one password for all access. Finally, the other system—being a standalone server—may have more robust authentication and password storage than the remote access server is capable of.

  The disadvantage is that if any aspect of the user list is compromised, it's compromised for your entire network instead of a single device. Also, you run the risk of changing access privileges on the file server that inadvertently affect the privileges on the remote access server. You need to consider the full effect of any changes before making them.

- **Third-Party Security**   In this case, you set up a robust security method outside of the remote access server that is then used to authenticate any incoming connections. This method allows you to use such features as token-based or one-time-use passwords, where the password changes regularly and the user has a way to know which password to use at any given moment (such as a SecurID token). This is the most secure authentication you can use for dial-in access. The only disadvantage is that it requires more work for the user to determine which password to use, but that's a minor inconvenience.

Setting Up Dial-In Network Access

For the simplest form of dial-in network access, you may already have the components you need to set up a remote access server. If you are using a Windows NT server, you can configure it for remote access services (RAS), hook up a modem and telephone line, and go. Your Windows users most likely already have Dial-Up Networking installed on their computers and can begin dialing in right away. Users of other platforms probably also have dial-in PPP software already installed or readily available and can dial in just as easily.

However, if you don't want to increase the load on your NT server, or if you don't want people dialing in to a computer that may also have sensitive data stored on it, you can set up a standalone remote access server:

- **Commercial Remote Access Boxes**   Many of the top companies producing routers and firewalls also produce remote access servers, including Cisco, Intel Networking Systems (formerly Shiva Corp.), Lucent Technologies Internetworking Systems (formerly Ascend Communications), Sonic Systems, and 3Com.

- **Combination Remote Access Routers**   A number of products on the market are officially network routers but include additional features such as remote access (and others, including firewalls). The advantage is that you can buy a single product that handles multiple network functions—but be sure it doesn't compromise on necessary features. To be a secure dial-in server, it must be able to support multiple methods of authenticating users, have a way to restrict network access on a per-user basis, and so on.

- **Software-Based Remote Access Servers**   Some network operating systems support dial-in access. For example, you can install Routing and Remote Access Services on Microsoft Windows NT to provide dial-in access using any authentication method Windows NT supports. Similarly, you can set up PPP servers on most UNIX-like operating systems, and the MacOS has the optional Apple Remote Access Server software.

Regardless of the method, any remote access server supports some standard dial-in protocol, usually PPP or less often the older Serial Line Internet Protocol (SLIP). PPP uses the Internet Protocol (IP) but is designed to handle others as well, such as NetBEUI or IPX/SPX.

You'll generally follow these steps to set up the remote access server:

1. Install the necessary hardware on your network, usually the remote access server box or computer on which the remote access software will run.

2. Install as many modems as you want to use for dialing in.

   Note that many remote access servers support some sort of multiline PPP, which allows a single dial-in user to connect over multiple lines using multiple modems, effectively getting a wider bandwidth (and therefore faster) connection.

3. Set up a user list that includes the user ID, default password, and access level (which network protocols to allow, which IP address to give the user, and so on).

   Remember that you can use authentication methods other than the one built in to the remote access server. See the following "Authentication" section for more information.

4. Disable all unneeded network protocols, accounts, and features.

   For example, if the remote access server provides Telnet and Web-based methods of configuring it, you may want to disable the one you don't plan to use. Remember that any active service on a server is a security risk. Some servers allow you to Telnet in and then Telnet back out again to a new location, perhaps providing additional network or server access in the process or at least a way to mask the source of an attack.

5. Activate the server for dial-in and test your configuration.

How you perform each of these steps depends on the details of your particular remote access server. See the documentation included with your server for details.

Authentication

Authentication is the process of determining a user's identity to determine whether to allow access and what level of access to provide to your network. How your dial-in server determines which users have access depends on the kind of authentication you set up.

Internal User Lists

All remote access servers provide some kind of internally stored static authentication list, including the user ID and password feature for basic authentication. This list should include as many of the following features as possible:

*   Complex user IDs and passwords, including high numbers of characters and a combination of numbers, letters, and punctuation
*   Requiring the user to change the password on next login
*   Requiring the user to change the password at regular intervals
*   Setting a minimum password length (at least 8 and preferably 12 to 16 characters)

In addition, other features, such as the ability to share a user ID/password list with other remote access servers of the same type, may be available for convenience.

The disadvantage of using the internal user list is that if the remote access server is in any way compromised, the user and password list becomes available to the cracker.

Also, this approach is subject to the same weaknesses as other password-based authentication, because a password that is too short, too simple, or too easily guessed can be cracked. If you use this method, be sure your users are selecting robust passwords that will better withstand crack attempts.

External or Third-Party Authentication

Many remote access servers support the use of an external or shared authentication list. For example, suppose you have several remote access servers (A, B, C, and D) from the same vendor on your network. You might store the user and password list on server A, whereas servers B, C, and D all consult server A to authenticate a dial-in user.

The advantages here are mainly in convenience, because you can make a change to the user list in a single location and have it take effect immediately throughout your network. The other advantage is that any cracker compromising server B, C, or D (in this example) would not have access to the user list. If server A is *only* a user list server and not actually used for dialing in, this setup could protect the user list more thoroughly.

Although this approach is more robust and protected than using the server's internal list, it's still subject to the same weaknesses as any other password-based authentication.

Another (and usually more robust) kind of external authentication involves a standalone server whose sole purpose is to house the authentication information. These options include RADIUS, TACACS+, and Kerberos.

> **Note:** These authentication servers support some mixture of authentication, authorization, and accounting.
>
> *Authentication* is the process of determining whether a user is who she says she is, based on information such as user ID, password, source (network address or Caller ID number from which she's connecting), and so on.
>
> *Authorization* is the process of determining what, exactly, a user can do once she's authenticated and connected. This process is similar to an operating system's access control list or access privileges.
>
> *Accounting* determines and reports how the user spent her time, such as how many minutes the connection lasted, which services were used during the connection, and so on. This process is similar in concept to activity logs.

- **RADIUS**   The Internet Engineering Task Force (IETF) developed the RADIUS (Remote Authentication Dial In User Service) standard for a centralized authentication server. When the remote access server needs to authenticate a user, it contacts the RADIUS server and proves that it's authorized to ask by sending a prearranged "secret." When the RADIUS server responds with its own prearranged "secret," the remote access server requests and receives encrypted user ID, password, and privilege information from the RADIUS server. If the information received indicates that the user is allowed to dial in to the network, the remote access server proceeds to make the connection. RADIUS supports authentication, authorization, and accounting. (The secret generally consists of an encryption key that both verifies the sender and renders the connection and authentication process more difficult, although not impossible, to spy on.)

- **TACACS+**   Developed by Cisco Systems but widely implemented in other products, TACACS+ is the latest generation of a family of authentication standards that began with Terminal Access Controller Access Control System (TACACS) and Extended TACACS (XTACACS). This authentication method requires the user to enter a user ID and password, and (as with the other two authentication servers) encrypts this information in the process of checking it to verify that it's valid.

If so, the user is connected. TACACS+ supports authentication, authorization, and accounting.

- **Kerberos**   Kerberos is an authentication server that acts as a "trusted third party" and assumes almost nothing about the security of the network. When a client (the dial-in user) wants to connect to a server (the remote access server), the client contacts the Kerberos server and provides a password, receiving a "ticket" to use the server along with information to prove the ticket is valid. When the server gets a copy of this information, encrypted so that only the server can read it, it establishes the connection. Note that Kerberos supports only authentication, not authorization. As far as Kerberos is concerned, an authenticated user can do anything (although the remote access server itself may have some control over the user's abilities once logged on).

These authentication servers are a big improvement for allowing users to log in, because they use encrypted connections from beginning to end while checking the user's credentials. Because the authentication process is encrypted, the user's password can't be sniffed; because the authentication can be tied to a number of criteria (user ID, password, source IP address, and so on), it's difficult for a cracker to intercept the connection by pretending to be the authenticated user.

Smart Cards and One-Time Passwords

None of the authentication solutions mentioned here is worth anything if the user's password is compromised. If the user is careless and allows someone to see the password, if the password is too easy to guess (such as the user's spouse's name, or the user's own initials), or if a cracker gets hold of and cracks the password list, the accounts are compromised.

You can change passwords regularly, require a certain amount of complexity in passwords, and educate your users thoroughly on how to create complex passwords, in order to alleviate (if not eliminate) much of this particular risk. However, another solution involves the user carrying a token of some kind that provides a different password each time the user connects, or that provides a calculated password too difficult to remember or spoof.

Smart cards are small devices—usually about the size of a credit card—containing microprocessors and a limited amount of data storage. These cards can be configured with the holder's security information, such as security certificates, public and private encryption keys, passwords and other keys for server access, and so on. When the user wants to connect to your remote access server, for example, she'll instruct the smart card to send the necessary authentication data up a serial link with the computer she's using to log in. A smart card provides a way to carry around extremely complex and robust security keys that the user has no need to memorize or copy. The card is protected by a PIN or other kind of password to prevent its use in the wrong hands.

A *security token* is a small device—in the form of a credit card, a keychain or fob, or something similar—with an LCD readout that generates a unique passcode every minute or so. Figure 5.2 shows a typical security token. The authentication server on your network is synchronized with these tokens. When a user needs to log in to your network, she takes out the token, perhaps enters a PIN to see the code, and then enters that code combined with the PIN as the login password before it expires and is no longer valid. Similarly, a *software token* runs on the user's computer and requires the user to enter a PIN before seeing the temporary passcode needed to log in to the network.

FIGURE 5.2
An example of one style of hardware security token.

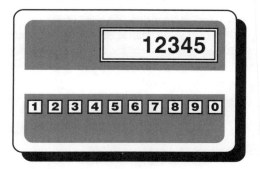

These options have a huge advantage over regular passwords that can be stolen, guessed, or cracked. A constantly changing password cannot be guessed or cracked and, if sniffed off the network, compromises your network only for a very brief time (usually less than a minute).

The only risk is that the token itself will fall into the wrong hands, at which point the PIN becomes your only barrier to its use. However, assuming you are notified of the token's change in status, you can disable its access at the authentication server.

Authentication Recommendations

If your dial-in server provides access only to a small subset of your network, or if the information on your network is not very sensitive, a strong educational plan can bring your users up to a fairly secure set of password practices. You can encourage these practices by causing even their complex, random, unguessable passwords to expire (with notice) at regular intervals.

However, you'll probably want to keep the remote access server's password list somewhere other than the server itself, or even use a third-party authentication solution.

However, if your network contains sensitive information, you should consider the stronger authentication methods, especially the one-time password tokens or smart cards. Short of requiring retinal scans or sending encrypted fingerprint data across the link, one-time passwords are your strongest authentication method to date.

Virtual Private Networking

Virtual Private Networking (VPN) is one of the easiest and most versatile of the secure solutions you can implement. Once a user has set up a secure VPN connection, all internally available network services (printers, file servers, databases, and so on) are available to the remote user as if her computer were physically connected in your office.

As discussed in Chapter 4, "About Firewalls," a LAN-to-LAN VPN connection is set up when the VPN server (a firewall, router, or dedicated server, for example) on your local network contacts the matching system on the remote network over the Internet and sets up a secure "tunnel" between your site and the other site. Then, when your local VPN server receives data that is meant for the remote LAN (such as peer-to-peer file sharing connections, database access, or email server traffic), the VPN software on your LAN encrypts that data and sends it to the remote LAN's VPN server, where it is decrypted and forwarded to its intended destination.

For individual users to connect to your network, they need to use VPN client software that matches the protocol you're using on your VPN server. Figure 5.3 illustrates a VPN connection.

FIGURE 5.3
A typical VPN connection over the Internet.

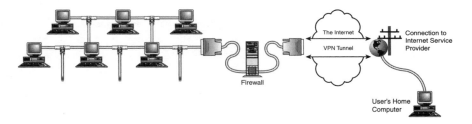

The user connects to the public network (usually the Internet, although you can use VPN over leased lines or other insecure ways of connecting) in whatever way is most useful. This can be any of the following:

- A dial-up account with an Internet service provider (ISP)
- A cable modem
- An xDSL connection (ADSL, for example)
- Internet access at another site, such as a company's or college's network

Once the user is connected, he can run a VPN client software package, such as Dial-Up Networking (built in to Windows), the free PPTP client available for Linux (with an L2TP client in development), or Network Telesystems' TunnelBuilder for MacOS computers. Usually, the developer or manufacturer of a VPN solution also makes available VPN client software or can provide information on finding some that is compatible with their system if necessary.

As with dial-in networking, once the user is connected to the network, all services are available to him as if he were physically connected to the network onsite. Because most VPN solutions can tunnel PPP over the public network, and because PPP can support many different networking protocols, the user connecting with VPN can use TCP/IP, NetBEUI, IPX/SPX, AppleTalk, and other networking services without difficulty.

Advantages and Disadvantages

For a user who has access to a public network already, a VPN connection is a secure and convenient way to connect to the remote network.

How secure the connection is depends on the protocols in use (as described in the next section). But for the most part, a VPN connection using a robust encryption method is not crackable directly.

As with any secure connection, however, there are risks that encryption can't solve. The user's password can be guessed, stolen, or cracked, for example. Any VPN encryption solution must be combined with robust authentication methods, as described earlier in the "Authentication" section.

Available VPN Encryption Methods

Most VPN solutions consist of encrypting a networking protocol—often PPP (Point-to-Point Protocol)—and decrypting it at the other end. PPP is used in most implementations because it's IP based and can be configured to carry multiple networking protocols, such as NetBEUI, IPX/SPX, AppleTalk, and so on.

Here's a quick listing of the major protocols, or encryption methods, in use.

Point-to-Point Tunneling Protocol

The main implementation of Point-to-Point Tunneling Protocol (PPTP) is by Microsoft. Windows NT 4 Server supports PPTP connections, and Windows 2000 is also expected to do so (in addition to more secure methods of connecting). Although PPTP has been proposed as a standard, the growth behind the PPTP specification is already slowing as Microsoft turns its attention to other technologies. Microsoft's implementation of PPTP has been widely criticized by networking security experts as having weak encryption methods that can compromise passwords, as well as being susceptible to denial-of-service (DoS) attacks. This may be one of the reasons that Windows 2000 will support additional VPN protocols that are more secure than Microsoft's PPTP.

Also note that PPTP uses TCP packets to transmit data, which is slightly more reliable than UDP packets but can be slower. Speed becomes more of an issue when you configure your firewall to allow VPN traffic to pass through to your VPN server.

Layer 2 Forwarding

Layer 2 Forwarding (L2F) is an older VPN protocol developed by Cisco Systems and supported by some other companies as well. It provides a method of tunneling PPP that works well, but it never became an industry-wide standard and has mostly been replaced by L2TP.

Layer 2 Tunneling Protocol

In Layer 2 Tunneling Protocol (L2TP), the features of L2F and PPTP have been merged into an industry standard mechanism for tunneling PPP over all kinds of media, including a public network connection such as the Internet. Often combined with IPSec, L2TP is the most widely used VPN standard and provides the most interoperability between products from different vendors of all of the VPN protocols.

Note that L2TP uses UDP packets to transmit data, which is slightly less reliable than TCP packets but provides better transmission speed in most cases. As with PPTP, speed is important when you configure your firewall to pass L2TP traffic to your VPN server.

IPSec

IPSec is a relatively new standard that uses encryption to ensure private transmission of sensitive communications over any network.

Although IPSec isn't a purely VPN-specific solution, it can provide an IP-only VPN connection, or—combined with L2TP as it usually is—it can provide very strong security for a multi-protocol VPN connection. However, IPSec was designed mainly to secure traffic between routers and firewalls, so by itself it's not as flexible a solution for single-user VPN connections as L2TP.

SSH

SSH is a secure shell technology designed to replace such client utilities such as Telnet, FTP, rsh, and so on. However, because SSH can be configured to encrypt and forward PPP, as well as other protocols, it can be used to set up a VPN connection. (After all, one kind of VPN connection is simply a secure, encrypted PPP connection that creates a virtual tunnel.)

Encryption Recommendations

Given that you can use L2TP with IPSec for maximum security over your VPN connection, L2TP seems to be the best choice for single-user VPN connections. The only reason to use PPTP is if your VPN server requires it, which is true in cases such as Microsoft Windows NT 4. Once Windows 2000 is released, this problem will disappear, too, because Windows 2000 is expected to support both PPTP and L2TP connections.

However, read on to see how technologies such as SSH are still useful and necessary for a secure network.

Setting Up a VPN Server

You may already have the components you need to set up the simplest form of VPN access. If you are using a Windows NT server, you can configure it for VPN RAS (remote access services), give your users a PPTP client, and go. Your Windows users most likely already have Dial-Up Networking installed on their computers and can begin connecting right away. Users of other platforms can install software to connect almost as easily.

However, if you don't want to increase the load on your NT server, you don't want people connecting through a computer that may also have sensitive data stored on it, or you don't want to use a PPTP implementation that may not be as secure as your other choices, you can set up a standalone VPN server:

- **Firewalls** Many firewall packages, whether hardware based or software based, include VPN functionality. The advantage to enabling VPN on your firewall is that you can depend on the firewall's security features to prevent unauthorized entry. Any other solution requires placing the VPN server inside the firewall and opening access to VPN connection attempts on your network, which can be an added security risk.

- **Routers** Just as routers can offer firewall functionality, they can also function as VPN servers, with all of the features provided by other VPN servers. Be sure that the router's VPN connection uses a protocol that supports one user-to-LAN connection; many router-based solutions support only LAN-to-LAN connections. In particular, many solutions based on IPSec alone (not IPSec integrated with L2TP, which is a different story) support only LAN-to-LAN connections. Ask the manufacturer if it provides an IPSec-based client for single-user VPN connections before implementing its VPN product.

- **Software Solutions** Barring any of the above solutions, you can place almost any server on your network (inside the firewall, usually) and install a software-based product to handle incoming VPN connections. The most commonly available solution is Microsoft's Routing and Remote Access Services (RRAS), which can provide a PPTP VPN connection on any Windows NT server. (Eventually, when Windows 2000 ships, the servers will be able to handle PPTP or L2TP, according to Microsoft's advance literature.) However, you can also set up PPTP, SSH, L2TP, and other protocols for most UNIX-like operating systems.

Tip: As with dial-in connections, you'll need to implement strong authentication for the users who will be connecting over VPN connections. Be sure to read the "Authentication" section earlier in this chapter before making a decision on which authentication to implement.

Also note that, with VPN connections, you may be able to use additional information to authenticate a user who isn't available for dial-in connections. For example, some VPN systems let you restrict access to users coming from a certain IP address range. If the user's home system has been assigned a static IP address of, for example, 192.168.7.2, you can set up the user's VPN connection to be cancelled unless the user's IP address matches that static address.

continues

> If the user's IP address is assigned dynamically by the user's Internet provider, you can improve the security somewhat by allowing the connection only if the user's IP address matches a particular range.
>
> The user's IP address isn't adequate for VPN authentication alone but, taken along with the other authentication methods you implement, it can provide one more level of protection against crackers.

Regardless of the kind of VPN server you implement, you'll generally follow these steps to set up VPN access:

1. Determine the user list and access privileges for all users who will be connecting using VPN. This information should include their user ID, password and, if possible, the IP addresses from which they'll be connecting.

   Remember that you can use authentication methods other than the one built in to the VPN server. See the "Authentication" section earlier in this chapter for more information.

2. Install the necessary hardware on your network, which generally requires a router or firewall with VPN services enabled, or a computer on which the VPN host software will run.

3. Disable all unneeded network protocols, accounts, and features. For example, if the VPN server provides Telnet and Web-based methods of configuring it, you may want to disable the one you don't plan to use. Remember that any active service on a server is a security risk. Some servers allow you to Telnet in and then Telnet back out again to a new location, perhaps providing additional network or server access in the process or at least a way to mask the source of an attack.

4. If the VPN server is inside your network (and not part of the existing firewall), configure your firewall to allow incoming VPN connections to reach the VPN server. If the VPN server is outside the firewall, set up some authentication between the VPN server and the firewall so the traffic forwarded by the VPN server can enter your network.

   This process usually involves finding out from the VPN server's documentation which TCP or UDP ports carry the connection and then configuring the firewall to allow incoming traffic on those ports to be forwarded *only* to the VPN server.

5. Activate the server for VPN and test your configuration.

How you perform each of these steps depends on the details of your particular VPN server and firewall. See the documentation included with your server for details.

Other Internet Services for Outside Users

A dial-in or VPN connection can provide access to all network services from inside your local network, just as if the user plugged in to a network port in your office.

However, you may not want to set up this kind of access to your network for several reasons, including

- **Hardware costs** An existing server can run some services, but if you don't already have a server capable of adding VPN or dial-in network access, you'll need additional equipment.

- **Network load** A VPN connection running on a firewall or router can add an unacceptable load that will slow everybody's network access. This speed reduction becomes more of an issue when larger numbers of users connect to your network.

- **Security** If, in spite of all the precautions described in this chapter, a cracker gets in on your dial-in connection, that cracker will have the same access privileges as whichever user she's pretending to be.

If for these reasons or others you'd rather not set up dial-in or VPN access to your network, you can enable individual network services your users may need, instead. These individual services can be just as secure as a full dial-in or VPN connection.

> **Note:** Be sure you talk to your users about their remote access needs before implementing a service. Remember that a large part of security consists of closing the doors that don't need to be open, which usually means disabling services that nobody is requesting. However, you don't want to shut down access your users need, or they'll look for ways around your restrictions that may not be as secure as the approaches you'll implement.

The following sections describe some additional remote services and the issues involved in implementing them.

Shell and File Access

Administrators of UNIX-like operating systems in particular may need to provide their users with command-line access to some systems inside your network. From a command line, users can perform almost any task: read and write email, create and edit documents, transfer files, browse Web sites, and so on.

Most UNIX-like operating systems include Telnet—a service that provides shell access to the system on which it's running. There are even Telnet hosts available for Windows and Windows NT, although they are used much less commonly on the Windows platform. However, Telnet is not a particularly secure service. In its standard form (as included with most UNIX-like operating systems), it uses no encryption or extra authentication; it simply uses the standard user list for the operating system. This lack of authentication leaves a Telnet connection open to numerous cracks, and Telnet is generally considered to be insecure.

In the same way, UNIX file transfers have typically used FTP (File Transfer Protocol), which is widely used on Windows NT servers as well. However, FTP has the same (or similar) weaknesses as Telnet, in that it uses no encryption and has only basic authentication and access privilege protection.

For these reasons, secure alternatives have been developed. As part of securing your systems, I recommend that you disable the Telnet and FTP services on any machines on your networks that don't absolutely require them.

> **Note:** This recommendation does not apply to anonymous FTP. If the only FTP access a machine is providing is anonymous, then authentication and encryption become moot. In this case, FTP should still be used, especially because it is so widely supported in FTP clients and Web browsers as a way for users inside and outside of your network to download files.

As an alternative, if you need to provide secure shell or file access to a computer, look for the following technologies.

SSH

SSH (secure shell) is a protocol that lets you log in and execute commands on another machine over a network, as well as transfer files. In the UNIX world, SSH can replace Telnet, FTP, rlogin, rsh, and rcp. It currently exists in two versions (SSH 1 and SSH 2), so it's helpful to know which version you're using (SSH 1 clients don't work with SSH 2 servers, and vice-versa).

> **Peter's Principle:** More Uses for SSH
>
> As an added bonus, you can also use SSH for TCP and X11 (X windowing) forwarding, which lets you set up secure tunnels (a VPN connection) and secure X servers. But that's a discussion for another section.

SSH uses RSA for authentication. RSA is a public/private key system of authentication. When you first set up an SSH server, it generates a new public key and a new private key. The private key is used only locally, while the public key is shared with all who connect to the server.

When a client connects to the server, either it has the host's public key (received from a trusted source) or it receives the host's public key directly from the host (less secure, but only a risk at that one moment). Here's what happens then:

- The client wants to verify that it's talking to the correct host, so it sends a random message encrypted with that public key. Only the holder of the matching private key can read a message encrypted with the public key.

- The client then receives back the encrypted message. The client knows that the message was decrypted successfully and that it is therefore talking to the correct host.

- The reverse happens so that the client is likewise uniquely identified to the host.

Once the host is authenticated, the user authenticates himself by exchanging an encrypted user ID and password.

After the connection is authenticated, the flow of data is encrypted using one of several encryption standards (IDEA, DES, DES3, Blowfish, and so on). Because these encryption methods are so strong, the most a cracker can do with an SSH connection is interrupt it, but the data inside the SSH connection is secure from eavesdropping. Even using a packet sniffer, the most the cracker will get is a stream of encrypted packets that are difficult or impossible to crack.

Although SSH servers generally run on UNIX-like operating systems (including Linux, Solaris, FreeBSD, and so on), a Windows NT version (and presumably Windows 2000, although that may not be the case) of the server and client is available. It's called SSH for Win32, and it requires the UNIX shell Cygwin to run.

However, client software is available for numerous other platforms, including

- **Windows 95/98/NT/2000**   Includes numerous options, including F-Secure from Datafellows (http://www.datafellows.com), SecureCRT from Van Dyke Technologies (http://www.vandyke.com/), and several free offerings, such as TTSSH (http://www.zip.com.au/~roca/ttssh.html), an add-on for the terminal emulator Tera Term Pro.

- **MacOS**   Includes F-Secure from Datafellows (http://www.datafellows.com) and freeware alternatives for shell access only in the form of NiftyTelnet (http://www.lysator.liu.se/~jonasw/freeware.html).

- **Java**   A very flexible SSH client is available for Java (and therefore any platform with a Java Virtual Machine) in the form of MindTerm (http://www.mindbright.se/mindterm/). MindTerm is available as an applet that can run from within a Web page and as a standalone Java application.

New SSH clients are appearing all the time, so fire up your favorite search page and start looking. As of this writing, an SSH client has even appeared for Palm handheld devices: http://www.isaac.cs.berkeley.edu/pilot/.

> **Caution:** Not all countries allow the use of every secure authentication and encryption technologies, either because of political or often copyright and licensing reasons, and these restrictions may include SSH. Be sure of the laws in your location before downloading and using SSH.

Secure Socket Layers (SSL)

SSL is a security protocol developed by Netscape Corporation that sits above the TCP/IP layer but below the "higher" protocols (HTTP, FTP, LDAP, and so on). As with SSH, SSL provides a standard way for a client to authenticate itself to a server, as well as a way for the client and server to encrypt their communication. The client and server authenticate through the use of public keys and the use of security certificates from trusted sources.

> **Note:** A newer protocol than SSL, Transport Layer Security (TLS) is being developed by the IETF and is based on SSL.

Although Netscape developed this protocol to secure interactions mainly between users and Web servers, it is a flexible protocol that has been put to use for other tasks as well.

In particular, SSLeay is a free implementation of Netscape's Secure Socket. Using SSLeay, a whole suite of secure utilities has been developed for secure connections, including SSL MZtelnet, a Telnet server and client package that provide encrypted shell connections similar to that provided by SSH.

SSL MZtelnet interoperates with conventional Telnet utilities. If a standard Telnet application tries to connect to an SSL MZtelnet server, the server recognizes that the client can't handle encryption and "drops down" to allow a standard connection. (Of course, you can disable this "drop down" to prevent the less secure connection.)

Similarly, the MZtelnet client can connect to either SSL encrypted servers or standard servers, always negotiating the highest level of security possible.

See http://www.psy.uq.oz.au/~ftp/Crypto/ for the latest information on these utilities, and where to find them if they are available for your computing platform.

Secure File Transfer Options

For transferring files, FTP is just as insecure as Telnet: No encryption is typically used, and anybody with a packet sniffer may be able to collect your user ID and password as you connect.

Fortunately, alternatives exist to provide your users with FTP-like file access without compromising security. To be safest, you should disable FTP access (except for anonymous FTP, if that service is necessary) and replace it with one of the following.

SCP

SCP is part of the SSH protocol and provides the same method of authentication and encryption described earlier for SSH. SCP is served by SSHd, the daemon on (mainly) UNIX-based servers. The SCP clients appear on multiple platforms, although with less availability than the SSH shell clients.

You can install SCP on Windows 95 and NT with version 2.0 or later of the DataFellows SSH client (http://www.datafellows.com or in the packages found at http://bmrc.berkeley.edu/people/chaffee/winntutil.html). You can also go to any of the FTP sites listed on http://www.ssh.fi/sshprotocols2/download.html and look in the contrib directory. The Win32 version you find there will run in a Windows shell using the Cygwin UNIX-like environment for Windows (found at http://www.student.uni-koeln.de/cygwin/).

FTP over SSH

If your users are in a UNIX-like environment and are already using SSH to connect to your network, they may want to run FTP *through* the SSH tunnel. The drawback to doing so is that you have to run an FTP server in your office. But the benefit is that connecting with FTP through the SSH link encrypts all stages of establishing the FTP connection and therefore renders an insecure utility (FTP) more protected.

To set up FTP through an SSH connection on a UNIX-like system, follow these instructions. First, from the user's remote computer, set up an SSH connection to the SSH server inside your network (sshserver.example.com) with a forwarded connection to the FTP server inside your network, using the username *stockman*:

```
ssh sshserver.example.com -l stockman -g -L 4000: ftpserver.example.com:21
```

This line sets up a connection for user *stockman* with the following options:

- **-l** Lets you specify a name other than the user's local login name, in case we're not already logged on locally as *stockman*. .
- **-g** Tells SSH to allow remote hosts to connect to local port forwardings.
- **-L** Tells the local SSH client to listen on port 4000 (a random port number of your choosing that should be anything above 1024).

Once the tunnel is set up, the user can open a new terminal window on the local machine and enter the following command to launch FTP:

```
ftp 127.0.0.1 4000
```

This command opens an FTP connection to the local host (indicated by 127.0.0.1) on port 4000, which is already forwarded through SSH to the remote FTP server on your internal network (on ftpserver.example.com). The user can then enter the regular FTP user ID and password for your FTP server and transfer files as usual.

SSL FTP

This FTP client is similar to the Secure Socket Layer Telnet program described above. The FTP server can connect to a standard FTP client or an SSL-based secure FTP client, or you can disable the less secure standard FTP altogether for the highest security. With the SSL FTP client, a connection is authenticated using public keys and by exchanging security certificates from a trusted source. Once the connection is authenticated, all file transfers are encrypted to prevent packet sniffing, interception, and so on. As with SCP, a connection secured with SSL can at most be interrupted, but not cracked, by an attacker.

See http://www.psy.uq.oz.au/~ftp/Crypto/ for the details on how SSL FTP works and where to find the utilities for your computing platform, if they're available.

Secure Email

There are two concerns with the security of email: making a secure connection to the email server and securing the email itself.

Any mail you send out over the Internet without any encryption is, by its nature, insecure. One saying heard among computer professionals is "Never send anything by email that you wouldn't write on a postcard." However, you may have an office email system (such as Microsoft Exchange Server, Lotus Notes email, cc:Mail, or QuickMail) that is used internally but may also have a link for sending and receiving mail from an Internet mail server.

This section does not discuss the security of Internet mail. Rather, it discusses how users who are at home or on the road can make connections to your *internal* email system to read and send their mail to others in your organization, as well as any other locations your mail server can reach.

Of all the possible solutions to reaching an email server from outside your network, I recommend three in particular: VPN or Dial-In Network connections, dialing in to the mail server directly, or placing some email security on your firewall and mail server.

VPN and Dial-In Network Connections

You've already read about how the user can connect to your network securely from outside and have access to all network services inside your protected LAN. Virtual Private Networking (VPN) and dial-in networking using a remote access server both provide this kind of secure connection.

The benefit for your users who need to read email is that once they are dialed in or connected by VPN, they can simply run their email client software as they would from a desk in your office, plugged in to a physical network port.

The advantages to this method are that the user does not need to learn any new connection method for the mail server; she simply launches and logs in the same way she would onsite. With most mail systems, the email can be left on the central mail server, allowing the user to read and manage mail from any machine that can connect; or the email can be downloaded to the user's local machine, allowing her to work with the mail even after disconnecting from your network.

The disadvantages to this method are that a modem connection can be annoyingly slow, not only because it's a slower connection than being in your office, but also because the modem is handling the network connection (VPN or dial-in) as well as the mail server connection, all over the same bandwidth. That can be a lot of overhead for the modem to handle, and a simple email connection can slow to a crawl.

However, in spite of the possibly slow connection (not an issue if the user is on a high-bandwidth network connection, such as another site's network or a cable modem/xDSL connection), this method proves the easiest to learn for most users who want to retrieve email.

Mail Server Dial-In

Many dedicated mail servers can be configured to allow a direct dial-in connection, allowing the user to connect and manage email without providing access to any other network services.

For example, many mail servers can be configured with a collection of modems connected to telephone lines, allowing users to dial in from wherever they happen to be to collect and send mail.

Mail servers can usually be configured either to accept the user's email name and password to dial in or to interact with a third-party security server (such as SecurID) to require a more sophisticated ID and password, such as one offered by a smart card or one-time use password token.

When you use this method to retrieve and send email, you don't need to implement full dial-in networking on your network, which can require a significant hardware and infrastructure investment (server hardware, phone lines, reliable modems, and so on). The other advantage for users is that instead of having to manage a complete dial-in networking connection, they can simply tell their mail program to retrieve mail remotely, and the mail program handles the rest of the connection.

The disadvantage to using this method is that your mail server may not support dial-in mail connections. There's no reason to implement a different mail server simply to have this functionality, when the other solutions will work as well.

However, if your mail server supports a dial-in connection—and especially if it supports robust authentication methods—dialing in to the mail server is a convenient way to retrieve email without changing anything about your network configuration.

Firewall and Mail Server Secure Access

The simplest way for users to access their email from outside your network is for your standards-based mail server (POP or IMAP, for example) to be accessible to anyone on the Internet. You can accomplish this arrangement by placing the email server on the DMZ, alongside your publicly accessible Web and file servers. Or, you can place it inside your firewall and set up firewall rules to authenticate incoming connections and route mail traffic to the appropriate server.

However, don't rely completely on firewall-based authentication to protect your mail server. Remember that crackers can be inside your network as well as outside, and using simple user IDs and passwords on your mail server can leave you at risk. Fortunately, many mail servers support advanced authentication protocols, such as Kerberos, RSA, or OpenPGP. These protocols allow only authenticated users to connect to your mail server from inside or outside of the network. Many email client programs support advanced authentication methods, including Qualcomm's Eudora Pro, which supports Kerberos.

You may also want to implement mail encryption standards, such as S/MIME (a secure implementation of the multipurpose Internet mail extension protocol that uses RSA algorithms for authentication). Doing so provides strong authentication and encryption between the mail server and the user's mail client, rendering the mail virtually untappable by crackers between the two sites.

The advantage to using this method is that users can retrieve mail from anyplace they have an Internet connection, including another organization's network, a cable modem or xDSL connection, or the user's dial-up ISP. However, unlike a VPN connection, the user simply configures her email program to connect to the public IP address of the email server. (If your network is using internal IP addresses only, as it might if your network is behind a NAT router, the user would provide the IP address of the router instead.)

You can run additional mail server security software to encrypt the user's email connection, although you'll need to make sure the users all have email programs that can handle the kind of encryption you're using. Although S/MIME is still a new method of encrypting email, more and more mail clients are being released that support it, including Microsoft Outlook and Outlook Express, as well as Eudora Pro (with the addition of a plug-in).

There aren't any noticeable disadvantages to this method, as long as your users have email applications that support your chosen authentication and encryption methods.

Summary

If your users need network access to perform their tasks, locking them out will serve only to make them resentful and less productive. There are secure ways to provide almost any network access your users need without opening yourself up to any appreciable security risks, for email, command shell, file transfers, and most protocols on the entire network.

The key is to make it as easy as possible for your users to connect, while implementing secure authentication and encryption methods to keep out crackers. The final goal is to make the connections so secure that the best any cracker can do is interrupt—not intercept—the flow of data.

About Authentication and Passwords

As described briefly in Chapter 5, "Letting Users Connect Securely," *authentication* is the process of verifying a user's identity to determine what level of access (if any) to allow to services on your network, or to the network itself. The authentication method you choose depends mainly on how strong you want your network restrictions to be and how convenient you need access for your users to be.

For example, the simplest authentication I've encountered was a call logging system where the user (an internal support representative) had to enter a name to use the system. The call system was set up to require a name for access, but no password was required. This system worked for the company because the identity of the user was important, but if the wrong identity were to be assigned, no real damage was done.

It's hard to define exactly what the strongest authentication available is, because at the high end of authentication products there are so many options. Authentication can require any of the following (including combinations) to prove a user's identity:

- Something the user knows, usually a name and password combination. This category can also include one-time passwords that require a correct answer to a challenge, usually calculated based on some agreed-upon algorithm.

- Something the user has, such as a key stored in a smart card or a calculated value that changes at regular intervals from a hand-held security token or piece of software.

- Some physical characteristic of the user, including voice, retinal, or thumb scan patterns, often called "biometrics." A recent release, Mac OS 9, provides voice authentication to desktop computers, for example, where saying a predefined passphrase provides access to the system.

The problem with the basic name-and-password combination is that it is subject to eavesdropping. A potential cracker could be looking over the user's shoulder, sniffing packets from the network, running a keystroke recorder on the user's system, and so on as a way of stealing the password.

Peter's Principle: Never Underestimate the Gullibility of Users

Your users aren't stupid, but inexperienced or uneducated users can be fooled, and you should not underestimate their ability to walk into clever traps.

America Online, for example, long ago started including a warning on every email and instant messaging form to remind users that AOL employees would never, ever ask for their password, and nobody else should ask for it, either. A friend of mine received an email asking him to go to a "special" Web page that pretended to be an official AOL contest, requiring only that he enter a screen name and password to enter the contest.

Internet users are regularly asked to download free games or other utilities that are actually trojan horses, pretending to do something useful while actually capturing names and passwords and sending them to the crackers.

Users occasionally fall for phone calls (from outside of their organization, no less) from people claiming to be their network administrator, telephone service representative, and so on. They are often asked for information such as user-names and passwords "to check the account for trouble" and other unlikely notions.

Enough users fall for these scams to make it worth the crackers' while to continue trying them. The solution is a strong authentication system for your network and regular, thorough user education to keep your users from being too gullible.

Regardless of the risks, however, a password is by far the most popular method of authenticating users, because it is convenient. The user can connect from anywhere simply by having a name and password and doesn't need any additional hardware, software, or knowledge. Requiring a smart card, token, or other additional utility to connect adds inconvenience.

Note: Passwords and authentication are areas in which the larger security risk comes from *inside* your network, not outside. To use a packet sniffer to pick up user login sessions, the cracker must be on your local network. To "shoulder surf," or watch a user entering security information from nearby, a cracker has to be inside your facilities.

One of the advantages of following the security precautions in this chapter is that all the users on your internal network will *know* that you're implementing these precautions. Knowing how vigorous you're being and the strong measures you're taking to provide robust authentication may prevent a would-be cracker from wasting her time.

For this reason, this chapter first describes how to make passwords as secure as possible for authenticating users, before addressing the less-convenient alternatives to passwords.

Building Secure Passwords

If you choose to use standard passwords for authenticating services on your network, you need to make sure that users, voluntarily or enforced by software, are using robust passwords that are resistant to easy cracking. As discussed briefly in the "Passwords and Authentication" section of Chapter 3, "Identifying Risks to Your Network," the strength of passwords is affected by their length and by how complex they are.

There are numerous methods of cracking passwords, and the amount of time each method takes depends on the computer speed and the complexity of the password being cracked.

It's important to note here that most passwords are stored and handled in encrypted form, and that the encryption algorithm is one way and not reversible. That is, you can take a word and encrypt it, but you can't start with the encrypted version to get the word. This arrangement is useful because as long as both ends of the authentication process are using the same encryption method, they can send the password back and forth between them for anyone to see, and it won't be very useful. Even if the person in the middle gets a copy of the encrypted password, the encryption algorithm doesn't provide a way to get the password from the encrypted value.

However, if the encryption method is known—and it usually is for most commonly used networking services—there are several ways a cracker can attempt to crack the password.

With password encryption methods, a given word taken by itself will always yield the same encrypted result. Taking advantage of this fact, the cracker (or more accurately, the cracking software) encrypts potential passwords and compares the results to the encrypted password stolen from the network or a system. When the two encrypted passwords match, the cracker has found the correct password.

There are numerous methods of doing this, including

- **Dictionary Attack**   Working on the assumption that the vast majority of users will choose real words from their own language for passwords, the dictionary attack uses a standard list of words to crack the passwords. The software then encrypts the list of words, one by one, using the same one-way encryption algorithm as the password list. When the encrypted version of the dictionary word matches the encrypted password, the password is identified.

- **Brute Force Attack**   This method is time consuming but extremely effective. The password cracker, running any of the freely-available password cracking utilities, uses alphanumeric characters and attempts to match every combination of those characters to the password, either by trying to connect or by encrypting the combinations and comparing the results to the encrypted password. This method can take anywhere from no time to forever, depending on the length of the passwords, but eventually, a brute force attack will succeed.

What the Experts Say

Well-known security organization L0pht Heavy Industries says this on its Web site about brute force attacks:

"Really complex passwords that use characters that are not directly available on the keyboard may take so much time that is not feasible to crack them on a single machine using today's hardware."

Note that they don't say it can't be done; they simply say it's not feasible. They go on to make a valuable point that a password only has to take longer to crack than the amount of time you have set until the password expires.

With computer hardware getting faster with each passing year, the amount of time required to crack passwords goes down. However, if your organization uses complex passwords (that don't use dictionary words) and makes them long enough, you can ensure that only a brute force attempt can crack your passwords. If you force your passwords to expire at reasonable intervals, the cracking attempts won't be completed quickly enough to be useful.

Follow the guidelines described here to build a robust password.

Password Length

The longer a password is, the longer a brute force cracking attempt will take. At a minimum, make sure passwords are at least eight characters long. With an eight-character password, the number of possible combinations (if the passwords are truly random) is 7.2×10^{16}, which would take considerably more time to crack than a five-character password that matches a word in the dictionary.

Although you can't force every user to set up a 16-character password, you *can* set a minimum length on most services. For example, on a Windows NT server you can specify it in the Account Policy dialog box of the User Manager, as shown in Figure 6.1.

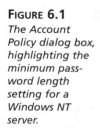

FIGURE 6.1

The Account Policy dialog box, highlighting the minimum password length setting for a Windows NT server.

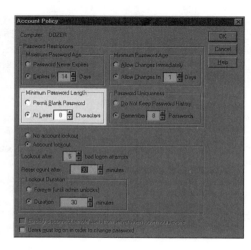

For basic security, require a password length of at least six characters. If the software you're using doesn't allow you to force a password length, be sure to set the policy inside your organization and inform your users that if they don't choose a long enough password, one will be assigned for them.

See "Testing Password Complexity," later in this chapter, for information on how to check whether your users are following the rules.

Password Complexity

As described earlier, be sure that passwords used in your organization cannot be found in any dictionary. The less like any real word a password is, the longer a cracking attempt will take, up to a point.

Remember that your users will be willing to use only passwords they can remember easily. If you force them to use passwords that are too complicated, they'll end up writing them down somewhere, which is a worse security risk than using simpler passwords.

Passwords shouldn't be too closely associated with the person using them, but they must have some kind of built-in mnemonic so that even if the user forgets the password itself, she can still re-create the password using the original method. Follow these methods to create passwords that are complex yet easy enough to re-create as needed:

- Include letters, numbers, and punctuation as much as possible, while keeping the password memorable. One technique is to join multiple random words with punctuation (as in *door%wet* or *wander?politics*) or to combine two words with a number (as in *force206blue*, or *ring12ding*).

- Use the first letters of a long phrase you can remember. For example, the phrase "Four score and seven years ago, our fathers brought forth" would yield a password of *FSASYAOFBF* or, even better, *4SA7YAOFB4th*, where the numbers appear literally instead of by their initial letters or function as mnemonics for words that sound like numbers (such as *to/too for two*, *fore/for instead of four*, *wan/Juan to replace one*, and so on). The advantage is that you can remember the phrase, but the password is a seemingly meaningless string of characters.

- Use a familiar store's name, interspersed with the number from its street address, as in *To2y4s5R8Us*.

- Drop vowels and replace letters in a memorable word. For example, a user in the organization's Documentation department might take the word *publications* and make it *publicat10ns* or some other mangled variation, as long as the user can remember how to mangle it.

Also, remember to explain clearly to your users not to include personal information in creating passwords, including addresses, telephone numbers, family or pet names, and so on. The first thing a cracker with any personal knowledge of a user will try (and personal knowledge is relatively easy to find) is to apply passwords based on that information.

The goal in creating passwords is to combine letters, numbers, and symbols to make lengthy nonsense. Lengthy nonsense is the hardest and most time-consuming password to crack, and the harder you can make the job for the crackers, the better your security will be.

Testing Password Complexity

If you have an organization full of cooperative users who will always follow your security-related instructions no matter how complicated or inconvenient, you can skip this section.

However, if you live in the real world, users may not follow your instructions carefully enough or reliably, especially when doing so might be too inconvenient. Given that your entire organization's network security can be compromised by just a single user who sets his password to *password*, what can you do to make sure this aspect of your setup is secure?

That situation (among other, less honorable reasons) is why password crackers were invented. Just as a network security scanner is designed to probe your network for weaknesses by attempting to break in, a *password cracker* is a program designed to test for password vulnerabilities by attempting to decode the passwords. If the password cracker can decode the passwords, so can anyone trying to break in to your network by hijacking user accounts.

Make it part of your policy to periodically scan your password files with a password cracker to identify weak or simple passwords that your users may have chosen.

Some Windows NT password cracking utilities include

- **L0phtCrack, from L0pht Heavy Industries (`www.l0pht.com`)**   This utility can gather hashed passwords from the NT Registry or a Security Accounts Manager (SAM) database file (where NT domain controllers store passwords on disk) or by capturing them as they are entered over a local network.

- **NTCrack**   This is another utility to run a dictionary attack on a hashed password file at a speed close to 2 million attempts per second, according to the author. The original author's Web site is no longer available, but using any Web site search engine to look for "NTCrack" should yield its location.

The best-known UNIX password-cracking utility is Crack, from `ftp.cert.org/pub/tools/crack/`. Crack attempts dictionary and brute force methods of cracking the `/etc/passwd` file.

In addition, many of the network security scanners include password cracking utilities so that you can check the complexity of the passwords on your network. For example, BindView's HackerShield (`www.bindview.com`) provides this feature, as does ISS System Scanner (`www.iss.net`) and ISS's other scanner utilities.

Frequency of Change

You can set up many network services to allow passwords to *expire*, requiring the user to select a new one. The main reason this action improves your security is that expiring a password forces any cracker to start over. If any of your user accounts have been compromised, forcing a password change will do one of two things:

- If the user changes the password, the cracker is locked out of that account until she can crack it again.
- If the cracker changes the password, the account's legitimate user is locked out and should notify you.

In either case, the cracker is foiled, because you should have a policy in place that no user who is locked out of an account should have his account unlocked without a new password.

> **Tip:** Remember that frequency of change is not enough to provide security. You also have to ensure password quality. A friend of mine had a UNIX shell account for years with the same password. How? Because every time the system forced him to select a new password, he simply entered the old one. Because the system hadn't been configured to require a *unique* password, the user defeated a well-intentioned security feature every 30 days.

You should never simply provide a user with the existing password on an account. Doing so can allow an account's password to remain compromised, opening you and your department up to social engineering attempts to gain passwords by crackers pretending to be legitimate users. In any situation where a user finds himself locked out, provide a new password for the account via regular channels (memo, face-to-face meetings, or other verified circumstances that resist social engineering).

Using Server Tools to Require Regular Changes

There are two scenarios in which you can force passwords to expire:

- **Users can change their own passwords**   In the first and easier scenario, a user receives a notice that his password has expired. He then selects a new one (subject to length, complexity, and other security factors you have in place).

  The advantage to this method is that it's easy, requires no intervention from you or your group, and is mostly secure, because the user must know the current password to set a new one.

  The disadvantage of this method is that the cracker may respond to the request to change the password instead of the user. For an account that is idle or seldom used, the cracker's change might go undetected for weeks.

- **Users are assigned passwords by the network administrator**   In this scenario, the user must be issued a new password by your organization at regular intervals, preferably before the old password expires. Most systems provide the option of allowing users to change their own passwords but, for those that don't, this scenario provides your only option.

The advantage to this method is that the cracker can never change the password without the user's knowledge. In addition, if passwords are always assigned and not chosen by the user, you can guarantee a certain level of complexity, length, and so on to prevent the user from selecting too simple a password.

The disadvantage of this method is that it's less convenient for you and the user. You must provide a secure method of notifying users of new passwords that is not subject to social engineering (crackers pretending to be users to receive the new password information) or other interception. The only truly safe method of providing a user with a new password would be face-to-face (after seeing identification) or encrypting a notice about the new password with the user's public key, which only the user would be able to decrypt.

If you choose to allow your users to choose a new password at regular intervals, you then need to configure your system to expire the old password and ask the user for a new one. For example, on a Windows NT server, you can specify password expiration settings in the Account Policy dialog box of the User Manager, as shown in Figure 6.2.

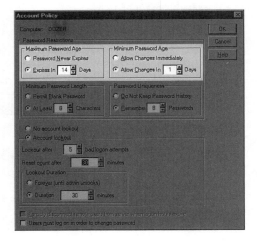

Figure 6.2

The Account Policy dialog box, highlighting the password expiration settings for a Windows NT server.

In the Windows NT example, you can specify how many days until the user must change the password. You also can specify how long the user must keep this password before changing it.

Why should you restrict users from changing a password too frequently? If you are preventing your users from using duplicate passwords (the same password as was used as the last login password), the user might set up a throwaway password when forced to change it then immediately set up the old password again. However, if you set a minimum password age of, say, two days, the user would be forced to use the new password for two days before changing it back.

If you have a restriction that prevents reusing a password for five password changes and there is a two-day password minimum, you're placing ten days between when a password expires and when the user is able to use it again, effectively eliminating the risk.

Avoiding Duplicate Passwords

Users often have favorite passwords and like to use them on multiple accounts, even at different organizations. Often, in the absence of any password restrictions, a user will accept the default password initially created with his account and begin using it on other accounts as well.

This tendency is understandable; given how much information we're all expected to memorize in day-to-day life, passwords are something that users feel they should simplify to avoid confusion or inconvenience. As long as the user is the only one who knows the password, why should it matter if he's been using it for years or on seven different accounts in your organization?

Unfortunately for your security needs, this is the kind of reasoning that leads a user to keep *password* as his password of choice or to continue using his birthday, Social Security number, pet's name, spouse's middle name, and other simple passwords over and over again. A good friend of mine who has always enjoyed snack foods uses a variation of "Twinkie" for almost every password he's allowed to choose. Fortunately, his current network administrators don't leave it up to his whims.

The only way to implement complex, unique passwords without annoying your users too much is to educate and work with them to create passwords that are easy to memorize but still complex enough to provide your network with adequate security.

> **Note:** Another solution is to use a third-party security solution that doesn't involve any user memorization or inconvenience, such as security tokens or one-time password programs. See "Adding Extra or Third-Party Authentication," later in this chapter, for more information.

In case you still need incentive to prevent the practice of repeating passwords, the risks of using the same password for too long include the following situations:

- Password cracking utilities with access to a user's encrypted authentication information can take minutes to find a simple password, but even a complex password may be cracked in a couple of weeks of trying. If a password is cracked in two weeks but your passwords don't expire for thirty days, that leaves the cracker two additional weeks to use the password unimpeded.

- The longer a password is in effect, the more people may see it entered over a user's shoulder, written on the inside cover of a user's notepad, or taped to the user's monitor. Changing passwords frequently means that even compromised passwords are a risk for less time.

Using a password more than once opens your network up to all of these risks. I recommend that you prevent users from using any password that has been used as any of the past five passwords.

Rules for Your Users

As mentioned throughout this book, educating your users is a key component to any security policy. Included in the educating you need to do is informing users about your password-setting policies and making sure they know the rules for creating a robust password.

Include the rules and the other password requirements mentioned in this chapter in your employee handbooks, network policy documents, user account booklets, and so on, and reiterate them whenever you provide network or security presentations to users in your organization (new user orientation, for example, if you provide it).

Rule 1: Never Write Down Passwords

As discussed in Chapter 1, "Networking and Security Overview," users will inevitably write down passwords on notes attached to their monitors, on the inside of desk drawers, on the underside of keyboards, in their wallets, and in other obvious places a cracker moving through your offices might look. If your users absolutely *must* write something down, you might suggest that they write down a hint, rather than the password itself.

For example, instead of writing down the password made from the phrase "Try to take over the world!" (*T2TOVRTW!*), the user might write down "Why, what are we going to do tomorrow night?" This animated cartoon catchphrase on the paper might provide a hint to a potential cracker as well as the user, but to make use of the note the cracker would not only have to know that the paper holds a hint (and not the phrase itself), but she'd also have to guess the correct phrase and then determine the correct password based on the phrase.

Any hints that are written down should be as obscure as possible, and ideally they should be meaningful only to the user. However, the best option is still to write down nothing and memorize the necessary clues to the password.

Rule 2: Always Use More Than One Word to Make a Password

A dictionary crack is useful only if the password consists of words. A single-word password is easily cracked by most utilities. A better option is to string several words together, joined by numbers or symbols, as in *$Jump5Cat#* or *&@Elephant!@soap$radio*.

The addition of symbols (as opposed to just numbers) adds to the complexity of the password and makes a brute force password attack much less likely to succeed in a reasonable amount of time.

Rule 3: Use Phrases to Build a Password

As shown in other examples in this book, a strong password doesn't even contain words. If you use the first or last letters of the words in an easy-to-remember phrase, replacing characters with numbers or symbols, you eliminate the possibility of a dictionary crack succeeding. You force any cracking attempt to use the much more time-consuming brute force method of discovering the password.

The phrases you use might be famous quotes, song lyrics, or advertising slogans (from organizations other than your own). Examples of passwords made from phrases might include "You Ain't Nothin' But A Hound Dog," which leads to the password *YANBAHD*, or better yet, *YA'N'BAHD* (with the addition of the apostrophes from the original phrase to make it more complex).

Rule 4: Never Enter a Password with Anyone Else Facing the Keyboard or Screen

Again, this seems obvious, but often a user will log on while working closely with another user, or he will log on to give a demonstration to someone who is staring intently at the computer.

In those circumstances, it's easy for the observer to pick up some or all of the characters a user is typing and remember them for future use.

Make it a policy in your organization to politely turn away while any user is entering a password at a computer. This practice will help remind users that others shouldn't look at them entering a password at all and can encourage the good habits of hiding this step.

Rule 5: Change Your Password Frequently (Even if the System Doesn't Force You To)

If your network servers don't allow you to set expiration dates for passwords, you'll need to set up a policy for users to voluntarily change their passwords at regular intervals, such as every 21 days or so.

See the "Using Server Tools to Require Regular Changes" section earlier in this chapter for an explanation of why users should change their passwords regularly, then educate your users on when to change passwords without being reminded.

Rule 6: Change Your Password if You Even Suspect a Leak

If your systems allow the user to initiate a password change, encourage your users to change a password if they have even a suspicion that the account has been compromised. The wrong modification date on a file might be enough of a clue to suggest to a user that it's a good time to choose a new password.

Rule 7: Never Tell Anyone, Even Me, Your Password

As the person administering security for your network, you'll never have a reason to know a user's password. You have the power to clear any password from a user's account and assign a new one if you require access. For this reason, you'll never need to ask the user for the password itself.

Use this policy to avoid social engineering attempts of the worst kind: a cracker's attempts to gain the user's trust and exploit it. A cracker may try any number of creative attempts to get a user to reveal a password, such as a phone call to the user, pretending to be a network consultant testing the configuration, a Web page asking the user to enter the name and password to activate more advanced account features, or other such tricks.

If your users are in the habit of refusing all requests for a password, no matter how reasonable they sound or what authority asks, social engineering attempts of this kind will always fail.

Using Built-In Authentication

Most servers of any kind provide their own built-in authentication. This consists of a user and password list stored locally. On UNIX systems this may be found in the /etc/passwd file, on Windows it could be in the SAM files in the system directory, and so on.

The built-in authentication may range from simple names and passwords stored in clear text form to an encrypted set of information that then points to another set of encrypted data elsewhere on the same system. However, the results are generally the same:

1. The user connects to the server and requests a connection.

2. The server asks for authentication data.

3. The user sends a user ID and password.

   On more secure systems, this information is encrypted before it is sent, but for many systems, authentication information is sent as clear text.

4. The server compares the password received to the locally stored authentication data and tries to find a match.

5. If there is a match, the user is granted access to the system.

Using the built-in authentication system is usually the easiest option, because it's installed with the server software, and it usually requires no configuration outside of providing user account information.

However, for many servers, the built-in authentication system is the weakest point. Why? Because the authentication data is stored on the same system to which users are connecting. A user wouldn't have far to go to get a copy of the password file to crack, and virtually all of the operating system and server software available has proven vulnerable to cracking their password files.

In addition, because each device has its own built-in authentication, that requires you to maintain multiple user lists and passwords and also provides multiple points of attack for a potential cracker.

The other disadvantage to using the built-in authentication is that you're restricted to the features provided. If the developers provided no way to force passwords to expire, you would have to clear them manually at regular intervals. If the software accepts only clear-text password authentication, you're left with a security hole that anyone on your network can exploit.

If you use operating system and server software that supports additional authentication methods, the possible ways to strengthen user access expand immensely. (See the next section for more information about adding external authentication.) For example, an AppleShare server uses clear text or a simple random number encryption algorithm to send authentication data across the network. If you add a Kerberos user authentication module (UAM), you're suddenly using the MD5 encryption algorithm, which is considerably stronger. You're also bypassing the process of sending a password between the client and the server, reducing the chances of a packet sniffer finding anything useful.

I recommend that whenever possible you implement servers that support third-party or external authentication. If the built-in authentication turns out to be secure enough for your needs, you're no worse off. But if it turns out that you need something more robust, it's better to have the option to expand.

Adding Extra or Third-Party Authentication

Many of the systems available that require user login are compatible with add-on, or third-party, authentication tools. Third-party authentication is the process by which a server consults something other than its own default authentication method to determine whether a user has access or not.

You may set up a standalone server whose sole purpose is to house the authentication information, and all other services on your network may look to that server to authenticate users. These options include TACACS+, RADIUS, and Kerberos.

> **Note:** These authentication servers support some mixture of authentication, authorization, and accounting.
>
> *Authentication* is the process of determining whether a user is who she says she is, based on information such as user ID, password, source (network address or Caller ID number from which she's connecting), and so on.
>
> *Authorization* is the process of determining what, exactly, a user can do once she's authenticated and connected. This is similar to an operating system's access control list or access privileges.
>
> *Accounting* determines and reports how the user spent her time, such as how many minutes the connection lasted, which services were used during the connection, and so on. This is similar in concept to activity logs.

RADIUS and TACACS+

RADIUS (Remote Authentication Dial In User Service) and TACACS+ (Terminal Access Controller Access Control System) are centralized authentication services designed specifically for remote access systems, such as dial-in networking servers.

RADIUS was originally proposed by the Internet Engineering Task Force (IETF) and is now a standard described in RFC2058. RADIUS supports authentication, authorization, and accounting.

TACACS+ (not really related to the now-defunct TACACS and XTACACS protocols) was originally developed by Cisco Systems and continues to enjoy wide use. TACACS+ supports authentication, authorization, and accounting.

Using a RADIUS or TACACS+ authentication server follows this basic pattern:

1. The client connects to a dial-in server and provides a user ID and password.

2. The dial-in server bundles up the user ID, password, and other identifying information (the dial-in server's ID and the incoming connection port), encrypts this bundle of information, and sends it to the authentication server.

3. The authentication server decrypts the bundle of information and compares it to a database of authorized users (such as the database of whatever system it's running on, a Kerberos authentication server, and so on).

4. The authentication server sends authorization back to the dial-in server to allow the user in, specifying the kind of access and necessary services the user is permitted to have. The authorization sent to the dial-in server is encoded with a digital signature to verify that it comes only from the authentication server and not from any other entity.

   Note that the information that a RADIUS server returns to the dial-in server contains both authentication (verifying who the user is) and authorization (indicating what the user can do or has access to) in a single user profile. TACACS+ separates authentication from authorization and can provide either individually.

The advantage to using these authentication protocols for dial-in authentication is that passwords are all stored in a central location that is more easily managed than providing each dial-in server with its own user list. Because the authentication process is encrypted, it is secure from prying eyes. Another advantage is that the authentication server can tap into almost any existing security system you're using to authenticate the user, such as Kerberos, Windows NT domain controllers, UNIX passwords, and so on, providing another single-location password source.

The disadvantages are minor; one is that, if the authentication server is compromised, the entire dial-in network can be infiltrated. If you implement RADIUS or TACACS+ authentication for your remote access services, be sure to take all necessary precautions to limit access to the authentication server on your network.

Another potential disadvantage is that RADIUS authentication travels your network using User Datagram Protocol (UDP) packets, while Transmission Control Protocol (TCP) packets are considered more reliable in reaching their destinations. TACACS+ travels over TCP packets, which may provide a slight advantage to using this protocol.

Ultimately, if your remote access server offers RADIUS or TACACS+ authentication, you should consider using it if you don't need something stronger, such as token-based or one-time password–based authentication.

Kerberos

Kerberos (currently at version 5) is an open-source authentication system developed by the Massachusetts Institute of Technology (MIT) to provide a secure way to authenticate over an insecure network, such as the Internet.

> **Note:** Among other commercial products, Kerberos version 5 is the standard method of authentication on Microsoft Windows 2000 networks, rendering the login process much more secure than in previous Windows server releases. See http://www.microsoft.com/Windows/server/Technical/security/kerberos.asp for more information.

Kerberos runs on its own system, as a trusted third party that the client and the server can look to for authentication information.

From the client, your system contacts the Kerberos server and exchanges encrypted authentication information to prove your identity. In exchange, Kerberos gives your client a token, often referred to as a *ticket*. You can then use that ticket to prove to other servers on the network that you have authorized access. Note that Kerberos supports only authentication, not authorization. As far as Kerberos is concerned, an authenticated user can do anything (although the server itself may have some control over the user's abilities, once he is logged on).

The advantage to this is that your authentication information crosses the network only once—and in encrypted form—to the Kerberos server. After that, you use the ticket to connect to services, and your password cannot be compromised. Because the authentication process is encrypted, the user's password can't be sniffed and, because the authentication can be tied to a number of criteria (user ID, password, source IP address, and so on), it's difficult for a cracker to intercept the connection by pretending to be the authenticated user.

The only risk to this method is when the Kerberos server is compromised in any way, so you need to be sure that the access privileges to that server are robust (and preferably that no other service is running on a dedicated Kerberos server).

For complete information about using Kerberos authentication on your network, see http://Web.mit.edu/kerberos/www/.

Public-Key Cryptography

Briefly, public-key encryption consists of a public key and a private key. With the public key, anyone can encrypt messages that only the owner of the private key can read, but the public key cannot decrypt those messages. Similarly, the private key can create a digital signature that the public key can verify but not create. This means that only the owner of the private key can digitally sign a message, which is therefore guaranteed to come from that owner, but anyone with the public key can check to see if the digital signature is valid.

The result of this, as far as authentication is concerned, is that a system can use public-key cryptography to verify a user's identity. The server can test the user's identity by encrypting a brief message or a string of random numbers with the user's public key and send it to the user's machine. All the user must do is decrypt the message and respond correctly. When the correct response arrives, the user is authenticated and allowed access.

This is essentially one of the methods used to establish secure connections using SSH, which is a shell, file transfer, and tunneling protocol available at `www.ssh.fi` or from `www.datafellows.com`. Once the server has the user's public key, the user can connect to the server without using a password at all, simply by exchanging encrypted challenges. (Note that the user is still asked for a password to unlock the local private key, but that password is not sent over the network.) Other technologies that use public key encryption to authenticate users include SSL, the Secure Sockets Layer used to set up secure Web transactions, and S/MIME, a standard for encrypting and authenticating email.

Smart Cards and One-Time Passwords

The authentication solutions mentioned in this chapter are useful and powerful ways to verify a user's identity while protecting the authentication information (the password, in particular) from detection by those inside or outside of your network. However, these methods aren't worth much if the user's password is compromised. If the user is careless and allows someone to see the password, if the password is easy to guess (such as the user's spouse's name or the user's own initials), or if a cracker gets hold of and cracks the password list, the accounts are compromised.

You can change passwords regularly, require a certain amount of complexity to passwords, and educate your users thoroughly on how to create complex passwords, and this will alleviate, if not eliminate, much of this particular risk. However, another solution is for the user to carry a token of some kind that provides a different password each time the user connects, or that provides a calculated password too difficult to remember or spoof.

Smart Cards

Smart cards are small devices, usually the size of a credit card or so, with microprocessors and a limited amount of data storage. These cards can be configured with the holder's security information, such as security certificates, public and private encryption keys, passwords and other keys for server access, and so on. When the user wants to connect to your remote access server, for example, she instructs the smart card to send the necessary authentication data up a serial link with the computer she's using to log in. The smart card allows a portable way to carry around extremely complex and robust security keys that the user has no need to memorize or copy. The card is protected by a PIN or other kind of password to prevent its use in the wrong hands.

From an authentication point of view, a smart card is no more than an extension of the user's memory. To avoid forcing the user to memorize a password lengthy enough to be secure, that lengthy password is stored in the smart card, with a shorter password required to make it available for use.

The disadvantages to using a smart card are the added expense of providing security hardware to each user of your network and the inconvenience to the user to need a physical card each time she connects. If the user doesn't have the card at a particular moment, there's no way to connect at all.

Smart card authentication systems are available from numerous companies, with more coming out every year. Microsoft is providing information on integrating smart cards into Windows 2000 and other areas at http://www.microsoft.com/windowsce/smartcard/.

Other companies that are embracing the smart card concept include IBM, Hewlett-Packard, and Litronic (www.litronic.com).

Security Tokens

A security token is a small device—in the form of a credit card, a keychain or fob, and so on—with an LCD readout that displays a unique passcode every minute or so. Figure 6.3 shows an example. The authentication server on your network is synchronized with these tokens. When the user needs to log in to your network, she takes out the token and perhaps enters a PIN to see the code, then enters that code, combined with the PIN, as the login password before it expires and is no longer valid.

A similar *software token* can run on the user's laptop or handheld computer and similarly requires the user to enter a PIN before seeing the temporary passcode needed to log in to the network.

FIGURE 6.3
A typical portable security token.

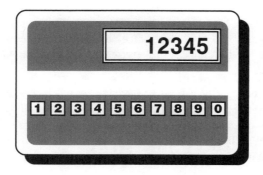

These options have a huge advantage over regular passwords, which can be stolen, guessed, or cracked. A constantly changing password cannot be guessed or cracked and, if sniffed off the network, compromises your network for a very brief time, usually less than a minute.

The only risk is that the token itself will fall into the wrong hands, at which point the relatively weak PIN becomes your only barrier to its use. However, assuming you are notified of the token's loss, you can disable its access at the authentication server.

The best-known security tokens come from the SecurID product line from Security Dynamics (`www.securitydynamics.com/products/authentication.html`) and AXENT's Defender product line (`www.axent.com`).

One-Time Use Passwords

One-time use passwords often consist of a shared key that both you and the server know. Unlike a regular password system, however, the shared key is never transmitted between you and the server, when it could be captured in transit. Instead, the server asks for your username, receives it, and sends a challenge in response from a predefined password list (and that particular challenge is never used again). On your local system (not over the network), you run a program that performs a calculation based on the challenge and your shared key. You then send the server the result of that calculation to log in. Figure 6.4 illustrates this process.

Figure 6.4

A sample S/Key dialog box, showing server challenge, user response, and reply (in two formats).

Note that in this example, the user's response is shown as bullets to prevent *shoulder-surfing*, or someone behind the user viewing the screen. The calculations performed are considered a *one-way hash*, meaning that the calculation of the key and password values provides a result, but the result can't be reversed to provide the original values.

Because the password is never transmitted over the network, it's safe from eavesdropping. A cracker could get the password from this process, however, by collecting the information exchanged between the user and the server and running a dictionary attack through the same calculating program until the same result is found. For this reason, it is still essential that the user implement a strong, complex password (as described earlier in this chapter) that is not easily cracked through a dictionary attack.

The best-known one-time password utility is S/Key (available at `www.telcordia.com`), which was made freely available by Telcordia Technologies, Inc. (formerly Bellcore, Inc.), but which is now unsupported. You can find the files necessary to use S/Key at `ftp.telcordia.com/pub/nmh/`.

Other options include OTP (One-Time Pad Generator) from `www.fourmilab.ch/onetime/otpgen.html` and One-Time Passwords In Everything (OPIE), developed by the U.S. Naval Research Laboratory (NRL) and based on RFC1938, available at `ftp.inner.net/pub/opie`.

Also, in case you thought that only desktop computers could use one-time passwords, a utility for Palm handheld computers called `pilOTP` provides S/KEY and OPIE one-time password generation in the PalmOS. See `http://astro.uchicago.edu/home/web/valdes/pilot/pilOTP/` for details.

Summary

Users can be authenticated on a system by entering memorized information, using a security token, or displaying a unique attribute such as voice or retinal pattern. In most cases, memorized information is the method of choice.

Operating systems provide ways to make passwords more robust by enforcing length, complexity, expiration dates, and so on. Take advantage of these features to keep your passwords up to the job.

Passwords are the most misused security feature available in most organizations, mainly because users sacrifice security for convenience. In their efforts to use memorable passwords, they choose passwords that are too short, too simple, too obvious, too common, or too easily cracked.

It's up to you to come up with a way to convince users to follow the rules for strong passwords that will frustrate even the most determined cracker.

Barring that, you may need to implement other authentication methods, including security tokens, one-time use passwords, or public key cryptography.

Regardless of the solution you choose, monitor the situation carefully, listen to your users' needs, and change the passwords often.

PART III

The Strategies/Implementation

Planning Your Network

As we discussed in Chapter 1, "Networking and Security Overview," the search for networking security is always a tradeoff between safety and convenience. If you're just starting to plan a network, either because you're setting up a new one or you're replacing a network already in existence, you'll constantly run up against this tradeoff.

The users want convenience, which means being able to connect anything, anywhere, anytime, going in or out of your network, with the least amount of effort.

As the person planning the network, you'll probably be leaning towards disconnecting everything, taking out all of the networking cards, and telling the users to exchange data by hand-carrying floppy disks from cubicle to cubicle.

Clearly, there's a common ground between enabling everything and shutting down the whole thing. You can enable some services without opening your organization up to attack, and allowing users to connect from the road or home isn't inviting crackers into view your accounting data.

This chapter describes the questions you should ask yourself about the nature of your network, the tasks you need to perform with it, and what the answers indicate you should do. Each network is different, and each situation calls for different answers, but there's no reason you can't make users happy and efficient and protect them and your data at the same time.

Questions to Ask Before Setting Up a Network

When you sit down to plan a network, the first question you need to ask about any aspect of the network is "Why?" Why do you need to hook that computer to the network? Why do you need to set up a print server? Why does the accounting system need network access?

Sometimes the answer will be that you don't need to add connectivity. In that case, your security needs for that particular user, device, or service become much simpler (although they never disappear completely).

However, that's becoming less and less common as software companies are building Internet access into word processors, text editors, graphics editors, and so on.

> **Note:** One of the more common overlooked features built in to software packages is the ability to update the software directly from the manufacturer's Web site. Assuming you have decided to trust the manufacturer to do this (the likelihood of an established commercial developer using this link to crack your network is slim), you need to configure your network to allow for this service.

What Services Will Be Running on the Network?

This is the most important question you need to ask, because each service you run on your network is, potentially, a service that can be cracked. It is very difficult to gain illicit FTP access to a server that isn't running FTP, and it's nearly impossible if FTP software isn't even installed on the system.

To use an analogy, if there are five keys to your house, is it safer to carefully hide the keys you don't need or to get rid of them altogether? Crackers can't exploit a "house key" that doesn't exist.

The way to answer this question, then, is to start at zero and count upward from there. Assume that you do not need any services at all; turn off everything, including the fundamental networking protocols. Then, using the answers to the questions asked here, enable only the services (and underlying protocols) that are absolutely needed.

Enable the services in as minimal a way as possible; if you discover that you must enable Microsoft Windows networking, don't throw open the gates to enable Windows networking over IP, NetBEUI, and IPX/SPX all at the same time. Reading the sections that follow, determine which of the protocols best suit your needs, then enable the fewest possible protocols and services required to provide Windows networking. (For a Windows workstation, for example, that could be a single protocol, say, NetBEUI, and file sharing only, without printer sharing or other additional services.)

Unfortunately, fewer services is only the beginning. You also need to consider how risky each service is when deciding to enable it. For example, numerous security flaws have been discovered in Microsoft's Internet Information Services (IIS) recently. More will undoubtedly be discovered as the security industry continues to hammer at IIS. For now, at least, you may want to consider turning off IIS, unless it provides an Internet service that you cannot live without. Third-party Web servers, such as Apache, may provide a safer alternative.

As another example, running FTP services may not be necessary, given that FTP may be badly configured or contain security holes, and other more secure options may be available to replace it.

If you decide a service provides too many security flaws to use, consider finding a more secure replacement for it. Available options include choosing another manufacturer's product, choosing an open-source product over a proprietary one, or choosing a more secure technology that provides the same features as the insecure option.

For example, you might replace IIS with the open-source Apache Web server, replace FTP with the scp or SFTP options available with Secure Shell (SSH) technology.

See "Insecure Services and Their Secure Replacements," later in this chapter, for options for some network services.

Which Physical Sites Need to Be Connected?

This question applies to everyone, whether your organization is contained in a single room, floor, building, or world. In the past few years, connectivity has gone beyond hooking up offices in two different cities over leased lines and has expanded to connecting a single office to 20 different "remote nodes" operating out of people's homes. Organizations everywhere have come to realize that an infrastructure already exists with which to connect users from home and from satellite offices: the public, chaotic, Internet.

Fortunately, the technology exists to connect remote sites securely over public connections, as described in Chapter 5, "Letting Users Connect Securely." Virtual private networking can connect a single node (a user's computer) to your network, or it can connect an entire remote network to your network, so that they appear to users to be a single large connection.

One of the big issues with connecting remote sites will be the speed of the connection. Even if you are connecting the sites through a high-speed line, such as a cable modem, DSL, or even a T1 or T3 connection, the hardware on each end will provide a bottleneck. Remember that the VPN connection provides a *virtual* tunnel, by encrypting the data strongly between the two points of connection to the public network. Strong encryption is very processor intensive, and a computer, firewall, router, or VPN server with a slow processor will be quickly overwhelmed by the task of encrypting too much data.

The solution is to use a fast system to handle the VPN connections and to avoid overloading the system with other tasks. A dedicated VPN server will always be more efficient than a firewall with VPN services built in, especially as you add more sites and users.

Also, note that the services you run on your networks can affect the efficiency of the connection between two networks. NetBEUI and AppleTalk, for example, both broadcast packets regularly, announcing their presence to the network. If those announcements are regularly sent across a VPN or other remote connection, they are encrypted along with all other traffic, which can slow things down. If you can disable a protocol or service from the remote network link, do it.

For example, a user making a VPN connection using Microsoft Windows Dial-Up Networking software has the option to enable TCP/IP, NetBEUI, and IPX/SPX across the connection. If the user is communicating only via TCP/IP from the remote location, disabling the other protocols can provide a speed boost.

Finally, be sure to use the most secure methods of connecting the networks that are available. If a private leased line is feasible, it is safer than relying on the public Internet for connectivity. Remember that the fewer public connections you open, the safer your network will be.

Which Operating Systems Will You Be Using?

The security questions you need to answer and the precautions you need to take depend heavily on the operating systems you need to use.

To use an extreme example, if you plan to use nothing but MS-DOS, you have few networking security worries, because there is no networking built in to DOS. If you decide to add NetWare or a TCP/IP stack, it is at that point that things begin to get more complicated.

With modern operating systems, there is a great deal more networking functionality built in right from the beginning. To secure your network, you have to know exactly how each operating system you're using is communicating so that you can either turn it off, secure it, or watch it for intrusion:

- **Microsoft Windows**   Out of the box, Windows may have (depending on the questions answered during installation) NetBIOS, NetBEUI, IPX/SPX, and IP all listening to the network and sending out packets that announce their presence. IP is the most likely candidate for intrusion, as usual, but NetBIOS (if carried over IP or IPX) is a close runnerup.

- **UNIX**   IP is the lifeblood of UNIX-like operating systems, available and intricately tied to almost every function of the operating system. Rather than disabling networking, you'll more likely want to trim any unnecessary services and secure the system as well as you can. Other networking protocols are also available and may be installed by default, depending on the flavor of UNIX you are using, including SMB (also known as CIFS, which is a fundamental protocol of Windows networking), AppleTalk (provided by the netatalk package), and other protocols. In particular, Linux and NetBSD, two flavors of UNIX that are constantly being updated, may provide a better margin of safety because bugs and weaknesses are quickly eliminated, provided you keep up with the latest versions.

- **Macintosh OS**   Macintosh currently has AppleTalk and IP enabled out of the box, either or both of which can be disabled without affecting the system. Prior to version 9.0, MacOS runs very few IP services by default but, with MacOS 9 and higher, IP is replacing or duplicating the features of AppleTalk in many instances, including file sharing and printing.

- **Others**   Other desktop operating systems, including BeOS from Be Incorporated (www.be.com) and OS/2 from IBM, all speak IP fluently, and may have other networking protocols running as well.

Pay close attention to the networking protocols in use by the desktop operating systems and other networking devices you install. You'll want to disable any protocols you don't need and set up the proper monitoring and detection systems for the protocols you leave running.

Setting Up Services and Disabling Unnecessary Services

Building your physical network is beyond the scope of this book, but network services are vital to the cause of network security. As described earlier, you need to determine what you need to run, which versions you need to use, and what you should disable (presumably, everything else).

Many of these issues are described here from a server and desktop point of view, but the same questions apply to any network-capable device, including printers, routers, backup devices, and so on. Disable what you don't need to use, and secure whatever you do need to use. Follow the guidelines here to help decide.

Protocols You Need to Run

Determining the protocols you need to run depends entirely on how you answered the questions in the previous section, "Questions to Ask Before Setting Up a Network." If you aren't running services that use IPX to communicate, you clearly don't need to enable IPX on your network, and that means that nobody can enter your network through the doors opened by that protocol.

Use the guidelines in this section to question your assumptions. You don't need to enable a protocol simply because it's installed on each desktop and server by default. A MacOS computer will run perfectly well without ever using the AppleTalk protocol. A UNIX system will crunch numbers happily for years without any networking services at all, if that's the system's most important task.

Again, start from zero. Assume you don't need any networking protocols at all, and then enable them one by one only if you have a genuine need to do so.

When You Need TCP/IP

Clearly, IP is the most common networking protocol in use today, being the language of the Internet, UNIX systems, and almost all cross-platform (Mac to Windows to UNIX to Amiga to BeOS to any other platform). Even within a single platform, operating system developers are moving in the direction of IP as their common networking protocol, such as Apple Computer's Mac OS (moving away from AppleTalk in favor of IP) and Windows (encapsulating NetBIOS over IP instead of or in addition to NetBEUI).

However, as blasphemous as it might sound, a network could very well be configured and operate smoothly without any TCP/IP running at all. If your network is completely based on Microsoft Windows, for example, and your file servers, printers, and databases can all accept connections over NetBEUI, why would you need to enable IP?

AppleTalk networks may never need to enable IP either. Printing, file sharing, interapplication communication, and other services run well over AppleTalk.

However, as soon as you add Internet access, Web servers, or communication between platforms, you need IP as a protocol running on your network.

When You Need IPX/SPX

IPX (Internetwork Packet Exchange) and SPX (Sequenced Packet Exchange) are part of the collection of protocols used by Novell NetWare. Starting with NetWare 5, IP is the default protocol, although IPX and SPX are still available and supported. Outside of NetWare, some games use IPX/SPX, and other applications exist that use this protocol to communicate as well.

IPX and SPX are routable, meaning that someone on a network on the other side of the router could use this protocol to connect to a service inside your network, if your router is configured specifically to allow it. Be sure that routers on your network are configured to pass this protocol only if absolutely necessary.

However, note that public routers on the Internet are not configured to route IPX/SPX, so there is virtually no chance that anyone outside of your network can connect using these protocols.

If you have the choice between running your NetWare services IPX/SPX or IP, use the protocol that best suits your current and future network needs. However, there is a slight security advantage to using IPX/SPX, all other considerations being equal, because IPX/SPX will not be accessible outside of your network.

When You Need AppleTalk

AppleTalk has traditionally been the default protocol on which all Macintosh applications communicated, including AppleShare file and printer servers, database access, email, and so on.

However, with the popularity of more open standards such as IP, even Apple is moving away from AppleTalk as a default protocol. AppleShare servers can be configured to support connections over IP, as can database programs, email servers and, with Mac OS 9, even peer-to-peer file sharing can operate over IP instead of AppleTalk.

AppleTalk is a routable protocol, and very large wide area networks are possible using AppleTalk. Routers can carry AppleTalk from network to network over an entire campus or office complex, while each user's computer appears in a *zone*, which is similar in concept to an IP subnet.

However, given that routers on the public networks are not configured to carry AppleTalk, there is virtually no chance of anyone outside of your LAN or WAN breaking in over this protocol.

Note that AppleTalk can also be configured to travel in IP packets (called *tunneling*) using the IPTalk or KIP (Kinetics Internet Protocol) protocol. This requires that the AppleTalk routers at each end of the connection "wrap" and "unwrap" the AppleTalk packets from the IP packets. If you don't configure your routers specifically to handle IPTalk, this method of connecting will not be useful to crackers.

If you have the choice between running your Mac OS computers over AppleTalk or IP, use the protocol that best suits your network. However, there is a slight security advantage to using AppleTalk, all other considerations being equal, because AppleTalk will not be accessible outside of your network.

When You Need NetBIOS

NetBIOS (Network Basic Input/Output System) is the application-level protocol by which Microsoft Windows networking communicates. Unlike the other protocols discussed here, NetBIOS doesn't travel your network independently; it travels *encapsulated* in other protocols. NetBIOS can ride on, or be encapsulated in, IPX/SPX, NetBEUI, or IP.

If you are using any of the built-in Microsoft networking features, including peer-to-peer file and printer sharing, most Windows NT networking services, database access, and so on, you need to include the NetBIOS protocol in your plans. However, the protocol on which you allow NetBIOS to ride determines your other network needs, including security concerns.

For example, if you configure NetBIOS to be encapsulated over IP and your firewall is not blocking the ports on which NetBIOS connects, the people outside of your network will be able to see and attempt to connect to your NetBIOS services. If you configure NetBIOS over NetBEUI, on the other hand, nobody outside of your network will be able to connect, because NetBEUI is not a routable protocol. However, if you have multiple networks in your organization with traffic routed between them, using NetBEUI could limit your connectivity options, because all NetBEUI traffic would stop at the router.

Chapter 9, "Security on the Desktop," discusses the options for binding NetBIOS to different protocols. Once you determine that your network must carry NetBIOS, consider carefully which protocol should carry NetBIOS around your network.

When You Need NetBEUI

By default, Microsoft Windows workstations have the NetBEUI (NetBIOS Extended User Interface) protocol installed, which is Microsoft's proprietary networking protocol intended for small networks (fewer than 200 systems or so). NetBEUI is one of the protocols that can carry NetBIOS around your network, and it's very easy to configure and use. Once NetBEUI is enabled on the systems on your network, they can automatically browse the network for available services. You don't have to assign any special addresses or gateways, nor do you have to have a central server handling the traffic. NetBEUI is very plug-and-play–oriented, especially compared to something like IP, which requires much more configuration to use.

NetBEUI is generally supported only by Windows systems. Even the Windows networking clients for other platforms use IP and not NetBEUI to handle the networking traffic. You may not want to use NetBEUI alone if you have to support clients on other platforms.

From a security standpoint, NetBEUI is very safe from outside attack because it is not routable. Nobody on the other side of a router (including those on other networks within your organization and those on public networks such as the Internet) can see or connect to any NetBEUI-based services on your network.

The disadvantage to using NetBEUI is that, for very large networks, it is much slower than other protocols such as IP. Consider performance as well as security when you decide which protocol to use for Windows networking. However, if your main concern for Windows networking is outside attackers, NetBEUI should be your choice for carrying NetBIOS traffic.

Insecure Services and Their Secure Replacements

In every operating system, there are networking services running at a very low level that provide the basic networking services that users depend on. However, not all of those services are necessary, and many of them can provide assistance to crackers intent on gaining access to your network hosts.

At the risk of sounding repetitive, *disable all unnecessary services* but, in particular, disable the ones discussed here.

However, this section assumes that for many services, you'll want to retain the features, even if you disable the risky service. For that reason, I suggest secure alternatives where they are available.

Telnet and FTP

The problem with Telnet and FTP is that, by default, they exchange their authentication information as clear text, and the authentication methods are very basic (username and password). (Anonymous FTP service also provides potential crackers with access to a system that may be compromised, depending on the version of the FTP server you're using.) Standard Telnet and FTP daemons can't handle third-party authentication methods or encrypted password exchange at all.

The danger in this is that FTP uses the standard user list to provide access so, if the account is cracked, any files to which the user has access are at risk. Telnet allows the user to connect to a shell account to the host, which not only provides file access but may also allow the user to execute programs and utilities. Any cracker who could capture an FTP or Telnet account would have a strong base from which to launch attacks on your system or to relay attacks on other systems.

For this reason, you should consider disabling Telnet and FTP (at the very least, disable anonymous or guest FTP access if it's not needed) and replacing them with some of the alternatives:

- **SSH**   SSH (from www.ssh.fi, and commercially from www.datafellows.com), which stands for Secure Shell, can provide a Telnet-like shell interface as well as other services, such as scp (secure copying for files) and sFTP (secure FTP, in SSH2). These services all use encrypted authentication methods set up using public key encryption, which provides a virtually (although perhaps not absolutely) unbreakable process of verifying access.

- **SRP-enhanced Telnet and FTP**   SRP (Secure Remote Password, available at srp.stanford.edu/srp/) is a relatively new protocol using encrypted authentication and cryptographic key exchange to establish a secure connection.

The Stanford site also provides links to free, SRP-enhanced versions of Telnet and FTP servers and clients so you can replace your existing software with secure versions.

- **SSL-enhanced Telnet and FTP**   SSL (Secure Sockets Layer) is the session encryption standard first developed by Netscape Corporation (`www.netscape.com/eng/ssl3/`) but now also available in the OpenSSL standard (`www.openssl.org`, which in turn is based on the SSLeay library developed by Eric A. Young and Tim J. Hudson, available at `www.ssleay.org`).

- **Kerberos-authenticated Telnet and FTP**   Kerberos authentication, developed at MIT, provides an encrypted method of authenticating users, which can make Telnet and FTP sessions more secure. Clients that support this kind of authentication include a Kerberos Telnet and FTP (KTELNET) client for Windows, available at `http://www.stacken.kth.se/~thn/ktelnet/index.html`.

Note that for most versions of Microsoft Windows, including Windows CE, the free Tera Term terminal client software has been extended to support SSH, SSL, and other secure terminal session standards. See `http://hp.vector.co.jp/authors/VA002416/teraterm.html` for more information about Tera Term.

Also, the commercial product SecureCRT handles SSH and other shell connections. See `www.vandyke.com` for details.

Another commercial SSH option for Mac OS and Windows computers is Data Fellows, at `www.datafellows.com`.

Solely for Mac OS computers, NiftyTelnet has been released to support SSH shell sessions. See `http://www.lysator.liu.se/~jonasw/freeware/niftyssh/` for details.

Finally, a free Java SSH client that will run on any Java-enabled platform is MindTerm, available at `www.mindbright.se/mindterm/`.

Sendmail

Sendmail is the most commonly used UNIX-based mail transport agent for sending and receiving mail on the server (working independently from the actual POP or IMAP mail server). As a large and complex program, Sendmail has a checkered history from a security perspective and has been updated and patched regularly over the years as security holes have been discovered. If you use Sendmail, be sure you always have the latest version installed (available from `www.sendmail.org` or, for the commercial version, `www.sendmail.com`).

Note: In addition to providing some security holes, Sendmail may also be exploited for relaying unsolicited commercial email, or spam, as well as relaying viruses, trojans, and other malicious code using the email protocols. Many administrators simply disable Sendmail relaying from all domains other than their own to address these problems. Otherwise, your network may be blamed as the source of attacks on others.

There are those who argue that, precisely because Sendmail has been around for so long and had so many security flaws discovered, it is therefore a secure product to use. Ultimately, you'll need to judge for yourself, but at the very least you can assure yourself that, because of the large installed base of Sendmail users in the world, any flaw will be quickly publicized and just as quickly patched.

However, if you decide to replace Sendmail, there are alternatives that claim to be more secure, including

- Postfix, which is Wietse Venema's (remember? The inventor of TCP Wrappers) secure alternative to Sendmail. See www.porcupine.org/postfix-mirror/ for links to the Postfix site closest to you.

- qmail. Details of qmail (written by Dan Bernstein) are available by following any of the links at www.qmail.org. If you currently run Sendmail, qmail is a good, secure alternative.

Commercial alternatives to Sendmail include products from Innosoft International, Inc. (www.innosoft.com), Post.Office from Software.com (www.software.com), and others.

Mail Servers

POP (Post Office Protocol), in the form of POP3, is probably the most commonly used mail server protocol on the Internet, as well as on many private networks. Unfortunately, the POP3 protocol sends authentication information as clear text, meaning that anybody between the mail client and the mail server could see something like this:

```
+OK InterMail POP3 server ready.
USER mstockman
+OK please send PASS command
PASS clearpass
+OK mstockman is welcome here
STAT
+OK 0 0
QUIT
+OK mstockman InterMail POP3 server signing off.
```

The italicized lines in this example are those sent by the mail client, while the plain text is the response from the server. The line that starts *PASS* is the mail client sending the password in a clear, unencrypted format that anyone could read who runs a packet sniffer on the same network.

One alternative to clear text authentication in a POP server is to use APOP (Authenticated POP). Most modern email clients that support POP support APOP. Using APOP, the mail client encodes the password using a one-way hash, rendering it much more difficult to capture with a packet sniffer.

IMAP (Internet Message Access Protocol) is an alternative to the POP standard. IMAP supports a model in which the user leaves his mail on the IMAP server and uses his email client to read, write, organize, and delete mail in place instead of downloading it to a personal computer. IMAP has many of the same clear text password vulnerabilities as

POP, but numerous secure authentication methods are available, including MD5 hashing of passwords, SSL encryption, Kerberos, and others.

If you are running an IMAP mail server, contact the developers of your server to determine which authentication methods are active by default and which you can add separately. Be aware that your IMAP client software must be able to support the authentication method you use on each platform that your users connect from.

Finger

Remember that one of the first things a cracker needs to attack your network is information. The Finger daemon, available on most UNIX systems, can provide information that you might prefer to restrict.

The Finger daemon can provide information about a server or about just a particular account. For example, this is the result of Fingering a particular account on a server:

```
-User-      —Full name—            Idle TTY -Console Location-
Stockman . Mike Stockman           Login Sat 21-Aug-99 5:25PM from
hostname.example.com
  [2875,2875]  </home/others/Stockman>;  Group: Advanced  Shell: /bin/tcsh
  Groups: Advanced

  Stockman has no new mail, last read Sat 21-Aug-99 5:25PM
  [New mail is forwarded to mstockman@aol.com]
```

This result confirms *at least* the following useful information:

- That the account is active and therefore still has login privileges.
- That the account has been used recently, so new activity on the account won't stand out.
- The host from which the user is connecting, which might provide a means to intercept or sniff packets.
- The user's full name, which can often (in the absence of a strong password policy) provide clues to the user's password.

In other words, the information provided by Finger can compromise the security of the account and therefore the entire system. Remember that anything you can do to make a cracker's job harder is worth doing. You can either disable fingerd (the Finger daemon on a UNIX system) altogether or configure it to refuse connections from outside of the host on which it's running.

You might also simply configure your firewall to refuse traffic on the ports used by Finger (TCP port 79, usually).

TFTP (Trivial File Transfer Protocol)

TFTP is an unauthenticated file transfer protocol that may be needed to provide unattended downloads, such as downloading configuration information to a server, upgrades to network routers, and so on.

If you don't need it, however, it could compromise security on the server, yielding access to sensitive files such as password files or user activity logs.

If you must run TFTP, you may want to consider running it on a small, dedicated server that contains no other sensitive information.

Others

There are numerous other services and protocols that you should either disable or replace. Chapter 8, "Security Overview for the Major Network Operating Systems," describes many of these services for each platform and offers secure alternatives where available. Remember to always turn off whichever services you're not using.

Scanning Your Network for Security Holes

Once you have your network up and running, with the systems and services you need running behind a good, strong firewall, you need to scan your network for any remaining security holes and vulnerabilities.

Recap of Network Scanning

As described in Chapter 3, "Identifying Risks to Your Network," you can use different kinds of network scanners to identify the services that are listening to your network. For example, an FTP server listens for a network connection on TCP port 21 of the system on which it's running.

A simple port scanner can attempt to make connections to each TCP and UDP port on a host and report back on any port that appeared to be accepting connections. However, the port scan doesn't tell you everything. In particular, it fails to tell you

- Whether all attempts to connect on that port will be logged by the host
- How strong the security is on the open ports
- Which product and which version of that product is listening for connections, and whether that version is safe

For this kind of detailed information, you need a network security scanner, such as nmap, HackerShield, Kane Security Analyst, and so on. Many of these packages are summarized in Chapter 3.

Network security scanners not only discover the ports on which a host is listening, they also try to establish connections to those ports, using common or simple user IDs and passwords, known security holes, and insecure accounts (such as anonymous). Network security scanners may also attempt to launch denial of service (DoS) attacks, some known buffer overflows, and other attacks to see if the host is vulnerable.

One of the most important things the resulting report can tell you is whether a host is listening for services you may not have intended. Many operating systems and network devices enable services right out of the box as a convenience, but that convenience may also open a security hole you need to know about.

Other results the security scanners can provide include

- Recommendations for services to disable, if those services (such as Finger or Sendmail, for example) are known to have vulnerabilities.
- The overall strength of the underlying operating system. The nmap scanner, for example, can identify most common operating systems during a scan and tests for vulnerability to certain attacks based on predicting the TCP packet sequence.

    Essentially, the more unpredictable the TCP packet sequencing is, the less susceptible the system is to a certain type of connection hijacking. Microsoft Windows NT 4.0 (up through service pack 3) has very predictable TCP sequencing, and nmap (and possibly other tools) can point that out for you so that you can upgrade to service pack 4 or higher or, better yet, Windows 2000.
- How sensitive your system is to detecting intrusions. Any system that keeps a log of incoming connections should register the attempts by the security scanner to scan, connect, and attack the host. If any of the scanner's attacks are not logged, your intrusion detection system has a vulnerability that you should correct.

    For example, most scanners not only attempt to open connections (with the SYN, SYN-ACK, ACK sequence of packets), they also attempt to create "stealth" connections that won't appear to be connection attempts at all, such as sending a FIN packet to a port to close a connection that is not actually there. Based on the way the host responds to a request to close a non-existent port connection, the scanner can tell you whether the host is listening on that port.

    With a strong intrusion detection or logging system, even a stealth scan should register as a scan.

Once you have scanned your network setup and identified the holes, you can proceed to close them. Most security holes are closed by a combination of product updates and turning off services. Often, the network security scanning software will make recommendations on how to close the hole, so read the reports carefully.

Summary

Most operating systems provide a vast collection of protocols and services that you can install by default. Resist the temptation to start with these settings.

Instead, plan your network by eliminating all default networking protocols and services and then adding them little by little as your networking needs require. Don't enable a service or networking protocol unless you can demonstrate a clear need for it.

When you do enable a service, be sure you are using the latest version, with all known vulnerabilities patched. If a more secure product exists that provides the same features, as in the case of Telnet and FTP services, install the secure product instead.

Finally, be sure to include intrusion detection systems and security scanners in your network plan. Schedule regular security audits and lay out an expectation of how to monitor for intrusion regularly and what to do when an intrusion is detected.

Remember, as you plan network security, avoid complexity wherever possible. Simplicity is your ally.

Security Overview for the Major Network Operating Systems

There are numerous network operating systems in use around the world today, but they fall into a few well-defined categories:

- **Windows NT or Windows 2000**   As the name implies, these are network services based on the Microsoft Windows NT and upcoming Windows 2000 operating systems. Microsoft has worked hard to ensure data integrity and secure connections, with varied levels of success.

- **Novell NetWare**   Novell has been making the NetWare operating system available for many years now, and the current version, NetWare 5, is as powerful as ever and provides excellent safeguards for your clients and data.

- **UNIX-like operating systems**   The operating systems that power the Internet are also the network servers of choice within many organizations. UNIX-like systems include Solaris or SunOS, BSD, Linux, and others. UNIX provides great power and potential for secure connections. However, these systems also carry great complexity and can trip the unwary.

Other network operating systems include AppleShare, a lesser-used but powerful network operating system, IBM's OS/2 Warp server, Banyan VINES, Artisoft's LANtastic, and so on. Many of the concepts discussed here apply to all of these operating systems, although they are not discussed specifically in this chapter.

> **Peter's Principle:** C2 Certification
>
> You may have heard about C2 certification and how it's the highest level of security an operating system can provide. That's not exactly true, however, and you should not put too much faith in claims of C2 certification.
>
> "C2" is a level of certification that results from applying Trusted Computer System Evaluation Criteria (TCSEC), often referred to as the "Orange Book," to a product. The TCSEC is a standard developed by the National Security Agency (NSA) and the National Institute of Standards and Technology (NIST) to provide a standard way to determine how much the government could trust commercial products, such as network servers.
>
> *continues*

Class C2 is one of several possible ratings given to an evaluated system by the National Computer Security Center (NCSC) after a thorough evaluation, and it basically indicates that evaluation showed the security features of the product to be strong enough for the government to trust. This can be useful information, except that they evaluate the server on a particular piece of hardware, in a particular configuration, in carefully controlled circumstances. They don't say, for example, that Windows NT 3.51 has a C2 classification; instead, they say that Windows NT running on a particular piece of hardware, with an exact set of features operating, achieved that rating.

Before you decide that one OS is more secure than another based on its NCSC or Orange Book rating, see the NCSC Web site at `http://www.radium.ncsc.mil/tpep/` for details of the actual tests performed.

Steps to Secure Your Network Servers

The network server is the heart of a network operating system and provides the client system with such services as file serving, printing, centralized database access, Web services (for intranet Web servers), mail servers, discussion groups such as news servers and chat databases, and so on.

All the networking client needs is to have the correct software installed and the necessary information to set up an authenticated connection to the server. This software can be built into the client's desktop operating system, as in the case of Windows' built-in networking clients and the Mac OS AppleShare client, but often it needs to be added separately, as in the case of NetWare client software (for any platform) and Windows networking clients (for the Mac OS and UNIX systems).

Chapter 9, "Security on the Desktop," discusses how to make sure the desktop client software is secure, but there's a server side to this, too. For any given networking server providing files, printers, data, and other services to your network, you have to keep up with the following areas of security:

- Securing Access Methods
- Setting Appropriate Access Levels
- Applying Updates and Patches
- Enabling and Disabling Services
- Detecting Intrusion

As discussed in this chapter, these actions are part of setting up and maintaining any network server, and they can be time consuming. However, they're not nearly as time consuming as re-creating your servers and data from backups. (I'll assume you keep regular backups, although that is outside the scope of this book.)

Note: One thing you'll need to do regularly, regardless of the network operating system you're using, is to scan the server using any of the numerous free and commercial security scanning tools available for the task, such as nmap, ISS Internet Scanner, BindView's HackerShield, and so on. See Chapter 3, "Identifying Risks to Your Network," for more information.

Planning the Security and Access Levels

Before you can start securing any networking server, regardless of the platform on which it runs, you need to determine who will have access once it's up and running. Because you want to provide only the access users need to accomplish their required tasks, you need to plan carefully who will have access to which features before you even set up the server.

Why plan your security ahead of time? To help make the task manageable and clear, because without a security plan, access levels can be set up incorrectly, vital tasks might be overlooked, and dangerous security holes might go unnoticed.

Follow these steps to create a security plan for your network:

- Break down security needs
- Organize users into logical groups
- Set up a procedure for maintenance
- Educate your users

We'll examine these steps in the following sections.

Break Down Security Needs

Setting up security for your entire network or even an entire server is a big project, and if you try to do it all at once, it can quickly grow out of control. Take your security plan one step at a time by breaking it down into manageable steps:

- Plan what the network is used for, and determine the level of security each task needs. For example, access to your accounting data probably needs to be very carefully restricted, while access to printing on your network is likely to be wide open. (That may not always be true, especially if printing is a restricted resource or billable by department, but your needs may vary.)
- Describe the people who will need access to your network services. Don't list them at this stage; simply describe the groups and functions they'll need to perform and what tasks they don't need or that should be restricted from them.
- Identify each resource on your network and what it's used for. Include file servers, databases, mail servers, printers, modems, and so on—in short, anything that is shared by more than one person. Be sure to include individual workstations in this section, because they may be sharing files and other resources.

Remember, nothing is too small or insignificant to be a security risk, so leave nothing off your list of network resources. You can't depend on something being safe because it's obscure—crackers will find even the tiniest holes in your network, if you let them.

Once you (and your team of administrators, department representatives, and others, to have as much input as possible) have created this list, begin setting up the users and groups.

Organize Users into Logical Groups

Most server security is based on the group to which a user belongs, not who the individual user is. If the user's group has access to the print server, the user can print. This is a powerful and flexible way to set up user access, but it can get complicated, as shown in the following examples.

Example 1: The Simple Organization

In this example, a company of 12 people has a network that contains file servers, print servers, an email system, and a database of customer and sales data. The network administrator sets up all the users on the system and begins to organize them into groups. This being a small organization, the administrator picks an Administrators group, an Advanced Users group, a Users group, and a Guest group, with decreasing levels of access.

The Administrators group has access to everything, which makes it such a powerful group that it has only one member: the network administrator.

The Advanced Users group has access to every service on the network and has the ability to perform some advanced tasks (backing up servers, changing the ownership of some directories or files, and other quasi-administrative tasks). Membership in this group is restricted to four senior people.

The Users group contains everyone else in the company. They have access to files, printers, email, and so on, but they are not able to add or remove resources or change the security settings on the network at all.

The Guest group contains one user: a Guest account with no password, used for visitors to the company such as temporary workers and consultants. This group has access to the printers and a special directory on the file servers used for transferring data back and forth.

In this example, there is a simple hierarchy, where each group has its own level of access.

Example 2: Cross-Linking Chaos

In this example, an organization of 600 people, there are much more complicated security needs and therefore more complicated user and group configurations.

There is always an Administrators group, since there's always an administrator. Those in this group have full access to everything on the network. There may be several members of this group in a large organization.

There is a group for each department: Marketing, Accounting, Sales, Information Technology, Shipping, Administration (not to be confused with Administrators), and so on. Each of these groups has access to its own areas of the file servers, its own printers, and its own databases, but all have access to the email system and discussion forums.

There is a group called Department Admins, who are given some administrative power in order to manage security for their own departments.

There is a group called Users, which encompasses all the features and services that any user in the organization might need access to, such as the company-wide sections of the file servers and databases, the email system, discussion forums, and so on.

As always, there is a Guest group for visitors on the network.

The main difference between this organization and the previous example is that this group has people who are members of multiple groups. A user might be a member of Users, Marketing, and Department Admins, while another user may be a member of just Users (such as a floating administrative assistant who doesn't belong to any one department).

The rule to remember is that access privileges are additive. If a user is a member of Group A and Group 2, that user has the access privileges of *both groups*. If Group 2 isn't allowed to use the executive laser printer but Group A is, then the user has those privileges.

To assign secure access for users, therefore, you need to know what groups to place them in, and you have to be careful not to inadvertently promote a user's access by placing her in too many groups.

Set Up a Procedure for Maintenance

As time goes on, users come and go, organizations are reorganized, and resources are added and removed. All of this requires that your security plan have *maintenance* built in.

Your security plan needs to describe the following maintenance plans:

- Who will add and remove users? In a smaller organization, the network administrator can be in charge of the complete user list. In a larger organization, however, there may need to be a specially trained member of each department, or even a few members of the Human Resources department, to handle this task and document the changes to a central location.

- Who manages the groups? Remember, the groups are the core of your access control system, so modifying a group should be carefully restricted. Even adding or removing users from groups is sensitive, but creating or changing what a group can do should be restricted to the highest-level network administration group in your organization.

- How are resources distributed, and how are changes implemented? As user tasks change and as resources are added (printers, file servers, and so on), you'll need a plan for how changes are to be made.

- How will you respond to an attack or a crisis? You need a plan in place for handling unauthorized access to your network services. See Chapter 10, "When You've Been Cracked" for details on how to handle an intrusion.

Educate Your Users

Your security plan needs to include how you're going to educate users on their rights and restrictions, how passwords are assigned, and how they can protect their own work on the network. This includes helping them to understand peer-to-peer file sharing and all that it implies, if you plan to allow it at all.

Peter's Principle: Life Cycle of a Security Hole

Here's how a typical security hole scenario works:

- A cracker, playing around with his own system, determines that a hole exists in a commonly used networking service, such as a mail server or Web server.

- The cracker exploits the hole to launch subtle attacks on some networks, probably going undetected.

- The cracker shares the exploit with friends and fellow crackers.

- A careless cracker (or aspiring cracker) is detected using the exploit, and the target network's administrator begins tracking down how it happened (or reports the problem to CERT or other security task force to discover how it happened).

- A general announcement is made of the flaw, and software developers begin to work on a system patch that will correct the vulnerability.

- The patch works its way through the online community, making it less and less likely that the exploit will work. Eventually, nobody bothers to try it anymore, and the crackers move on to the next vulnerability.

In many cases, a hacker or security team will discover the flaw before a cracker does. They'll usually contact the manufacturer of the software at risk first, to provide the manufacturer with an opportunity to address the problem and release an announcement that the flaw exists, with a patch.

In cases where the manufacturer is slow to accept that a flaw exists or is slow to release a patch, some hackers or security organizations will publicize the flaw widely as a way of pressuring the manufacturer to move more quickly.

Some people (usually on the side of the large companies who must fix the flaws) label the release of security flaws as irresponsible and, indeed, the announcement of a new security flaw can lead to a brief upsurge in attempts to exploit the flaw. However, the glare of publicity is usually preferable to having a flaw worm its way through the cracking community while the users of the product remain oblivious to the risks.

Windows NT and Windows 2000

Microsoft has been making inroads into the network server market for years now, competing with and even surpassing many of the more established systems that were previously dominant. However, while Windows NT, and soon Windows 2000, does not yet own the server market, it is in use throughout the world because it has comparable power to other systems, and it integrates well with Windows and Macintosh networks, among others.

Your Main Security Concerns

Given the security built in to Windows NT and 2000, your security concerns are not extreme but are similar to any network server. You need to be concerned with setting file and directory permissions appropriately, applying operating system patches and updates as they are made available, and staying informed about the risks and vulnerabilities related to using this particular server.

However, with Windows NT, you run into an additional concern. Unlike the open-source world of UNIX, Windows NT is a proprietary system, carefully guarded by Microsoft, and the security organizations in the world have no access to the source code or a great deal of other proprietary information that might make it possible to identify security holes.

Why is that a problem? With an open-source operating system on your file server, or open-source applications and utilities, whoever identifies a security hole or vulnerability might also release a patch to fix the problem. If that person or organization doesn't, somebody else probably will in short order.

In the Windows NT world, many security organizations are looking at Windows NT for security flaws, just as with any other network operating system. However, once they identify a weakness in the system, they have two choices:

- Notify Microsoft and hope Microsoft fixes it
- Notify everybody else so that everyone is informed of the risk

In several cases, those discovering a security hole in Windows NT have publicized the flaw after indicating that they had notified Microsoft and seen no action as a result. However, whether the publicity was necessary for action from Microsoft, it is certainly necessary for you to close the holes in your own system while waiting for potential fixes to arrive. For example, when you hear about a flaw in the FTP service provided in Windows NT, you might turn off FTP service (if you can live without it) until a patch or update is made available.

For this reason, if you run a Windows NT server, be sure to stay on top of the news about flaws in Windows NT or other Microsoft products you are using. At the very least, subscribe to the Microsoft Product Security Notification Service, which provides regular email notices as security flaws or updates are made available. You can find information about this service at www.microsoft.com/security/services/bulletin.asp.

How NT Security Works

Windows NT security is very strong compared to that of desktop systems such as Windows 95/98, Mac OS, and so on. As a server, Windows NT has security that is more than adequate for normal use, although it has fallen under criticism in the security community for having some serious weaknesses compared to UNIX and others.

Windows NT takes advantage of user-level security, which indicates that the access to files, directories, and activities depends on the groups to which the user's account belongs.

Windows NT provides the following basic security features:

- User ID and password-based connections, with centralized domain-based authentication, although Windows 2000 adds authentication methods such as Kerberos
- Extensive user lists, including groups with inherited access privileges
- File and directory-level security through a powerful Access Control List (ACL), if the disk is formatted using NTFS (NT File System)
- Access rights that let you perform or not perform tasks based on the groups to which you belong

However, Windows not only uses the user ID to determine whether the user has access to the system, but it also determines on a file-by-file basis what the user can read, write, and execute. It does this using advanced security features built in to the NT File System (NTFS), the format in which an NT volume can be formatted. Under NTFS, each file may have its own assignment of ownership, access control, and auditing (logging what happens to it).

> **Note:** The set of access restrictions on a file, directory, or any object in Windows NT is called an *access control entry (ACE)*. A collection of access control entries is called an *access control list (ACL)*. When the user connects to a Windows NT server with a name and password, NT checks the ACL to determine which shared services the user may use.
>
> Windows NT and 2000 servers may have their own user accounts to determine access privileges, as would a single server on the network, or they may be part of a larger *domain*, which contains a Primary Domain Controller (PDC) and one or more Backup Domain Controllers (BDC).
>
> The domain controllers provide a centralized place to handle user accounts and machine accounts for an entire network, including usernames and passwords, as well as what privileges each user has. When a user connects to a workstation or server, that system contacts the domain controller and uses the centralized user lists, rather than its own, to determine that user's access. The relationship between a server and a domain controller is a *trusted relationship*, meaning that the workstations and servers on a network all know that the domain controller is the final authority on who can connect.
>
> Any Windows NT or 2000 server stores the basic authentication information in a Security Administration Management (SAM) database. The SAM, stored in Windows NT in `WINNT/system32/config/SAM`, is a sensitive file that only the administrator should be able to read or change.

Making Your Systems More Secure

The basic rules for securing a server are true for Windows NT as well, as described in "Steps to Secure Your Network Servers" at the beginning of this chapter. Provide fewer ways to connect to the system, and make the system as robust as possible. Here are some of the ways you can "harden" a Windows NT server.

Enabling and Disabling Services

Unlike UNIX, which is much more of a multiuser system than Windows NT, only one person has control over the operating system at any given time. However, an NT server can be running any number of services that provide access to the server. As with all security issues, the fewer services the better.

To see a list of the services the server is running (assuming you are logged on to the computer as Administrator or as a user with access to the list of services), open the Services Control Panel as shown in Figure 8.1.

FIGURE 8.1

*The Services
Control Panel.*

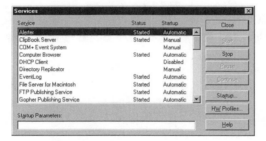

Services that start up whenever the NT server starts are labeled with Automatic in the Startup column. Any service that is currently running reads Started in the Status column.

Usually, a service is started as a result of some configuration change you make elsewhere on the Windows NT system. For example, you can configure the FTP, WWW, and Gopher services using the Internet Service Manager, usually installed in the Programs submenu on the Start menu.

However, you can always open the Services Control Panel, shown in Figure 8.1, select the service you want to stop, and click the Stop button. To prevent a service from starting the next time you restart the computer, click the Startup button and choose the Manual or Disabled button (instead of the Automatic button, which tells Windows NT to start the service automatically on startup).

You may want to disable any or all of the following services, depending on your networking needs:

- **FTP** If you have installed the Internet services, independently or as part of the IIS (Internet Information Server), Windows NT installs and starts an FTP server that you can configure or disable using the Internet Services Manager. The FTP service is a risk because of any of the following reasons:

FTP accepts passwords in clear text that can be collected from your network by a packet sniffer.

The FTP server can be misconfigured easily to allow users with access to a limited directory to navigate *upward*, gaining access to the parent directories that may contain sensitive information. The best choice, if you must run FTP at all, is to provide FTP access only to a separate partition that is dedicated to FTP access and nothing else.

Anonymous FTP can provide more access than you intend. Again, configure it carefully, but disable anonymous access if you don't need it.

If you can, disable FTP altogether. You may want to replace it with something more secure, such as the SSL-based EasyAccess 2000 FTP Server from Comm-Press Technologies (www.comm-press.com) or Cybernetica's Secure Sockets Agent (www.cyber.ee). If you must run an FTP server, make sure logging is enabled and, if possible, replace the Windows NT FTP service with a different FTP service that logs all access and can restrict connections based on the host address of the connecting user, such as the FTP server available from Ipswitch (www.ipswitch.com) or others.

- **Gopher**   Few people are using Gopher now, mainly because other technologies such as the World Wide Web have replaced it for information retrieval and display. While Gopher doesn't contain any specific risks, it listens for connections (on TCP and UDP port 70) and can provide access to crackers. Disable it unless you specifically need it.

- **WWW**   World Wide Web service may be useful or necessary to run your server, but be careful. A poorly configured Web server can provide unintended access. As with FTP, you should set up your Web server on a disk or volume that is dedicated only to Web services and doesn't contain any other information that could be compromised. Also, be sure not to set up the Web server on your boot volume (usually the C: drive), where a user bypassing the Web directories might gain access to other information, such as password files or the system Registry.

   Running the WWW server, if you don't need it, is an unnecessary security risk. Numerous security holes have been found and fixed in Microsoft's WWW server, and more will no doubt be discovered. If you must run it, however, be sure you update to the latest version so you can be sure that all currently known security holes have been patched.

- **NetBIOS over IP**   Windows file sharing runs over the NetBIOS protocol, which in turn is carried by NetBEUI (a Microsoft protocol that cannot be routed) or IP (the Internet standard protocol). If your server is accessible from outside your network, configure the protocol bindings (in the Network Control Panel) so that NetBIOS travels *only* over NetBEUI. If you must configure NetBIOS to operate over IP as well, configure your firewall to block TCP and UDP ports 137 through 139, which are the ports Windows listens to for a file or print serving connection.

To disable NetBIOS over IP, open the Network Control Panel, select the Bindings tab, and remove the NetBIOS binding from the TCP/IP stack.

- **Windows File Serving**   If Windows file serving (that is, the native Windows file sharing that operates over SMB or CIFS) is not required, such as when the server is specifically a Web or FTP server, you can not only disable the server itself using the Network Control Panel, but you can also disable NetBIOS altogether.

Setting Appropriate Access Levels

One of the strengths of Windows NT security is the NT file system, or NTFS.

The traditional format for disks in the MS-DOS/Windows 3.*x*/Windows 95 world has always been FAT (an acronym for File Allocation Table). There is no security built into FAT; if your operating system gives you access to a directory, you have access to all files in it. If you reboot from a startup disk that doesn't know who you are or which directories you should be able to see, you have access to all directories on the drive.

Windows 98 (and some releases of Windows 95) implements FAT-32, a more modern and efficient format, but still without any significant security features.

NTFS not only is a faster, more efficient file system than FAT, but it also provides file-, directory-, and application-level security. A user might place a document on an NTFS volume in a publicly shared directory that the world can see but, if the document itself is protected, nobody else will be able to see, open, or delete it.

Securing Access Methods

Windows NT supports some encrypted means of logging in for file sharing and other services, and these methods are usually sufficient to prevent the casual cracker from capturing user IDs and passwords from your network. Windows 2000 is expected to support additional methods of authentication, such as Kerberos, that are encrypted from beginning to end. (See Chapter 6, "About Authentication and Passwords," for more information on authentication.)

> **Note:** Using a packet sniffer, even an encrypted password can be captured off your local network. An encrypted password is harder to take advantage of than a clear-text password, but it can still be used. A cracker may be able to take the encrypted passwords and run a dictionary program against them to identify the weaker passwords, and in some cases he can send the encrypted password to certain services without even bothering to decrypt it first.
>
> Although encrypted authentication is much more secure than clear-text authentication, you may want to use better methods, such as one-time passwords, security tokens, or public-key encrypted authentication, that truly can't be broken in most cases.

Windows NT provides a great deal of control over user passwords, including the following capabilities, shown in Figure 8.2, when you choose Account from the Policies menu
in the User Manager for Domains utility.

- Password aging, which lets the password expire after a certain amount of time,
  such as when it is 14 days or 30 days old.

- Password length, allowing passwords to have a minimum length (such as 8 or 12
  characters).

- Password re-use. Windows NT can prevent the user from using the same password
  as the last *n* passwords. This forces the user to create a unique password each time
  the password changes.

- Minimum password age, which prevents a user from changing a password too often.

- Account lockouts. This is a powerful feature that can lock a user's account after a
  certain number of password attempts in a time period, such as more than five
  attempts in one minute or more than eight attempts in one day. Once the account
  is locked, you can have it remain locked until you (or another administrator)
  unlock it, or it can remain locked for an hour, a day, and so on.

FIGURE 8.2
*The Windows NT
Account Policy
dialog box.*

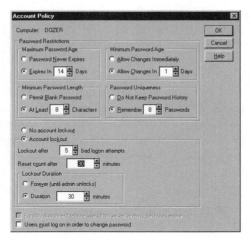

All these features help protect the key to a user's account. But what about crackers who
attempt to gain access in other ways?

Windows NT authentication is encrypted between the client and the server, so a casual
network packet sniffing attempt will not be able to identify a password from a regular
logon attempt.

As for other services on Windows NT

- FTP, as you know from other chapters, is insecure in its authentication method. If you
  are allowing anything other than anonymous FTP to your Windows NT server, you
  may want to replace it with another, more secure file transfer service. See "Enabling
  and Disabling Services," earlier in this chapter, for suggested replacements.

- Windows NT does not provide a Telnet service by default. If you implement a service that provides shell access to the NT server, be sure it's not using the simple Telnet protocol, which uses clear text authentication. Use a service that provides encrypted authentication, or something more robust, such as one-time passwords or security tokens for authentication.

- Web access. In addition to FTP and Gopher, Microsoft's IIS (Internet Information Server) also provides a powerful World Wide Web server. If you're providing Web access that requires any sensitive information to be entered, such as passwords, implement Secure Socket Layers (SSL) encryption.

  Also, make sure none of the sample applications and documentation included with IIS is installed on your server. Those files and sample applications are there for demonstration purposes and are not secured for active use. As such, they may provide a gap in your security.

Applying Updates and Patches

Given that Windows NT is a proprietary operating system, Microsoft is the only legitimate source of system updates and patches to close security holes. However, for information about security holes and vulnerabilities, there are several good sources:

- **Microsoft Security Notification Service**   This is an as-needed email distributed by Microsoft. It contains a description of known security holes and the fixes or workarounds that are available. For information on subscribing, see
  www.microsoft.com/security/services/bulletin.asp.

- **CERT Coordination Center (www.cert.org/)**   This site, hosted at Carnegie-Mellon University, provides a wealth of security information, but also includes a security advisory mailing list that provides warnings of vulnerabilities in most operating systems, including Windows NT. For information about the mailing list, see www.cert.org/contact_cert/certmaillist.html.

- **eEye Digital Security Team**   This security team discovers and publicizes security holes in many major operating systems, including Windows NT. See www.eEye.com/alerts.html for the latest information and vulnerabilities.

- **L0pht Heavy Industries**   Another security team dedicated to exposing vulnerabilities where they find them, including (and occasionally especially) in Windows NT. See www.l0pht.com/ for details.

These sites and others provide information on how people are cracking Windows NT servers and, if you're lucky, you'll find out before (or at least at the same time) as crackers so that you can close the holes before they are exploited.

For the latest Windows NT updates, see the Microsoft Web site.

Detecting Intrusion

Windows NT provides a number of powerful ways to detect intrusion that are already built into the operating system. In addition, you can add on utilities that provide even more information about who has been tampering, or trying to tamper with, your server.

Auditing and Logging

Windows NT provides a powerful logging utility called the Event Viewer. The Event Viewer keeps a continuous log of application-, system-, and security-related events that occur on the system for you to examine at any time.

To open the Event Viewer, choose Programs from the Start menu, then choose Administrative Tools from the menu that appears. In the Administrative Tools submenu, choose Event Viewer. Figure 8.3 shows the Event Viewer.

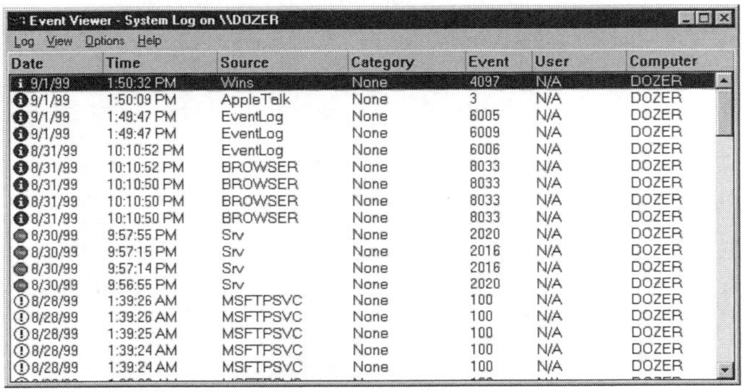

FIGURE 8.3

The Event Viewer Window, displaying system events.

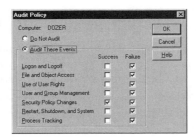

You can determine which events are logged to the Event Viewer using many of the administrative tools in Windows NT. For example, if you open the User Manager for Domains utility, you can choose Audit from the Policies menu to see a dialog box similar to that shown in Figure 8.4.

FIGURE 8.4

The Audit Policy dialog box.

The Audit Policy dialog box lets you specify which events are logged to the Security tab of the Event Viewer. You can specify the success, failure, or both of any of these events. (Note that recording successes for all but the most obscure of these events will quickly fill your event log with more information than you ever wanted. Select only the failures, except possibly for the Security Policy Changes events.)

Logging events can provide a way to identify some preliminary cracking attempts, such as when multiple logon failures occur in a short time period or when someone attempts to modify security policy settings but fails.

The Security log of the Event Viewer will be of the most interest to you in preventing or identifying crack attempts, although some security-related information is posted to the System or Application log. Be sure to save the logs to another location occasionally, such as a different server or workstation, or print them in order to have a complete record in case someone tries to tamper with the logs on your server.

> **Note:** If your server's volumes are formatted using Windows NT, you can set up auditing for each individual directory or file. This means that Windows NT can generate a log entry, for example, if any non-administrative user attempts to modify the WinNT directory, or the system Registry. I recommend that you audit your most sensitive files and directories to help identify and track cracking attempts.

IDS

As discussed in Chapter 10, "When You've Been Cracked," an intrusion detection system (IDS) can tell you a great deal about your network security, from the most tentative port scans of your servers to full-blown attempts to crack passwords or launch a Denial of Service attack.

Essentially, there are two basic kinds of IDS: host-based, which monitors the files and network activity on the server or other host system, and network-based, which works with your routers or firewall to identify suspicious network activity and stop it if possible.

Installing a host-based IDS on your Windows NT server can provide you with some early warning of an impending attack and can also help detect the signs of more subtle cracks, such as unauthorized modification of system files or changes to the user list or system Registry. Windows NT host-based IDSs include Security Dynamics' Kane Security Monitor (www.securitydynamics.com), AXENT's Intruder Alert (www.axent.com), and products from Internet Security Systems (www.iss.net).

Setting Up a Safe Access Control List Policy

Which files and directories a user has access to on a Windows NT system depends partly on how the server's volumes are formatted.

Which Drive Format to Use

Using FAT (File Allocation Table, common to DOS and earlier Windows operating systems) or FAT-32 (used in Windows 95 OSR2 and Windows 98) provides only directory- and volume-based access privileges. If a user has write or change access to a directory, the user has the same access to any file in that directory.

A volume formatted using NTFS (NT File System) provides much more security control than that. Under NTFS, each individual file can have its own unique level of security, just as on UNIX.

The dialog box in Figure 8.5 shows the Security tab that is added to a file or directory's Properties window under NTFS.

FIGURE 8.5
File Security options under NTFS.

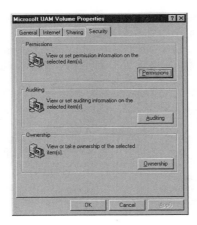

Using this tab, you can determine who owns the file, who can read, write, delete, execute, change permissions, or change ownership of the file, and (using the Auditing button) keep a log of any attempts to perform any actions at all with this file.

Given the overwhelming security benefits to using NTFS on your disks, there is no reason not to use it on any fixed volume on your server.

> **Note:** When an NTFS volume is shared over the network, any operating system with access to the server can use it. However, if you format a volume with NTFS and move it physically to another system (as you might with a Zip or Jazz volume or an external hard drive), you will not be able to use it when it is attached to a non-Windows NT system. Not even Windows 98 currently can read an NTFS volume directly. Format a volume as NTFS only if it will be used exclusively by Windows NT servers or workstations.

Setting Up Access Control Lists

Once you have determined which volume format to use, you can proceed to determine who has access to the files and directories on your server.

You can set up access control lists using the User Manager for Domains utility, which allows you to set up user IDs and the groups to which they belong.

As with UNIX systems, the group to which a user belongs determines most of the rights and privileges to the system. By default, Windows NT has an Administrators group, the members of which have full access to all features of the system, a Users group, which is the basic account for those who have access, a Guests account with minimal read access and very little write access, and other accounts of a similar nature.

To be safest, of course, users should have the least amount of access they need to a system, without being too restrictive.

> **User Account Tips:** The following tips for setting up users in Windows NT may make your system more resistant to cracking attempts:
>
> - Rename the Administrator account something else. Because it's the most powerful account on the system, it's an obvious target for password cracking attempts. Cracking an account is far easier if the cracker knows the account name. Because Administrator is a default name, crackers know it exists and therefore have half the information they need to gain access to the account (the other half being the password). Renaming the account eliminates even that slight advantage for the crackers.
>
>   Once you have renamed the true Administrator account to something else, you may want to create a new account named Administrator with no access privileges and log all attempts to connect to this account. This can provide some early warning of cracking attempts on your server.
>
> - Delete or rename the Guest account. Then try setting up a fake account named Guest and log all attempts to connect to it. This can provide some early warning of cracking attempts.

In Windows NT, the group to which a user belongs determines the following:

- Whether a user has read, write, execute, or delete access to a directory or the files in the directory.

- If the hard drive is formatted in NTFS, whether a user has read, write, execute, delete, change ownership, or change rights access to any individual file.

- Whether a user can perform certain system tasks, including creating and changing users and groups, assigning or modifying security for drives or directories, and so on.

There are a number of default groups that exist when you first set up a Windows NT server, and you can modify those and add more as needed. The default groups vary according to the installation (Windows NT Server standalone versus Windows NT Server as a domain controller), but the following groups are always created:

- **Administrators**   This group has complete power over the system, including all of the dangerous privileges: deleting or changing any file, modifying the system Registry, creating and changing anything to do with security, and so on. Very few users should belong to this group, but make sure there is more than one: yourself, and one or two trusted backup administrators, depending on the size of your organization.

- **Backup Operators**   This group is responsible for making backups of the system, and as such has access similar to the Administrators group for reading and moving files.

- **Power Users**   This group has a level of access that allows some administrative tasks, such as setting the system time, shutting down the system remotely over the network, and so on, as well as all the privileges that the Users group has.

- **Users**   The Users group can log on locally or access the computer over the network and use the system without having any access to system settings. This level (or possibly the Power Users level) should be the default group for those within your organization.

- **Replicator**   On a Windows NT domain controller, this group (like the Backup Operators group) has higher access for a specific purpose: to replicate directories across a Windows NT domain. Only users who need this particular ability should belong to this group.

- **Guest**   This designation provides limited access to the server, allowing only logon, logoff, and shutdown privileges.

- **Everyone**   This group encompasses all of the others, including Guest. Any privilege you assign to this group is also assigned to all of the other groups, because those groups are members of Everyone. For security reasons, you may not want to assign any privileges to this group, assigning privileges individually to specific groups instead. However, if you stay organized enough to know how a change here will trickle down to the rest of the groups, use this one as a shortcut for granting privileges you want everyone in the organization to have.

I recommend that a user belong to the minimum number of groups possible, and that you carefully monitor which groups belong to which other groups, so you can keep the access privileges straight.

To use an access control list to protect a file or directory

1. Right-click the directory you want to protect.

2. If the directory is accessible on an NTFS volume, click the Security tab, then click the Permissions button.

   A dialog box similar to the one in Figure 8.6 appears.

FIGURE 8.6
The NTFS Directory Permissions dialog box.

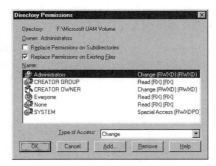

3. If the directory is on a FAT volume, click the Sharing tab, share the directory if necessary, then click the Permissions button.

   A dialog box similar to the one in Figure 8.7 appears.

FIGURE 8.7
*The Access
Through Share
Permissions
dialog box.*

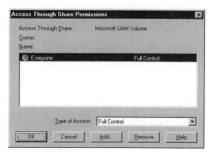

4. Specify which groups have access to the directory using the Add and Remove buttons.

5. Select a group and use the Type of Access drop-down list to specify how much access the group has to the directory.

   Depending on whether this is NTFS security or FAT sharing, you can specify whether the group can read, write, execute, delete, change permissions, or change ownership of the directory. NTFS gives you more of these options than FAT sharing.

6. Click OK to save your changes and close the dialog box.

> **Note:** In some cases, such as the `WinNT` (system) directory, you may need to provide read access for the group Everyone and then enter the directory to selectively override those settings by preventing even read-only access to some files and directories that you deem too sensitive, such as the `\system` and `\system32` directories.

Novell NetWare 5

Novell NetWare, which operated mainly over the IPX/SPX protocol in the past, now operates over TCP/IP by default (starting with NetWare 5), which greatly increases its functionality but also its security risks.

Fortunately, NetWare has been configured with extremely robust security, and most of the IP vulnerabilities result in Denial of Service attacks but very little actual cracked access. The security analysts reporting in so far seem to indicate that Novell NetWare 5 is one of the most secure network operating systems available, especially compared to Windows NT. Nonetheless, follow the instructions in this section to make sure your NetWare server is as secure as possible.

How NetWare Security Works

As with the other network operating systems discussed in this chapter, NetWare secures the server based on a combination of user rights and file system rights.

Once a user logs in, the NDS (Novell Directory Services) security rights determine which objects the user can see, use, or change. In addition, each file and directory has its own security settings to determine what the user can do with it.

NetWare also has some features that can provide digital signatures (called *NCP Packet Signatures*) to packets in a network connection. This offers stronger security and less likelihood of tampering, as well as features (such as user lockout after too many failures in a short time) to prevent some kinds of account cracking attempts.

NetWare provides the following basic security features:

- User ID– and password-based connections, with centralized NDS-based authentication
- Extensive user lists, including groups with inherited access privileges
- File- and directory-level security through a powerful access control list (ACL)
- Access rights that let you perform or not perform tasks based on the groups to which you belong

However, NetWare not only uses the user ID to determine if the user has access to the system, but it also determines on a file-by-file basis what the user can read, write, and execute.

When you create a new "user object," or user account, in NetWare, you specify the user's home directory (the directory the user "owns" by default), and you determine the groups to which the user belongs. The privileges you assign to a user determine which files the user can

- Read
- Write
- Create
- Erase
- Modify
- Change the access control of

Similar rights exist for directories as well. The user's setup and group memberships also determine the printers he can use.

Just as you can specify for any user which volumes, directories, and file structures the user can see and change, for any object on the system (file, directory, executable, and so on), you can specify exactly who is a "trustee," or valid user, of that object and whether to override any of the settings that are implied by that relationship.

For example, you might make user "Luis" a trustee of a particular file, with full access to see and change the file. Then, you can override Luis's ability to delete the file.

Novell NetWare 5 provides a great deal of control over the security of the entire system and very few unusual ways to compromise that security.

However, as with all systems, there are precautions you need to take to keep the system more secure from network intrusion. The following sections describe these precautions.

Making Your Systems More Secure

Many of the ways in which a NetWare server can be compromised require having physical access to the server. For this reason, and as is true with all network servers, you must make sure that the server is physically secure. The room or area in which the server resides must be lockable and monitored, and the server itself should be password protected in a way that can't be overridden easily, whether by cracking attempts or by booting the system from another volume, such as a floppy disk. Some computers even provide a way to place a locked barrier over the floppy and CD-ROM drives, so that you need an actual key even to insert a disk in the system.

NetWare provides a way to secure the server itself, by allowing you to load a security-related screen saver module (SCRSAVER.NLM) that blanks the screen and requires a username and password to display anything.

In addition to these physical precautions, take the steps described here to protect the server from compromise over the network.

Enabling and Disabling Services

Because NetWare is primarily a file and print server, albeit a very powerful and extended one, there usually aren't very many extraneous services running that you need to disable.

NetWare Loadable Modules (NLMs) are a powerful way to extend the capabilities of a NetWare server. NLMs are small pieces of executable code that are patched on to the existing server. Be careful not to load or run NLMs you don't need, or that provide remote access to any additional services on the server.

Note that although an NLM usually can only be installed and started from a console, which requires physical access to the server, the ConsoleOne utility and the REMOTE NLM provide a remote console (using either clear-text or encrypted passwords). Once the remote console is enabled, anyone on your network with the correct passwords can start a console and modify the configuration of the server. Disable remote consoles unless you absolutely need them.

Use the SECURE CONSOLE command at any console to prevent NLMs from being loaded from anywhere other than an approved path on the server; by default, SYS:SYSTEM is the only accepted path. See the NetWare documentation for complete instructions on using the SECURE CONSOLE command.

Securing Access Methods

As with all servers, one security risk depends on how securely users or administrators are connecting to the system. Insecure access methods or authentication methods can lead to compromised access.

Note: Unlike in Windows NT and UNIX systems, NetWare passwords aren't stored on disk, where they might be copied and cracked. NetWare passwords are stored in the Novell Directory Services (NDS) database, encrypted and protected, away from most prying eyes.

Fortunately, most of the services that can run on a NetWare server can be configured to accept encrypted passwords. The REMOTE NLM, which allows you to open a remote console directly on the server, can be started with the REMOTE ENCRYPT command, requiring an encrypted password for each connection.

The NetWare Web server (Netscape Fasttrack Server for NetWare) can provide administration access to the NetWare server, or it can provide standard Web services to an internal or external set of users. For either of these services, you can (and should) configure the Web server such that any connection that requires a login should encrypt the connection using Secure Socket Layers (SSL). You can also configure the access control to prevent the user's password from being saved to the user's browser cache for the next logon.

Note: Using a packet sniffer, even an encrypted password can be captured off your local network. An encrypted password is harder to capture than a clear-text password, but it can still be done. A cracker may be able to take encrypted passwords and run a dictionary program against them to identify the weaker passwords. In some cases he can send the encrypted password to certain services without even bothering to decrypt it first.

Although encrypted authentication is much more secure than clear-text authentication, you might want to use better methods that truly can't be broken in most cases, such as one-time passwords, security tokens, or public-key encrypted authentication.

Finally, note that the tools currently available to decrypt passwords in the NDS database take unimaginably long to crack a 12- to 16-character password and won't even try to crack an 18-character password. To be very safe, you may want to enforce a minimum-length password rule of 12 characters or higher on your users.

Peter's Principle: Signed Packets Can't Be Spoofed

NetWare provides an anti-spoofing, anti-packet-tampering technology that is intended to prevent packets from being hijacked over a network and subverted to purposes other than what the legitimate user intends. With this feature, called NCP Packet Signature or *packet signing*, the NetWare client and server agree on a 64-bit encryption key during the login process. For the duration of the connection, packets signed with that key are verified as coming from that client.

NCP Packet Signature is an optional feature and needs to be set on both the client and the server to work. There are four levels of NCP Packet Signature, and the levels must be compatible (that is, an allowable combination) between the client and server. The four levels are

- **0**   No packet signing.
- **1**   The server signs packets only if the workstation requests it.
- **2**   The server prefers packet signing but allows non-signing clients to connect.
- **3**   The server and client both must sign packets to allow a connection.

I recommend using at least level 2, to allow packet signing as often as possible without locking out any connections. However, if you require the most stringent levels of security, set the server and all clients to level 3 to prevent packets from being hijacked or spoofed.

Applying Updates and Patches

As with Windows NT, your main source of updates and patches to the NetWare operating system is the manufacturer, who in this case is Novell, Inc., at `www.novell.com`.

However, for information about security holes and vulnerabilities, there are several good sources:

- **Novell Security Mailing List**   This is an as-needed email distributed by Novell. It contains announcements of known security holes and the fixes or workarounds that are available, as well as other useful discussions of security issues. For information on subscribing, see `www.novell.com/corp/security/register.html`.

- **CERT Coordination Center (`www.cert.org`/)**   This site, hosted at Carnegie-Mellon University, provides a wealth of security information, but also includes a security advisory mailing list that provides warnings of vulnerabilities in most operating systems, including Novell NetWare. For information about the mailing list, see `www.cert.org/contact_cert/certmaillist.html`.

- **CIAC (Computer Incident Advisory Capability, `ciac.llnl.gov`/)**   This site, operated by the United States Department of Energy, contains security bulletins, virus and hoax warnings, and other information that can help you close holes before they're used against you.

- **eEye Digital Security Team**   This security team discovers and publicizes security holes in many major operating systems, including Novell NetWare. See `www.eEye.com/alerts.html` for the latest information and vulnerabilities.

- **L0pht Heavy Industries (`www.l0pht.com`/)**   Another security team dedicated to exposing vulnerabilities where they find them, including Novell NetWare.

These sites and others provide information on how people are cracking Novell NetWare servers, and if you're lucky, you'll find out before (or at least at the same time) as crackers so you can close the holes before they are exploited.

For the latest updates and software patches, see the Novell Web site.

Detecting Intrusion

As with other network operating systems, there are two strong ways to detect when a cracker has attained any kind of access to your server: log files that will show attempts to connect, whether successful or not, and intrusion detection systems (IDSs) that detect the changes that crackers make to your system and warn you to fix them before more damage is done.

Log Files and Auditing

NetWare provides a number of utilities to log activity throughout the server, from performance statistics to every console message that appears. These logs can be powerful tools for detecting intrusion attempts or intrusions that were successful.

For example, you can configure your system so that any message printed to the console, whether the physical console on the server or a remote console, is written to the CONSOLE.LOG file. Given that a cracker would likely have to gain access to the console at some time to gain useful access to the server, a record of his attempts and actions should appear in the CONSOLE.LOG file.

You can use the CONLOG NLM to manage these log files and copy them occasionally to other, more secure disks so that they won't be tampered with if the cracker is successful.

You also can set up auditing, a powerful tool implemented using the AUDITCON NLM, which lets you record information about how NDS, the file system, and volume events (down to the individual access of each file) are performing. Using audit logs, you can identify when sensitive files or directories are being opened, copied, or otherwise compromised, and you can take appropriate action or simply watch to see what happens. See the NetWare documentation for instructions on using the AUDITCON NLM.

IDS

As discussed in Chapter 10, "When You've Been Cracked," an intrusion detection system (IDS) can tell you a great deal about your network security, from the most tentative port scans of your servers to full-blown attempts to crack passwords or launch a Denial of Service attack.

Essentially, there are two basic kinds of IDS: host-based, which monitors the files and network activity on the server or other host system, and network-based, which works with your routers or firewall to identify suspicious network activity and stop it if possible.

> **Terminology Alert:** Novell's NetWare 5 documentation refers to one of
> NetWare's features as "Intrusion Detection." In fact, the feature they're talking
> about is only a small part of intrusion detection as the term is used in the com-
> puter industry.
>
> Novell's "intrusion detection" refers to a feature that locks a user's account
> after a certain number of failed login attempts. When the failed attempts are
> logged, the NetWare server records the network address (IPX or IP) from which
> the login attempt occurred.
>
> This is a useful and necessary feature for detecting intrusions into your network
> operating system, but it goes only part of the way. A true intrusion detection
> system would also indicate whether any key files were tampered with (indicat-
> ing a true intrusion, rather than simply an attempt) or other similar results,
> rather than simply one kind of attempt.
>
> Be sure to install a more feature-rich intrusion detection product on your
> servers rather than relying solely on that of NetWare 5.

The network-based intrusion detection systems are important to have, but to protect a
server specifically you need to install a host-based system.

Host-based intrusion detection systems that are compatible with NetWare are not as common as are those for other networking platforms, but there are several options, including

- Kane Security Monitor from Security Dynamics (`www.securitydynamics.com`)
- AXENT's Intruder Alert (`www.axent.com`)

UNIX Operating Systems

UNIX has been around seemingly forever and pioneered most of the networking features
that exist today. It's also the only open networking OS standard, and it has had input
from thousands of developers over the decades to make it the most complex and powerful operating system available, with the most security features—and needs—of all.

UNIX-like operating systems, for the purposes of this section of this book, include any
of the following:

- Linux
- FreeBSD
- NetBSD
- SunOS and Solaris from Sun Microsystems
- HP-UX from Hewlett-Packard
- Irix from Silicon Graphics
- AIX from IBM
- MacOS X Server from Apple Computer

This list is by no means exhaustive and, for some UNIX purists, may not be wholly accurate. For example, MacOS X Server is built on a UNIX foundation (specifically, BSD) but may no longer be UNIX-like enough for some people. However, for the purposes of security, it belongs on this list, because MacOS X server supports file and directory permissions the same way BSD systems do, as well as other aspects of networking security.

> **Note:** For brevity's sake, I'll refer to the entire class of UNIX-like operating systems as UNIX in this section.

Your Main Security Concerns

Because UNIX has security built in from top to bottom, you might think you don't need to worry about security as much as with other operating systems. This is partly true; most versions of UNIX are completely open systems based on open standards, which means that anybody can view the source code (the instructions that create the operating system) and examine it for weaknesses, vulnerabilities, and design flaws.

Don't be alarmed by this openness, however; an open system is generally considered a strength, not a weakness. An open standard does reveal everything to any interested party, including potential crackers, but it also allows a much wider variety of people besides the original developers to see how the system works, to identify flaws, and to develop better, more secure ways of doing things.

Peter's Principle: The Value of Open Standards

One of the common UNIX security tools is TCP Wrapper. TCP Wrapper is a low-level network logging package written by Wietse Venema, the same developer who wrote SATAN (one of the early security scanners).

Typically, when a client requests a connection on a UNIX server (such as Telnet, FTP, and so on), a daemon such as inet.d handles the request, running the appropriate server for which the client is asking.

With TCP Wrapper installed, the daemon runs the wrapper program instead of the requested server. The wrapper identifies and creates a log entry of the client's source (the host address) and some other information. This gives you a running log of all client attempts to connect to a service. Optionally, TCP Wrapper can use that client information to allow or deny access to the requested server, providing a basic form of access control.

TCP Wrapper exists because the various flavors of UNIX are based on open standards, allowing people to place a tool that enhances security into the existing system. With a proprietary system, such as Microsoft Windows NT, adding security tools can be much harder.

> Not only that, but TCP Wrapper is itself an open standard. It is released as source code, so you can see exactly what the software does once compiled and installed on your server. If you see a flaw or a needed enhancement, you can make changes to your copy. Not only that, each release of TCP Wrapper (as with many packages) is packaged with a PGP signature file that can be used to guarantee that the source code has not been tampered with after its release.

In the Peter's Principle "Life Cycle of a Security Hole," earlier in this chapter, I discussed how a security flaw is discovered, and how it gets fixed. For the most part, the UNIX community responds more quickly than the manufacturers of the other operating systems to news of security flaws. However, that is changing, as more companies realize the need for quick, responsive action when a flaw is publicized.

How UNIX Security Works

UNIX security is file based, with access privileges granted by the permissions assigned to each file using a complex and powerful set of authentication tools. This may remind you of Windows NT and Windows 2000 file security; that's because Windows NT and 2000 file security is based on the UNIX model.

The file security settings can provide the capability to read a file (or directory), to write to a file (or directory), or to execute a file (or files in a directory).

A user gains these privileges for a file by being the file's owner, a member of a group with privileges to that file, or everybody else, if the world has access to the file.

The system for setting the privileges (using the chmod command line utility or any number of tools in a graphical user interface) is beyond the scope of this chapter. However, the concepts for securing a UNIX file system involve

- Setting file permissions for all files, or setting the *file security*.
- Setting up users and groups with the correct access rights, or setting the *account security*.
- Implementing a secure authentication method to help prevent unauthorized users from gaining access to the existing accounts and staying ahead of bugs and security flaws in the system will help avoid cracks in your system. This provides *networking security*.

All these ways to strengthen security for UNIX servers are described here.

> **Note:** Don't forget to implement good *real world security*, or physical security, as well. Make sure you keep servers in private locations to which few people have access. While most of the methods of securing a UNIX server apply for network use as well as physical access, there are ways to crack a server that are much easier with physical access to the system.

Making Your Systems More Secure

As an open technology, UNIX has been modified, strengthened, and updated constantly over the years to the point where virtually any security technology is available for most flavors of UNIX. If a specific security technology isn't available for your particular platform, contact the developers to see if it can be compiled for your system, and look around for similar products that will work for you.

Follow the steps below to keep your UNIX server secure.

Enabling and Disabling Services

Throughout this book, I've been discussing the importance of enabling only the services you need on a server. This chapter in particular should make that point very strongly; all of the steps described here are multiplied by each network service you are running.

This means that, if you enable Telnet access on your system, you have to keep track of the version of Telnet daemon you're using to make sure all known security holes are closed. You have to set up who has access to the Telnet service and make sure those users have only the access they need. You need to make sure they're connecting with Telnet as securely as possible (through a VPN or ssh tunnel, for example). Finally, you need to check your Telnet logs regularly to make sure no unauthorized access has occurred and that no crack attempts have been made.

If you enable FTP access, you have to do it all over again, regularly.

The other reason to disable unnecessary services may be more obvious: If Telnet isn't running, crackers can't break into your system via Telnet. (This assumes that they can't enable Telnet through some other security hole, but that's still an additional major step to make them take.)

Here are some services you may want to disable that are part of most standard UNIX distributions, found in the `inetd.conf` file:

- **FTP (File Transfer Protocol) server**   If you don't need to transfer files using this protocol, disable it. Given that FTP is not particularly secure, replace it with something that is, such as ssh-based file transfers or SSL-enabled FTP.

- **Telnet**   If you don't need shell access to the system, disable it. If you do need shell access, replace it with something more secure, such as ssh- or SSL-enabled Telnet.

- **Echo**   This is a service mainly used for testing; anything you type to it is echoed back. Disable it unless you need to do that kind of testing.

- **Discard**   Again, this is generally used only for testing and debugging. Anything handed to the discard service disappears, as if you wrote it to `/dev/null`. Turn it off if you don't need it.

- **Chargen**   Kind of like Discard, except that it forwards or returns some predefined or random data. Used only for testing; disable it if not needed.

- **Date and Time**   Provide the current date and time in user-readable and machine-readable form, respectively. Disable them, unless they're needed.

- **R-Utilities: shell (rshd), exec (rexecd) and login (rlogind)**   The remote shell, remote execute, and remote login daemons provide access to the system using the concept of trusted hosts, which determines the user's access based on information such as the host address from which the user is connecting, the port on which the connection is coming in, and other information. Many security organizations recommend against using the R-utilities because the trusted relationship can be compromised in too many ways, but there may be solutions to make them more robust. If you don't need these services, or if you implement a more secure service such as ssh, disable these options.

- **talkd, ntalkd, dtalkd**   These services provide communication between UNIX systems in a real-time chat mode. This isn't particularly useful but, aside from some possible talk flooding and some Denial of Service attacks, it's not a major security risk. Nonetheless, there may be undiscovered weaknesses so, if you don't need to use these services, disable them.

- **Finger, systat, and netstat**   These services provide information to a remote host, such as information about who is logged in, which network connections are running, and so on. RedHat (one of the Linux vendors) has this to say about these services: "Finger, systat, and netstat give out user information which may be valuable to potential 'system crackers.' Many sites choose to disable some or all of these services to improve security." That should be sufficient warning for you to disable them, if you don't need them.

- **pop-2, pop-3, imap**   These are email servers, which you may or may not need. If you find that you need to use them, be aware that vulnerable versions of these tools have been released over the years with security holes that could provide root access and other dangers to your server. Be sure you have the latest versions of these daemons before enabling them and, as with all of these tools, stay aware of patches and new releases.

- **tFTPd**   Provides trivial File Transfer Protocol service that is usually needed only if the server is a boot server.

- **uucp UNIX-to-UNIX Copy Protocol**   Not needed by many modern applications, and therefore a good candidate for disabling.

There may well be others in your `inetd.conf` file or other configuration files that launch services. The rule is to disable unnecessary services, make sure the ones you are running are configured properly, and have the latest versions or patches installed.

Setting Appropriate Access Levels

Although being cautious in setting file and directory access levels may seem obvious, it can protect vital parts of your system from tampering. The default settings in most UNIX systems are to prevent access, rather than grant it, to any new user, but you need to plan your access levels carefully before setting up your user IDs and the groups to which they belong.

UNIX files are set up to provide different levels of access to their owners, the users in a specific group or groups, or the world (all users of the system). You can use any text editor to set up users, but most graphical UNIX interfaces provide tools to manage user and group lists.

These rules may help attain the safest access levels on your server:

- **Delete old or inactive accounts, and use account expiration dates**   Keep the user list as small as possible, and remove users from the list as soon as they should no longer have access to the system. If accounts periodically expire, this also can help eliminate unused accounts.

- **Keep superuser access to a minimum**   Don't provide any more access privileges to any user than is absolutely necessary.

- **Rename or delete well-known accounts**   For example, "FTP" is a standard user set up for the FTP service to use. Rename it to something less common to help prevent cracking attempts from using that account.

- **Prevent accounts from being used if there's no need to let users log in**   If an account is used only internally to the server, prevent anyone from using the account in whatever way you can. For example, on many flavors of UNIX, setting an account's password to an asterisk (*) assigns a null password, preventing log in. As another example, you can set a user's default shell to /bin/false, or similar non-shell, to prevent any shell login for that user.

- **Set restrictive default file privileges**   For example, on most systems you can use the umask utility to determine the file permissions that new files will receive. If the default is the octal 777, which is world readable, writable, and executable, that can be dangerous. You can include the umask command in each user's .login or other startup file to set a restrictive file permission default whenever the user logs in.

- **Set up password aging**   This feature require users to change their passwords at regular intervals (if you are not using one-time passwords, security tokens such as SecurID, or other authentication methods). Also, be sure to implement other password-strengthening measures, such as minimum-length passwords, a password generator, and user education.

- **Enforce a strong password policy**   In addition to requiring passwords of a certain length, you may want to run a password cracker periodically to verify that all users are using robust, hard-to-guess passwords. Password crackers (such as *crack*) have long been used by system administrators to identify users with weak or obvious passwords. At their simplest, password crackers use the dictionary and brute force methods to decode the /etc/passwd file. If the tools succeed, stronger passwords are needed.

  As another password-cracking precaution, you can implement *shadow passwords* on most variations of UNIX. Shadow passwords remove the passwords from the standard /etc/passwd file and place them into a more-restricted file (/etc/shadow) that is readable only by root. This allows any utility to read the /etc/passwd file for information such as the user's account ID but protects the password field, which is more valuable to potential crackers.

Finally, look into implementing stronger authentication methods than the built-in password system. For example, Linux supports Pluggable Authentication Modules (PAM) which make it easy to add on strong authentication methods, such as S/KEY, Kerberos, and so on. See Chapter 6 for more information on strong authentication methods.

- **Create a careful hierarchy of groups**   When you grant access to one group, all groups that are members of it gain the same access. Map out each group in your system and who belongs to which group, and know all of the ramifications of a change before you implement it.

These precautions should help provide reasonable access to all users of your UNIX server.

Securing Access Methods

Use encrypted logins wherever possible to avoid the use of packet sniffers. The more robust services you're using, the more likely a truly secure connection is.

Avoid using an .rhosts file. The .rhosts file is a way to specify that a user can connect to a service without authentication if that user is connecting from a known host. However, as convenient as that may be for users connecting frequently from the same host address, IP addresses can be spoofed, which makes this authentication method unsafe. Not only should you avoid setting up an .rhosts file on the server, but users should also be prevented from setting up an .rhosts file in their personal directories.

> **Note:** Even an encrypted password can be captured off your local network using a packet sniffer. An encrypted password is harder to take advantage of than a clear-text password, but it can still be used. A cracker may be able to take the encrypted passwords and run a dictionary program against them to identify the weaker passwords, and in some cases he can send the encrypted password to certain services without even bothering to decrypt it first.
>
> Although encrypted authentication is much more secure than clear-text authentication, you may want to use better methods that can't be broken in most cases, such as one-time passwords, security tokens, or public-key encrypted authentication.

Always look into the possibility of implementing any of these more-secure authentication methods, including Kerberos or one-time password systems such as S/Key. With a one-time password system, an attempt to log in is met with a challenge from the host; the challenge consists of a value that the host has calculated using a secret key. The user must then run the challenge through a calculation to find the proper response to the challenge.

Applying Updates and Patches

One of the most important tasks you can follow to keep your UNIX systems secure is to keep up to date on system updates and patches. The UNIX community in particular is very security conscious and quick to respond once a threat is identified.

- **Your UNIX Developer's Web site**   Don't underestimate the main site for your version of UNIX, whether it's www.sun.com or www.linux.org. The developers of your particular UNIX package are most likely to be the first to hear about a new vulnerability or security hole, and they'll also be a central point for distributing a fix, regardless of who develops it. Check there first, and if they offer a security mailing list, subscribe now.

- **CERT Coordination Center (www.cert.org/)**   This site, hosted at Carnegie-Mellon University, provides a wealth of security information, but also includes a security advisory mailing list that provides warnings of vulnerabilities in most operating systems, including UNIX. For information about the mailing list, see www.cert.org/contact_cert/certmaillist.html.

- **CIAC (Computer Incident Advisory Capability, ciac.llnl.gov/)**   This site, operated by the United States Department of Energy, contains security bulletins, virus and hoax warnings, and other information that can help you close holes before they're used against you.

- **eEye Digital Security Team**   This security team discovers and publicizes security holes in many major operating systems, including UNIX. See www.eEye.com/alerts.html for the latest information and vulnerabilities.

- **L0pht Heavy Industries (www.l0pht.com/)**   Another security team dedicated to exposing vulnerabilities where they find them, including (and occasionally especially) in UNIX.

Detecting Intrusion

To detect when someone has tried to crack your system is useful, especially if it helps you prevent any damage from being done, but you also need to be able to detect when the cracker has actually done some damage. This section describes both areas of detecting intrusions.

> **Note:** For more information on detecting intrusions and how to handle them, see Chapter 10.

Logging Activity

UNIX systems are full of activity logs, and these can be a valuable source of information when you're trying to prevent a crack. On most systems, the default location for log files of all shapes and sizes is /var/log.

The following shows a sample /var/log directory on a Linux system:

```
boot.log   htmlaccess.log    maillog.2    netconf.log.1  spooler    wtmp.1
cron       htmlaccess.log.1  messages     samba          spooler.1  xferlog
cron.1     httpd             messages.1   secure         spooler.2
cron.2     maillog           messages.2   secure.1       squid
dmesg      maillog.1         netconf.log  secure.2       wtmp
```

The files without any extension or with the .log extension are the most recent log files;
at regular intervals, a log file is closed and renamed with a numbered extension (the .1
and .2 files in this example), and a new log file is started.

Note that if a service you're interested in doesn't store its log file in /var/log, check the
documentation for that service to see how to enable the log or where the log is stored by
default.

The log files can provide valuable information about attempted cracks. For example, the
following section of the /var/log/messages file was created by a fairly unsophisticated
port scanning utility that attempted to see which ports the server was listening to by
opening connections to them, one by one:

```
Aug 13 13:50:32 10 proFTPd[1116]: FTP session closed.
Aug 13 14:06:43 10 sshd[991]: log: Closing connection to 10.19.0.6
Aug 13 14:07:06 10 proFTPd[1141]: FTP session closed.
Aug 13 14:07:07 10 sshd[1142]: connect from 10.19.0.6
Aug 13 14:07:07 10 sshd[1142]: log: Connection from 10.19.0.6 port 3048
Aug 13 14:07:07 10 sshd[1142]: log: Could not reverse map address 10.19.0.6.
Aug 13 14:07:07 10 sshd[1142]: fatal: Did not receive ident string.
Aug 13 14:07:08 10 Telnetd[1144]: ttloop:  peer died: Invalid or incomplete
multibyte or wide character
```

This series of failed connections, appearing so closely together in time, can indicate a
port scan (and indeed would have set off an intrusion detecting system). It's especially
noticeable if you know that the services showing these errors are listening to ports that
are in order, as indicated by a quick glance at the /etc/services file: ports 21, 22, 23,
25, 53, and so on.

Other telltale signs to look for are numerous failed login attempts and connections from a
host you don't know about or don't recognize.

> **Tip:** If your system does not have the TCP Wrapper installed, add it immediately.
> The primary function of the TCP Wrapper is to log connections to your system,
> even if the service in question isn't logging itself. See the beginning of the UNIX
> section of this chapter for a more detailed description of the TCP Wrapper.

If an attack does actually occur, the log files may be your only evidence of how the
cracker gained entry so that you can close the hole. Also, most services record the host
address making the connection to the service and, while that address is almost certainly
spoofed or otherwise misleading in the event of an attack, it can provide a trail that you
can follow in tracking down the true attacker's host system.

> **Tip:** Logs are not foolproof; a cracker who is thinking ahead will tamper with the log files after successfully tampering with your server to hide the evidence of the attack. To be safe, make sure the log files are written to a different, secured system, or that they are periodically copied over to another location (setting up a `crontab` job is a good way to automate this process).
>
> Another way to be more certain that the logs aren't tampered with is to have the important messages printed automatically to a secure location, so that a hard copy exists, in addition to the electronic copy.

Intrusion Detection Systems

As discussed in Chapter 10, an intrusion detection system (IDS) can tell you a great deal about your network security, from the most tentative port scans of your servers to full-blown attempts to crack passwords or launch a Denial of Service attack.

Essentially, there are two basic kinds of IDS: host-based, which monitors the files and network activity on the server or other host system, and network-based, which works with your routers or firewall to identify suspicious network activity and stop it if possible.

One of the powerful features of a host-based IDS, such as Tripwire, is scanning the files on a host and creating a signature, or checksum, to reflect their current state. When security-related files are changed, the IDS notices that the stored "signature" doesn't match the files' current state and notifies you. Reinstalling the affected files or restoring from a backup is usually your best option, although if the attack appears to be widespread, you may need to wipe the system and start over.

> **Note:** Before deleting or replacing files that have been tampered with, be sure to make a backup of the system that has been attacked. The modified files can sometimes provide valuable clues to help track down the attacker.

Only by staying vigilant and identifying when you might be attacked can you prevent the attack. Only by examining the results of an attack can you be sure of closing the holes to prevent it from happening again. Logs and IDSs are valuable tools in this fight.

Summary

Although no server can be made completely secure, any server can be made *more* secure. The practices recommended here can be summarized as follows:

- Disabling unneeded services

- Implementing good user access levels

- Replacing services or installing new services based on secure, encrypted authentication and communication standards instead of relying on clear text

- Applying updates and patches based on the recommendations of the operating system manufacturer and security organizations

- Installing a solid intrusion detection system on your servers

Once you have implemented the steps described here for your servers, you can be more confident that you not only don't appear as an easy target, but you actually have placed some serious obstacles between crackers and your servers.

Security on the Desktop

To maintain security within your organization (and with those outside of your organization who are legitimately connecting to the inside), you need to make sure the user's system is set up using the same secure configuration and products as any of the servers, routers, firewalls, and other devices on your network.

Here are a few examples of why the user's computer must follow the same rigorous security rules as any other device on your network:

- **Passwords for Workstation Access**   Windows can be configured to require a password to log on at startup, but this feature isn't useful if, as in many offices I've visited, users leave the password blank and don't follow the same password conventions here as everywhere else on your network.

- **Password Caching**   Dial-Up Networking, which gives the user remote dial-in access to your network (if you have a dial-in server running), can save passwords so that whoever has the laptop can connect to your network.

- **File, Web, and Data Sharing**   Many workstations can also share data, making them limited servers. As such, they can be taken over and used as the launching point for attacks on your network's other services.

> **Note:** Many of the Web servers in use today support some powerful extra features that allow them to execute code that they find on Web pages, including Microsoft's ActiveX controls and embedded JavaScript. Although these features are configured in the Web browser to provide some safety, numerous security holes have been found in both that can give crackers control over elements of the users' computers.
>
> If you enable embedded scripts or ActiveX in your users' Web browsers, be sure to monitor the Web sites for the browser's manufacturer as well as the security agencies mentioned in Appendix A of this book for information about security holes that are discovered and any patches that become available.
>
> Another solution is to simply disable ActiveX and JavaScript in all browsers on your network. This can disable some useful features and render some sites unusable, so the decision to disable these features must depend on how your users work and the sites they visit, as well as the security of your network.

- **Email Attachments**   Users may accept attachments from people they don't know or files they didn't expect from people they do know. Some macro viruses (such as the infamous Melissa virus) can use the address book of a trusted colleague to send copies of the viruses as attachments to friends, who are therefore not suspicious and execute the attached file. A cracker might also attach a disguised trojan horse, such as the remote control package Back Orifice, to take over the user's workstation.

  Unless you install antivirus and trojan horse software on your mail servers to scan incoming messages and install additional packages on each user's workstation for the same purpose, your network is at risk from these attacks.

These risks are not meant to scare you into locking down every workstation in your company and allowing only word processing and spreadsheet software to run. The networking services built into most operating systems are useful and productive features.

Your goal after reading this chapter should be to help users control who has access to their computers, both in and (especially) out of the office.

The section at the end of this chapter, "Overall Recommendations," describes some general precautions to take, but work with your users to determine which precautions will still allow them to accomplish their tasks efficiently and with a minimum of difficulty. If you don't, they may find ways around your precautions and put the entire network at risks you *don't* know about.

Concerns About Any User's Workstation

With most modern operating systems, features such as peer-to-peer file sharing and personal Web and FTP servers have made the line between workstations and servers a matter of capacity, rather than features. The main difference between an AppleShare server and a MacOS workstation running File Sharing is that the AppleShare server can handle more than 10 connections at a time.

For this reason, user workstations carry as much of a security risk as the servers on your network and, because their systems are listening for connections in the first place, they can become a launching point for attacks on the rest of your network.

Take this example: Suppose you run your entire Windows network using the nonroutable NetBEUI protocol. Because NetBEUI can't be routed to your external Internet connection (and you're careful not to configure Windows networking to run over IP), you figure you're not at much risk of attack from the Internet. Users can connect to the Web, but since you're not running any servers or programs that listen for incoming connections, you're not at risk, right? Wrong. That hotshot new guy over in Marketing just enabled the Personal Web Sharing services on his Windows computer and he's now running his own little Web server.

The first outsider to crack the Web server on your network now has control of a machine that is already running NetBEUI, just like all of the other computers on your network. The Marketing guy's computer is now the launching point for all kinds of attacks you weren't expecting. For example, the cracker might connect to the Marketing guy's Personal Web Sharing server and upload a copy of a remote-control package, such as Back Orifice. The cracker, controlling the Marketing guy's computer, might then log on to other systems on your network and install utilities that collect passwords as they're entered and email them back to the cracker, compromising not only your network but every network to which your users connect, and so the crack would continue to grow.

Even if you don't have users who enable Web servers on their systems, your users may accept malicious attachments in email messages without realizing it, and the same level of compromise occurs.

What should you do? First of all, don't expect that the configuration of the computers on your network eliminates the need for a firewall, packet filter, authenticating router, or other protective services described elsewhere in this book. Also, after you read this chapter, educate your users on how to avoid putting their systems at risk to others inside your network as well as attackers from outside.

> **Note:** Remember, a firewall keeps only *outside* people from attacking. Take precautions against insider mischief as well. While you're watching the firewall for intrusion, your users may be downloading your organization's financial data to take home, or that contractor you hired may be setting up backdoor passwords to exploit once the contract is done. Don't think that people inside your network can automatically be trusted, and take precautions against *all* cracking.

Users should know not to activate *any* servers or sharing on their systems without answering the following questions first:

- How do I limit the information I'm sharing?

  Sharing a folder isn't the same as sharing a whole computer or hard drive. Make that point as clear to your users as possible.

- How do I control who can read or change this information?

  Those controls can mean the difference between coming in to the office with the information missing or corrupted.

- How do I know who's been reading or changing this information?

  If there's no way to know, the user should share only data she doesn't care about.

- If I leave myself a back door, can anyone else find it?

  The answer, of course, is yes. Assume that any back door will be discovered, because it probably will. Users shouldn't leave themselves any more access than anyone else, even if that means disabling special "owner" access to the system. The next few sections describe some of the glaring security risks provided by user workstations, followed by sections on the major holes in each of the leading operating systems.

Sharing Too Much

One of the big risks created by file sharing becomes apparent when the user shares more than the necessary areas of his system. Usually, this involves sharing an entire volume (such as the entire startup drive) when only a single directory (say, the Budget directory in the Documents directory) is all that the other users need to see.

Whether the user provides read-only or read-write access is secondary to the risk of sharing private data with the entire organization. If the wrong people have access to C:\Documents\Salaries or the Departmental Reviews folder, more than simply your organization's security policy will need updating—perhaps your résumé will as well.

The security risk here is mainly internal to your network, rather than external. Your firewall should certainly be configured to keep out traffic that could carry file sharing connections (TCP and UDP ports 137 through 139 for Windows networking and TCP port 548 for AppleShare IP, for example) and, depending on the protocol you're using for personal file sharing, these connections may not even be routable outside of your network. (This is described more fully in the "Windows Networking over NetBEUI or IP" and "AppleShare over AppleTalk or IP" sections, later in this chapter.)

The solution to this problem is to make sure users have thorough instructions on how to share files and folders and how to provide others with the minimum access possible, so they don't attempt to figure it out themselves and possibly throw the door to their systems wide open.

Some vital file-sharing rules to follow:

- **Never, ever, ever share your operating system main directory**   This directory is set up by default on a Mac OS computer to the System Folder on the hard drive's root level, C:\Windows for Windows 95/98, C:\WinNT for Windows NT Workstation, and a number of areas on a UNIX-like operating system, most notably /etc for information such as password files and vital configuration information. Access to some files in the OS directory can lead to added control of the rest of the computer's drives.

- **Set up a special shared directory instead of sharing any working directory** Rather than sharing the C:\Documents directory, create a directory called C:\DropOff, provide full read-write access to everyone, and make sure that the only files it ever contains are those being exchanged with others.

As with other security holes, the less access the user provides, the less access there is to compromise.

Web and FTP Services

All of the operating systems in this chapter provide some kind of built-in Web server, either installed by default or available on the operating system's installation disk. The Web and FTP server is usually not enabled by default, but it's there for the user to activate with a simple click or command.

Both of these services communicate using IP, which as you know by now is the standard protocol on which the Internet is based. That opens each user's system up to the kinds of cracking attempts that Web servers and FTP servers are always prone to, including

- **Password sniffing** FTP servers generally do not encrypt their authentication process, so usernames and passwords can be captured by anyone on the same network with a packet sniffer.

- **Denial of Service attacks** Any system that is listening for connections over IP is subject to a Denial of Service attack, from connection flooding, bad packets or packet sizes, and other attacks that can lock up networking services on the user's system or crash the system altogether.

- **Buffer overflows** If a user installs any kind of script on her workstation's Web pages, a cracker could launch a buffer overflow attack that could load malicious code into the computer's memory and provide any kind of privileged access to the computer. Once compromised, the user's computer could become a launching point for other attacks on your network.

- **Unintended file access** A Web server or FTP server that's configured incorrectly can provide free rein over the user's hard drive, sharing data the user never meant to share.

Other, More Exciting Services

Operating systems are constantly being upgraded to include more and more interesting, useful, and potentially risky ways of connecting over a network. While this book doesn't cover them all, the sections below should help you become aware of the services your users *may* enable on their systems and what risk enabling each service creates.

For example, Apple has supported remote program linking since System 7 was released, and this service is expected to support connections over IP (in addition to the current AppleTalk connection) when Mac OS 9 is released. Program linking allows any authorized computer on the network to control applications running on the user's computer, supporting actions such as Quit, Print, Open, and Close, as well as many options that are more sophisticated.

This is a very powerful feature, allowing remote commands to be sent to an application, but of course this feature can be dangerous, too.

Don't panic, but do be aware that the more services a user's computer is listening for, the more doors there are open on that computer for attackers to use. Encourage your users to remove (not just close) all of the doors possible and to strengthen the locks on the doors.

Finally, be sure to scan incoming files that a user may download or receive in email messages that may be trojan horses. You can place a scanning program that can monitor all files received on your email server, if you provide one, and on each user's workstation to be sure they don't contain any *known* attacks. Of course, your users should be on guard against unexpected attachments or suspicious files to protect your network from *unknown* attacks as well.

Windows 95/98/NT Workstation

Windows 95 and 98 have networking services built in that provide access to file servers and printers, as well as peer-to-peer file sharing, so that users can exchange files with each other without any intervening system. Windows 95 and later and Windows NT support encrypted authentication, so passwords are unlikely to be seen by a cracker monitoring your internal network.

Also note that, beginning with Windows 95 Service Pack 1 and Windows NT Service Pack 3, encrypted passwords are required for logging on. Prior to these updates, connecting to older SMB (Server Message Block protocol, which is how Windows networking clients communicate) clients or servers could allow passwords to be sent in clear text, which could have been captured easily by someone on your internal network running a packet sniffer.

> **Note:** Windows NT Workstation users have the full weight of Windows NT security behind them. When they share files or folders for their peers to read or change, they have file-by-file, directory-by-directory access control (using NT's ACL [access control list] security). This provides much finer control over who can read or change files and directories and is too detailed to discuss in this chapter. Windows NT also supports third-party authentication, supporting such secure authentication standards as smart cards, tokens, and biometrics. See Chapter 8, "Security Overview for the Major Network Operating Systems," for details on how this works.

How Users Connect to Services

In a typical office with computers running various versions of Microsoft Windows, the Network Control Panel of each computer is configured with the protocols necessary to run the services you are using on your network. This can include

- NetBEUI, primarily used to carry Windows networking services such as Windows NT file and print servers, peer-to-peer file sharing, and so on.
- IPX/SPX, for Novell NetWare file and print servers, as well as other related networking services.
- TCP/IP, for virtually any networking services but certainly including Internet services (Web browsing, file transfers, email, and so on).
- Dial-Up Networking, which can carry all of these protocols over a remote connection that can include modem, ISDN, or VPN services.

Other networking services are available, but these are our primary concern right now.

> **Peter's Principle:** Fewer Protocols Means Greater Security
>
> Part of setting up a secure network is configuring as few protocols on users' computers as possible. Each protocol you enable on your network carries with it security vulnerabilities. Given that it takes time to secure your network and keep up with updates and security fixes for a single protocol, that job grows immensely with each additional protocol you install or enable.
>
> Identify the networking protocols you need on each computer to handle the services your users need, then disable or remove all others. If a protocol isn't running anywhere on your network, you can ignore any vulnerabilities that it contains, and you can ignore any updates to that protocol that are released for your systems.
>
> Fewer protocols means greater security, and greater security means more peace of mind.

The application-level protocol used to carry all Windows networking information is called NetBIOS (Network Basic Input/Output System), and NetBIOS can be carried across your network by any or all of the three communication protocols mentioned above (IP, NetBEUI, or IPX/SPX).

Once the appropriate protocols are installed on the user's computer, she can begin using any network applications (Internet utilities, database applications, client software for file and print servers, and so on) that she needs.

For example, once the protocols needed for Client for Windows Networking are installed, the user can open the Network Neighborhood icon on the desktop to browse for file servers and peer-to-peer file sharing from colleagues, as well as opening the `Printers` folder to set up the use of network printers.

Windows File Sharing Authentication

There are two kinds of authentication for a Windows workstation that is sharing files: share-level and user-level.

For a Windows NT workstation, all access is user level.

For a Windows 95 or 98 workstation sharing files or printers, if a Windows NT domain or name server is available, access can be either user level or share level. If no Windows NT authentication is available, access is only share level.

- Share-level access means that the resource is shared read only, read write, or both, depending on which password is offered. For example, if another user enters a password of `Big3l3fnt`, he would have read-only access. If another user enters a password of `Clrcu5Act`, she would have read-write access.

- User-level access means that the resource is shared to provide specific kinds of access to specific users or groups of users. For example, you might allow those in the Accounting group, plus your teammate Jean, to connect to the resource, without allowing any other groups or users access of any kind.

Windows' default authentication method is encrypted, so logging on cannot easily be captured over the network.

> **Tip:** If you're a Windows NT or Windows 2000 user, you may find it helpful to think of Windows 95/98's share-level access as a situation comparable to user-level access, but where all authorized users are members of only two groups, one with read (R) access and one with read/write/execute/delete (RWXD) access. All members of the first group have one password, and all members of the second group have a different password.

What's Enabled Out of the Box and What Security Precautions to Take

Fortunately, very little of Microsoft's networking services is enabled when you first install a Windows operating system. By default, all installed networking protocols are active, but they aren't listening on any ports until they are specifically configured to do so.

File and Printer Sharing

If you enable File and Printer Sharing in the Network Control Panel during Windows setup, the system is automatically listening for incoming connections on whichever net-working protocols you have installed (assuming you haven't changed the protocols to which the Windows Networking Client is bound).

Note that if you use Novell's network operating system on your network, your users may also want to install file and print sharing for NetWare Networks, also included with Windows 95 and later versions (but not installed by default). The security issues for file and printer sharing are the same for this service as for the Microsoft networking service, although some of the details may vary. Be aware that Windows supports file and printer sharing either for NetWare Networks or for Microsoft Networks, but not both at the same time.

> **Note:** Don't automatically select both options (I Want to Share Files or I Want to Share Printers) in the Network Control Panel under the File and Print Sharing button. If you don't need a service, disable it. If you have no printers attached to your computer, don't select the printer sharing option.
>
> Similarly, if you don't want to share files or printers, turn off both file and printer sharing options, and remove the File and Printer Sharing for Microsoft Networks option from the list in the Configuration tab. Any service you enable provides some risk, so if you don't need it, don't install it or turn it on.

However, even after you enable file and printer sharing, nothing on the system is available to others until you have specifically told Windows what you want to share.

For example, you could share an entire hard drive by right-clicking its icon in the My Computer window and choosing Sharing from the pop-up menu that appears. This is a bad idea, however, because you'll seldom want others in your organization to have access to your entire hard drive.

Instead, you should probably set up a file transfer directory, perhaps `C:\Transfer`. When you right-click that directory and choose Sharing from the pop-up menu that appears, you'll see a Properties window that indicates the directory is not currently shared. The configuration shown in Figure 9.1 provides a reasonable level of access to the `Transfer` folder (and no other part of the hard drive).

FIGURE 9.1.

File sharing properties for a transfer directory.

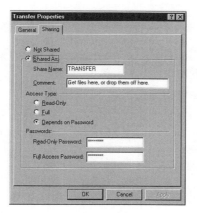

This configuration provides read-only or read-write-execute-delete access to the directory, depending on the password entered. No access to the rest of the hard disk is provided by this setup.

You may also want to share multiple directories, each with a different password, for different members of your organization to read and write files.

Compromised PWL Files

All operating systems that store local password files have the risk that those files can be copied and cracked, providing access to the user's complete set of security information. In the case of Windows 95 and 98, this includes files with a PWL extension. The original version of Windows 95 and Windows 95 Service Pack 1 (as well as Windows for Workgroups 3.11, for what it's worth) had a well-publicized weakness in the way passwords were stored in a local cache called a password list, or PWL file.

These PWL files were stored with a 32-bit encryption, which was apparently not difficult for some enterprising hackers (not necessarily crackers) to develop a way to decrypt. Microsoft responded by releasing an update that increased the encryption to 128-bit, which helped prevent the PWL files from being compromised but did not lock them up forever.

(See article #Q132807 in the Microsoft Knowledge Base, also available at `http://support.microsoft.com/support/kb/articles/q132/8/07.asp`, for details on this update.)

For this reason, users should take either or both of the following actions to protect their password lists:

- **Turn off password caching**   Microsoft has posted information in its Knowledge Base (article #Q140557), found at this location on its Web site: `http://support.microsoft.com/support/kb/articles/Q140/5/57.ASP`

- **Protect the operating system directory**   If you leave password caching enabled, make sure users never share their operating system directory (usually `C:\Windows` for systems that use PWL files).

This is a similar risk to someone stealing a copy of the Users & Groups Data file on a Mac OS computer or the `/etc/passwd` file from a UNIX-like operating system. You don't want these files to be copied and taken elsewhere to be cracked at leisure. Take all precautions that seem reasonable to prevent this from happening.

Web Sharing and FTP Services

Beginning with Windows 95 OSR 2, users with access to the Windows setup disks can install and activate a service called Personal Web Server. Once installed, this service provides the standard benefits and risks of any Web server and can be a considerable security hole for that computer. By default, the Web server provides access only to documents in the Web share directory on the root level of the user's startup disk, but the user can specify any folder as the Web server's root directory.

Personal Web Server can be configured to allow anyone to have read-only access (using the Allow Anonymous option), or it can be set up to use the more advanced privileges of Basic or Windows NT challenge/response authentication.

Personal Web Server contains the following basic security risks:

- **Network Access**   Personal Web Server runs over the TCP/IP protocol and is therefore vulnerable to attack both from inside your network and from outside, if Web traffic is allowed into your network by the firewall or other filtering device.

- **Folder Defaults**   If the user specifies that the Personal Web Server Control Panel should use a root folder that does not contain a valid HTML page (`Index.html`, `Home.html`, or a user-specified default page), Personal Web Server makes the contents of the folder available to any Web browser (depending on how the access was set up, as read-only or using more advanced privileges) for downloading. This is a considerable security risk because the directory specified and its subdirectories may contain sensitive information.

- **FTP Services**   Personal Web Server also provides an FTP server, which can, if not configured carefully, provide the same security risk as badly configured file sharing. This can leave the user's computer open to unauthorized access, especially if your firewall is not configured to keep incoming FTP connections out.

To avoid risks from Personal Web Server, I recommend the following:

- Install Personal Web Server only as necessary to provide browser access to files on the user's computer.

- Restrict Personal Web Server to read-only access to a limited directory of Web content. If you choose to use advanced access privileges for Personal Web Server access, be sure the privileges are restricted enough for both purposes.

- Leave the FTP server disabled (which it is by default) unless it is absolutely necessary, and enable it only with the most advanced authentication available. Follow the same recommendations provided above for file sharing to restrict FTP access to only a limited directory and not the entire system.

Connecting a Windows Desktop to Network Services

Once you have made sure that a Windows workstation isn't making any sensitive services available on the network, you need to take steps to be sure the system is connecting securely to other network services. These services include

- Windows NT servers
- NetWare servers
- UNIX-like operating system servers
- Dial-Up Networking

Each of these kinds of connections is described below.

Connecting the Client to Windows NT or Windows 2000 Servers

A Windows NT or Windows 2000 server can provide a number of services to a Windows client, including domain control for connecting to the network and file and printer sharing services. Windows NT can be configured to authenticate the user for all network access, not just access to the server, when logging on to the Windows workstation.

The regular Windows networking client provides complete access for logging on to a Windows NT server and encrypts the authentication process to prevent packet sniffing from being useful.

Windows NT also supports third-part authentication, including public key encryption products, tokens or smart cards, Kerberos (support for which is built in to Windows 2000), and other advanced authentication methods. If a third-party authentication method is in use, the Windows networking client requests the necessary information when the user logs on to the Windows NT or 2000 server.

See Chapter 8 for additional information on how to keep a Windows server connection secure.

Connecting the Windows Client to NetWare Servers

There are two ways to connect a Windows client to a NetWare server: using the built-in NetWare client available in Windows and using the NetWare client for Windows available from Novell.

In the past, NetWare used the IPX protocol. However, connecting a Windows client to a NetWare server has become slightly more complicated now that NetWare can run over either IPX/SPX or TCP/IP.

Only the Novell client can connect to a NetWare server over IP; the Microsoft client for NetWare operates only over IPX.

There is one noticeable security difference between the NetWare client included with Microsoft Windows and the client available from Novell: The client from Novell supports NCP Packet Signatures, and the Microsoft client doesn't. If you are requiring this added security feature on your NetWare servers, your users must install Novell Client32 for Windows instead of the Microsoft Client for NetWare. See Chapter 8 for an explanation of NCP Packet Signatures and why they're useful for securing your network.

Outside of this difference, both clients are equally secure. Both clients encrypt the authentication process to prevent the user name and password from being captured with a packet sniffer.

Connecting the Windows Client to UNIX-Like Servers

Most of the basic services used in the UNIX world, such as Telnet, FTP, and so on, are available to Windows users who are using the appropriate client software. For example, there is a built-in Telnet client with every copy of Windows. There also are numerous add-on products that perform the same task, such as HyperTerm 3 and higher, and other dedicated terminal programs with Telnet capabilities. All versions of Windows that have the TCP/IP protocol installed also include a command-line–accessible FTP client program, although there are numerous third-party FTP programs as well.

However, as discussed elsewhere in this book, many of these services are inherently insecure, including both Telnet and FTP, which typically send their authentication in clear text across the network, where any cracker can capture it using a network sniffer.

For this reason, use client software only to connect to secure UNIX services, such as the following:

- **SSH**   There are several SSH clients for Windows, including a product from DataFellows (http://www.datafellows.com), SecureCRT from Van Dyke Technologies (http://www.vandyke.com), and the free Java-based MindTerm (available at http://www.mindbright.se/mindterm/).

- **SFTP or SCP**   Part of the SSH package, SFTP can provide secure file transfers in a way similar to the standard FTP client. SCP can also provide secure file transfers.

- **Secure tunnels**   SSH can provide port forwarding through a secure tunnel, which effectively lets you use insecure utilities such as FTP, Telnet, and so on through a secure connection that renders them equally secure. For example, after setting up an SSH connection with a remote host, you might set it up to forward port 1501 from your computer to the remote host, at which point you could configure your local FTP client to connect to local port 1501. This can render virtually any Mac-to-UNIX client software secure, simply by carrying the connection wrapped in a secure shell.

Other tunneling products can provide the same protection, such as most VPN products.

- **Other Secure Telnet alternatives**   There are various clients available to make Telnet secure, such as Kerberos Telnet (making Kerberos authentication and encryption available to a Telnet client), available at `http://www.stacken.kth.se/~thn/kTelnet/index.html`. Also, Stanford SRP (Secure Remote Password) provides secure Telnet and FTP connections. See `http://srp.stanford.edu/srp/` for details.

Note that most UNIX-like operating systems can also run a Windows networking service to become very much like a regular file sharing server. One utility providing this service is called Samba. Once installed, the system appears to other computers on the network to be a Windows file or printer server. See `http://www.samba.org` for details.

Connecting Using Dial-Up Networking

Dial-Up networking service, while not a networking protocol specifically, is a client service that can prove a security risk to your network. The security risks come from the user's dial-up networking client and the dial-up networking server built into some versions of Windows.

The Windows dial-up networking client allows your users to connect from anywhere in the world over whichever carriers you make available on your network. This includes

- **Telephone or ISDN lines**   Using a regular modem on a telephone line or an ISDN terminal adapter on an ISDN line, a user can connect to a remote access server using the same kind of connection on your network.
- **Virtual Private Network (VPN) Connections**   If you set up a PPTP-compatible VPN server within your network, a Windows client can use dial-up networking to connect to your network from anywhere that a connection to the Internet is available, whether through a dial-up provider or another organization's network.

Once connected, the user can use the same networking services that are available from inside your network. This can be either risky or safe, depending on the security measure you put into place on your network. These measures are discussed in detail in Chapter 5, "Letting Users Connect Securely."

However, from the client's perspective, the biggest risk to your network security comes from how this dial-up networking client is used. If the user selects the Save Password check box in Windows 95 dial-up networking, then anybody who uses that computer may be able to connect to the remote network without specifying the password. Even if the Windows logon feature is being used (with user profiles authenticating the user logging in to Windows), anybody with physical access to the computer (at the user's home, hotel room, and so on) may be able to crack the locally cached password from the PWL file, allowing that cracker to log on to your network.

The best option is to instruct users not to cache dial-up networking passwords and to disable password caching on any individual Windows computer by modifying an entry in the Windows Registry, using the Policy Editor (`poledit.exe`).

The other risk occurs if the user installs the optional Dial-Up Networking Server software, available starting with the Microsoft Plus! Pack for Windows 95 and included with later versions of Windows. This configures the user's computer as a point of access to that particular computer and possibly to other services on your network as well.

For your users whose computers have modems connected to telephone lines that are accessible from outside of your organization (either by direct dialing or by entering your switchboard and transferring to the modem), restrict your users from installing or enabling Dial-Up Networking Server. Actually, no user's computer should ever be configured to answer an incoming modem line.

Windows Networking over NetBEUI or IP

The networking service that carries Windows networking is called NetBIOS (Network Basic Input/Output System), which is the application-level protocol. NetBIOS can travel your network riding on one of three communications protocols: Microsoft's proprietary NetBEUI (NetBIOS Extended User Interface) , the industry standard TCP/IP, or IPX/SPX, which is also used for NetWare networking.

NetBEUI was originally intended for use on smaller networks with fewer than 200 or so devices. The significant feature from a security standpoint is that NetBEUI is not routable, so only devices that are on the same physical network can communicate using NetBEUI. What this means is that, by setting up all systems on your network to carry NetBIOS over NetBEUI, you're protecting the Windows networking services from being attacked from outside your network.

The disadvantage to using NetBEUI instead of TCP/IP is that on a large network or a wide area network, NetBIOS services usually run faster over TCP/IP than they do over NetBEUI. However, on a small network, that speed difference is much less noticeable.

Note for Cable Modem or DSL Users:

When you get a cable modem or DSL service, the box that your provider installs is, effectively, a router between your computer and the provider's network. One easy way for you to protect your Windows networking systems from outside cracking is to follow the directions here to use NetBEUI, and not TCP/IP, for your Windows networking. Note that if you're running any other TCP/IP services, such as a Web server, FTP server, and so on, you are still at risk from outside your network. You should still install a firewall between your computer and the outside network. However, if you take this precaution, your Windows network setup will not be the source of any attacks.

For example, you might have a router and firewall connecting your internal network to the Internet. All of your internal systems might be running TCP/IP for Internet access without running any services that listen for connections over TCP/IP. Internally, all of your Windows-based servers and workstations might be connecting and listening for NetBEUI services for file sharing, printing, and so on.

This is somewhat more secure than having all of the internal systems connecting and listening for connections over TCP/IP but, with a properly configured firewall, this should not be much of an issue.

> **Note:** TCP/IP, NetBEUI, and IPX/SPX (used mainly for Novell NetWare services) can all carry the NetBIOS protocol on your network. The descriptions here for using NetBIOS over NetBEUI also apply to using NetBIOS over IPX/SPX. If you use IPX/SPX on your network already, you may want to bind NetBIOS to that protocol instead of installing NetBEUI at all. In the instructions below, substitute IPX/SPX for NetBEUI and you'll achieve essentially the same result.
>
> The only added step is to be sure to open the properties for the IPX/SPX protocol and select the Enable NetBIOS over IPX/SPX check box on the NetBIOS tab.

To disable NetBIOS over TCP/IP and use only NetBEUI in Windows 95/98

1. In Windows 95/98, open the Network Control Panel.
2. If you need only Windows networking and no Internet or other TCP/IP services, select TCP/IP and click Remove. Then skip to step 5.
3. If you need to keep both Windows networking and TCP/IP, select TCP/IP and click Properties.

   The dialog box seen in Figure 9.2 appears.

FIGURE 9.2
The Bindings tab on the TCP/IP Properties dialog box.

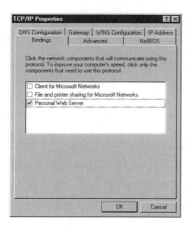

4. Click the Bindings tab if it is not already visible.

5. Deselect the Client for Microsoft Networks check box and the File and Printer Sharing for Microsoft Networks check box.

6. Click OK to close the TCP/IP Properties dialog box.

   When you leave this tab or close the dialog box, Windows warns you that no drivers are bound to TCP/IP and asks if you would like to go back to select some. This situation is fine, and you should answer No to the question. TCP/IP is still available for other programs to use; it's simply not bound to any installed networking components.

7. When Windows indicates that you must restart the computer for your changes to take effect, click Yes to restart.

After you restart your computer, it will no longer be listening on TCP or UDP ports 137 through 139, which are the NetBIOS over TCP/IP ports.

> **Note:** Once you configure a computer to use NetBIOS only over NetBEUI or IPX/SPX, that computer can browse only other computers configured the same way, and the list of computers displayed in Network Neighborhood will reflect this. No computers configured to carry NetBIOS over TCP/IP will be visible or available to the computer configured according to these directions.

There is a disadvantage and a risk to using this method to protect your network, however. The disadvantage is that NetBIOS is slower over the other protocols than over TCP/IP so, if you have a large network, you may want to consider this tradeoff carefully.

The risk is that if even one system on your internal network is compromised over TCP/IP, it will be a fairly simple matter for the cracker to use that system as a launching point for attacks inside your network. For example, if an outside cracker were to trick one of your users into installing a trojan horse, such as Back Orifice or NetBus, the cracker could then take control of the internal system. Since the internal system has full access to your network over NetBEUI, the cracker would then have the power to roam your internal network at will.

Recommendation

Ultimately, security isn't a matter of choosing the "correct" protocol, but rather securing the protocols you use. If your networking services require TCP/IP services, implement TCP/IP services and then concentrate on securing TCP/IP as best you can.

For small networks, such as small offices and home offices, NetBEUI can provide a simple way to reduce, but not eliminate, some risk.

For larger networks, you can find some security from outside attack by eliminating TCP/IP altogether and implementing only NetBEUI on your internal network. However, the tradeoffs are usually too great to allow this strategy (as more and more services are supporting TCP/IP as time passes), so I don't recommend this method.

Mac OS

The Mac OS doesn't currently provide very much in the way of advanced security features for using the computer, and therefore any information stored on the computer can be considered vulnerable to anyone with access to it. However, the Macintosh supports networking and connectivity options that are just as secure as any other platform, and you'll want to be sure to implement the secure options to provide your Mac OS users with the same access as your other users.

How Users Connect to Services

Using the built-in features of the Mac OS, users can use their computers to connect to a number of networking services. Passwords for networking services may be sent in clear text for any network sniffer to pick up, or they may be DES encrypted, which makes it difficult (if not quite impossible) to decrypt. With third-party features, additional password authentication methods are available as well. How all of this works depends on the network services in use and how they're configured.

Note: Although some security groups have recently published information about the algorithm used to store Mac OS file sharing passwords (a very simple scrambling technique), most Mac OS functions encrypt the file sharing passwords during authentication, making it difficult or impossible for a sniffer to detect them. The real risk of the simple algorithm lies in two places:

Insecure Physical Location   If a Mac OS server (or workstation with file sharing enabled) is physically available to a cracker, the cracker can steal a copy of the computer's Users & Groups Data File and unscramble the passwords elsewhere at leisure. Once the cracker has the passwords, he can log onto that computer from anywhere on your network. Note that a Mac OS 9 or higher computer can be protected from unauthorized physical access through the use of a user configuration password, voice code, or other added authentication. If a Macintosh is in a location that cannot be physically secured, you should at least enable the access restrictions available in Mac OS 9.

Sharing Too Much   If the server or workstation has the System folder or Preferences folder shared, a cracker may be able to copy the Users & Groups Data File over the network, at which point it is a simple matter to unscramble it to see the passwords.

Obviously, it would be better if the Mac OS encrypted its passwords file more securely. However, you can solve the two vulnerabilities listed here through some basic precautions described later in this chapter, and the strength of the encryption of the data file can cease to be a worry for your networking security needs.

Mac OS computers can communicate natively using two networking protocols: AppleTalk and TCP/IP. With third-party add-ons, a Macintosh computer can use additional protocols, including IPX/SPX (NetWare networking) and NetBIOS (Windows networking).

What's Enabled Out of the Box and What Security Precautions to Take

When you first set up a computer running Mac OS, networking services are turned off, but they can be enabled by running any of the networking wizards made available. Here are the networking services built in to a Mac:

Apple File Sharing

The Mac OS has had peer-to-peer file sharing services built in to the operating system since Macintosh System 7 was released. Called File Sharing, it currently allows up to 10 users to connect to the user's Macintosh and read or write files, depending on the access privileges provided.

In Mac OS versions 8.x and earlier, File Sharing runs over the AppleTalk protocol, Apple's proprietary networking protocol that can run over LocalTalk (a cabling system unique to Macs, except for some rare exceptions), EtherTalk (using the same ethernet connection as other networking protocols), a variety of dial-up connections, and other similar methods. Because AppleTalk is not normally routed to your Internet connection, AppleTalk services on your internal network are not visible to outsiders, although this still provides a security risk for crackers on your internal network.

In Mac OS 9.0 and later versions, File Sharing is expected to run over TCP/IP as well, which opens the user's desktop Macintosh to the risk of outside crackers, especially if the network is not protected by a firewall or other methods of filtering out incoming connections.

By default, File Sharing is not active on a new Mac OS system, but it is easy to turn on and configure, using the File Sharing Control Panel, seen in Figure 9.3.

Figure 9.3

The File Sharing Control Panel.

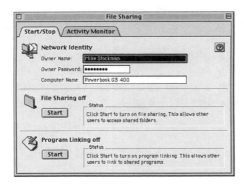

File Sharing contains the following basic security risks:

- **Owner Access** Regardless of which other users and access privileges the user defines, the owner of the Macintosh has complete access to the system (similar to root or superuser privileges in UNIX-like systems) by default. You can turn this option off by opening the Users & Groups Control Panel, opening the owner's privileges, and deselecting the Allow User to See All Disks option. However, since this option is on by default for the owner, it presents a significant security risk.
- **Password** When File Sharing is first activated, the File Sharing Control Panel requests an owner password, and displays a warning if the password is left blank. However, a blank password is accepted, which can leave the system wide open to the entire network.

  Also, there is no way to force passwords of a particular length or complexity, nor is there a way to force passwords to expire after a certain amount of time.
- **Access Privileges** The user is responsible for setting up access privileges, which consist of users and groups of users who may connect to the system using File Sharing, whether those users or groups can change their own passwords, and other options. There is currently no way to set up File Sharing to use a centralized access list or authentication system to provide file sharing access.

The risks of compromising a desktop computer may not be obvious, but there are several. The first, of course, is that the user may have confidential documents or data that is at risk of being compromised, either by having a cracker steal it or by someone changing or corrupting the information.

Another slightly less obvious risk is to the security of the rest of your network. As described earlier in this section, the Mac OS currently stores user and group passwords in a file in the Preferences folder, and the information is only lightly scrambled, not heavily encrypted. Any cracker who gains access to the computer may also have access to the Preferences folder and can therefore steal a copy of the Users & Groups data file. Because cracking this file is a trivial task that has been widely publicized, any user ID and password in that file is therefore available to a cracker who steals it. If the file contains user IDs and passwords that are unique to that Macintosh, there's not much of a problem. The cracker gains access to all accounts on that computer, but nothing more. However, if you have users who use the same password for multiple accounts on your network (a bad practice but one which is all too common), cracking this local file puts other, possibly more vital resources on your network at risk.

This is by no means the limit of the risks to which insecure file sharing can place your network, but it should be sufficient to encourage you to close this security hole.

To avoid risks to the user's computer, I recommend the following:

- Educate users on the dangers of enabling file sharing if it's not absolutely necessary.

- Enforce your standard rules for creating strong passwords, even on these desktop computers. Test this regularly by trying to connect to random computers using a blank owner password.

- Turn off file sharing if it's not absolutely necessary. You can identify shared Mac OS computers on your network by opening the Mac OS Chooser and clicking the AppleShare icon or by opening the Network Browser. The servers listed include all AppleShare servers on your network and any personal Mac OS computers shared using File Sharing.

- Turn off the Allow User to See All Disks option in the Users & Groups Control Panel for the owner account. This option provides little benefit compared to the greater security risk.

- Turn off Guest access by opening the Guest icon in the Users & Groups Control Panel and deselecting the Allow Guests to Connect check box.

- If a user needs to enable File Sharing at all, encourage her to share only a specific folder that contains the shared information, not the entire hard disk.

- Regardless of all other shared folders on the computer, make sure a user's System folder and its contents are *never* shared to any user. The System folder contains the password file for File Sharing, which is an easily cracked key to the entire computer.

- In the File Sharing Control Panel, be sure the Program Linking feature is turned off. This feature allows programs elsewhere on the network to communicate directly with programs running on the Macintosh, but this provides a risk that a cracker will send malicious commands to the Finder or other application running on the Macintosh.

As with other security measures, the best option is to disable all unnecessary services on the Macintosh computer.

Program Linking

Beginning with Macintosh System 7, the Mac OS has supported a feature called Program Linking, which allows applications to send Apple events to other applications, whether they are running on the same computer or elsewhere on the computer's network. For example, you might use a program on one computer to send a Quit command to a shared program on another computer on your network.

This feature has always been restricted to AppleTalk networks but, beginning with Mac OS 9, Program Linking is expected to work over IP as well.

This is a very powerful feature, clearly, but fortunately Apple has placed numerous steps in the way of enabling it to protect users. To enable Program Linking for, say, the FileMaker database program, you'd have to follow these steps:

1. Turn on Program Linking for the computer in the File Sharing Control Panel.

2. For each user created in the Users & Groups Control Panel, select the Allow Users to Link to Programs on This Computer check box.

3. Share the FileMaker application by selecting it in the Finder and choosing Info, then File Sharing from the File menu, and selecting Allow Remote Program Linking check box in the window that appears.

Each of these steps is required to share programs and, even then, only the authorized users and the shared applications are susceptible to this kind of control.

> **Note:** The Finder—which is an application that provides the Mac OS desktop, as does the Windows Explorer application in Windows—is shared for program linking by default.
>
> Once you enable Program Linking in the File Sharing Control Panel, any user who is authorized to link to programs can control the Finder, without any additional step being taken to share the Finder. Given that the Finder can execute all manner of actions based on received Apple events (such as deleting, shutting down, and so on), this is a risk that occurs whenever Program Linking is started.

While this is a powerful feature that is potentially very useful, it's also a risk and therefore should never be enabled without a clear need. Once it is enabled, be sure to provide only users who absolutely need it with access to Program Linking (as described in step 2 above).

Web Sharing

Beginning with Mac OS 8.0, all installations include a Web server called Personal Web Sharing. This service is off by default but can be enabled using the Web Sharing Control Panel. Once activated, this service provides the standard benefits and risks of any Web server and can be a considerable security hole for that computer. By default, the Web server provides access only to documents in the Web Pages folder on the root level of the user's startup disk, but the user can specify any folder as the Web server's root directory.

Personal Web Sharing can be configured to allow anyone to have read-only access, or it can be set up to use File Sharing access privileges as defined in the Users & Groups Control Panel, as shown in Figure 9.4.

FIGURE 9.4
The Web Sharing Control Panel.

Web Sharing contains the following basic security risks:

- **Network Access**   As a Web server, Web Sharing runs over the TCP/IP protocol, not over AppleTalk. For this reason, Web Sharing is vulnerable to attack both from inside your network and from outside, if Web traffic is allowed into your network by the firewall or other filtering device.

- **Folder Defaults**   If the user specifies that the Web Sharing Control Panel should use a Web Folder that does not contain a valid HTML page (`Index.html`, `Home.html`, or a user-specified default page), Web Sharing makes the contents of the folder available to any Web browser (depending on how the access was set up, as read-only or using File Sharing privileges) for downloading. This is a considerable security risk, because the specified directory and its subdirectories may contain sensitive information.

To avoid risks from Web Sharing, I recommend the following:

- Enable Web Sharing only as necessary to provide browser access to files on the user's computer.

- Restrict Web Sharing to read-only access to a limited directory of Web content. If you choose to use File Sharing privileges for Web Sharing access, be sure the privileges are restricted enough for both purposes.

Connecting a Macintosh Desktop to Network Services

Once you have made sure that a Macintosh desktop isn't making any sensitive services available on the network, you need to take steps to be sure the Macintosh is connecting securely to other network services. These services include

- AppleShare servers

- Windows NT servers (using a Windows networking, or SMB, client)

- Windows NT or Windows 2000 servers using the Windows NT/2000 Macintosh file services

- NetWare servers using a NetWare for Macintosh client

- NetWare servers using NetWare's Macintosh file services

- UNIX-like operating system servers

Each of these kinds of connections is described below.

Connecting the Macintosh to AppleShare Servers

Apple's native Mac OS file server is called AppleShare. Current versions of the AppleShare server software support AFP (Apple File Protocol) connections over IP and AppleTalk. The Macintosh client software connects to the AppleShare server in one of two ways:

- **Built-In Authentication**   By default, the AppleShare client and server exchange user ID and password information using DES encryption, which makes it difficult to impossible for a cracker on the network to capture and interpret the exchange, using either an AppleTalk or IP packet sniffing program.

- **User Authentication Modules (UAM)** AppleShare and AppleShare-compatible servers support the addition of third-party security modules called User Authentication Modules, or UAMs. The server can be set up to require the use of these modules or to allow the user to select a particular UAM when connecting. For the strongest security, you should require the UAM you deem the most secure and not permit users without that UAM to connect.

For example, you can install a UAM from the University of Michigan called AuthMan to support Kerberos authentication, the advanced user authentication protocol developed by MIT. Kerberos is time sensitive (meaning that access, once granted, expires after a period of time) and uses encrypted authentication, so the authentication process won't be picked up by crackers on your network. Microsoft's Windows NT and 2000 services for the Macintosh also support the use of a custom UAM, the Microsoft User Authentication Module (MSUAM), which also encrypts the exchange of the user ID and password.

Whenever possible, use the strongest authentication possible for all of your AppleShare-compatible servers, especially if they're accepting connections over TCP/IP (which is more likely to carry attacks from outside your network than AppleTalk).

To use a UAM on a Macintosh client, copy the UAM provided by the manufacturer of the server or authentication method you're using into the AppleShare folder in the client's System folder. The next time the user opens the Chooser or uses the Network Browser to connect to a server, a dialog box similar to the one seen in Figure 9.5 appears.

FIGURE 9.5
The Select UAM dialog box.

This dialog box lets you specify which UAM to use for authentication. Once the user chooses a UAM, the appropriate dialog box appears, in which the user can enter the authentication needed.

> **Peter's Principle:** AppleShare over IP Versus AppleTalk
>
> All AppleShare-compatible servers support connections over AppleTalk by default. AppleShare servers from Apple Computer, as well as AppleShare-compatible services provided by Microsoft Windows 2000, support connections over TCP/IP as well. Both methods work equally well, and both are equally secure. However, AppleTalk is generally not routed outside of your local network, while TCP/IP is, so this could reduce the chance of outside cracking. Ultimately, however, putting good security precautions in place (firewalls, strong authentication methods, and so on) should mean that you can choose whichever protocol best suits your other networking needs.

Note that with most methods of connecting to an AppleShare server, the server icon remains on the Mac OS desktop until the user puts it away (logs off). This provides a security risk if an unauthorized person starts to use the computer. Be sure your users know to log off of any sensitive servers whenever they're not at their computers.

Connecting the Macintosh to NT Servers

There are two ways to connect a Mac OS client to a Windows NT server, and both provide roughly the same level of security. The method you use depends mainly on the needs of your users and your networking configuration.

> **Note:** If these two connection methods aren't sufficient, you have other alternatives, such as running the FTP services that are built in to Windows NT or 2000. However, given that the security of most of those methods is discussed elsewhere in this chapter, this section discusses the two most common methods of logging on to a Windows NT or 2000 server from the Mac OS.

Using an SMB Client

Microsoft Windows networking operates using the Server Message Block (SMB) protocol, and a number of third-party SMB client packages are available for different platforms, including OS/2, various flavors of UNIX, and the Mac OS.

The SMB product available for the Mac OS is called DAVE, from Thursby Systems, Inc., available at http://www.thursby.com. Using DAVE, users can use the Chooser to connect to Windows 95, 98, NT, and 2000 servers.

DAVE is exactly as secure or insecure as any Windows 95 or 98 networking client. As with those clients, DAVE uses encrypted authentication, so it is unlikely to allow a user ID and password to be captured from your network.

Using Windows NT's Macintosh Services

As described earlier, a Windows NT or 2000 server administrator can enable a service called Services for Macintosh. This provides access to the server for Macintosh users via

AppleShare over AppleTalk or, under Windows 2000, over IP as well. Macintosh users can use the server volumes or the print queue on the server using their built-in networking software, including the AppleShare client and their network printing drivers.

Services for Macintosh can use the standard AppleShare authentication methods for logging in, or they can require that Macintosh users install the Microsoft User Authentication Module to encrypt the authentication process.

Windows NT services for Macintosh are relatively secure methods of providing a Mac OS user with file and print server access. Using the AppleTalk protocol to provide these services provides the added security of being restricted to your internal network (given that most network routers do not route AppleTalk to the outside network), making it less likely that any outside cracker will tamper with these services.

However, be sure to keep up with the latest Microsoft security updates and Windows NT service packs so that you can close any vulnerabilities as they are identified.

Connecting the Macintosh to NetWare Servers

As with a Windows NT server, there are currently two ways to connect a Macintosh client to a Novell NetWare server, and both provide basically the same level of security. The method you use depends mainly on the needs of your users and your networking configuration.

Using a NetWare Client

Once a free utility for NetWare users, NetWare Client for Macintosh is available for purchase from a company called ProSoft, Inc., which has entered into a partnership with Novell to develop this client software.

Similar to AppleShare or DAVE, NetWare Client appears in the Chooser as a MacIPX icon. Clicking this icon allows the user to see the available NetWare servers on the network and to connect to them as needed so that they'll appear on the desktop as standard Macintosh volumes.

NetWare Client for Macintosh uses the IPX/SPX protocol, which uses the same encrypted authentication as NetWare clients for other platforms. This encrypted authentication process cannot be picked up easily by packet sniffers on your local network.

Using NetWare's Macintosh Services

As with Windows NT servers, a NetWare server administrator can install a service called Services for AppleShare. This provides access to the server for Macintosh users via AppleShare over AppleTalk. Macintosh users can use the server volumes or the print queue on the server using their built-in networking software, including AppleShare Client and their network printing drivers.

Services for Macintosh can use the standard AppleShare authentication methods for logging in, or they can require that Macintosh users install the NetWare User Authentication Module to encrypt the authentication process further.

NetWare's Services for AppleShare are relatively secure methods of providing a Mac OS users with file and print server access. Using the AppleTalk protocol to provide these services gives the added security of being restricted to your internal network (given that most network routers do not route AppleTalk to the outside network), making it less likely that any outside cracker will tamper with these services.

However, be sure to keep up with the latest NetWare security updates so that you can close any vulnerabilities as they are identified.

Connecting the Macintosh to UNIX-Like Servers

Most of the basic services used in the UNIX world, such as Telnet, FTP, and so on, are available to Macintosh users who are using the appropriate client software on the Mac OS. For example, there are several Telnet clients for Mac OS, such as NCSA Telnet, NiftyTelnet, Telnet 3.0, and dedicated terminal programs with Telnet capabilities.

However, as discussed elsewhere in this book, many of these services are inherently insecure, including both Telnet and FTP, which typically send their authentication in clear text across the network, where any cracker can capture it using a network sniffer.

For this reason, use client software on the Macintosh only to connect to secure UNIX services, such as the following:

- **SSH** There are several SSH clients for the Mac OS, including a version of NiftyTelnet (available at `http://www.lysator.liu.se/~jonasw/freeware/`) and the Java-based MindTerm (available at `http://www.mindbright.se/mindterm/`). Both programs also support SCP for secure file transfers.

- **Secure tunnels** SSH can provide port forwarding through a secure tunnel, which effectively lets you use insecure utilities, such as FTP, Telnet, and so on, through a secure connection that renders them equally secure. For example, after setting up an SSH connection with a remote host, you might set it up to forward port 1501 from your computer to the remote host, at which point you could configure your local FTP client to connect to the local port 1501. This can render virtually any Mac-to-UNIX client software secure, simply by carrying the connection wrapped in a secure shell.

AppleShare over AppleTalk or IP

Now that AppleShare servers can support connections over AppleTalk or IP, which should you use? Functionally, there is little difference between the two protocols; users connect to AppleShare servers using the Chooser or Network Browser easily for either protocol.

TCP/IP carries a lot of advantages that arise from it being an industry-standard protocol, more easily supported on a network. Your routers can handle it easily, as can firewalls and other security devices on your network. Your users will also be able to connect to AppleShare servers from offsite more easily, assuming you have adequate safety measures in place to prevent unauthorized access.

AppleTalk may be a safer choice, because it is not routed on the Internet and so there is little risk of any incoming cracking attempt using AppleTalk. Users can connect to AppleShare servers from offsite only by first establishing a dial-in or VPN tunnel through which to carry the AppleTalk protocol, but this solution works well.

Recommendations

Ultimately, the benefits of using TCP/IP over AppleTalk may outweigh the slight increase in security risk, and if you take standard precautions (filtering incoming IP packets, configuring your firewall to protect your network, and so on), either protocol should provide a safe method of connecting to AppleShare servers. Allow your networking needs to determine which protocol you use, and be sure to put rigorous security precautions into place no matter which you choose.

UNIX/Linux

The advantage to UNIX-like operating systems is that they've always been designed on the server model, not the workstation. For this reason, they've always been designed with security, authentication, and controlled user access. Logging on to a UNIX workstation is almost exactly the same as logging on to a UNIX server.

For this reason, this section doesn't discuss the ways in which a UNIX-like operating system provides server access. That's assumed to be the case for any UNIX box, and making sure these services are secure on a UNIX box is discussed in detail in Chapter 8.

This section, therefore, discusses some kinds of client software used on UNIX-like operating systems and how to make sure it's the most secure software possible.

Connecting a UNIX Desktop to Network Services

A number of services exist to let UNIX-like systems connect to network services, and this section is *not* going to attempt to catalog them all. However, I will discuss briefly the more common basic methods of connecting over the network, and which security concerns you should examine when you allow your users to connect with these services.

These services include

- AppleShare, Windows, and NetWare servers
- Other UNIX-like operating system servers

Each of these kinds of connections is described below.

AppleShare, Windows, and NetWare Servers

Client software for the common network operating systems exists for most UNIX-like operating systems, including the following:

- **AppleShare**   AppleShare client software is not very common, but it is available, including Partner, from IPTech (http://www.iptech.com), the free afpfs

(AppleShare Filing Protocol File System, available at `http://www.panix.com/~dfoster/afpfs`), and possibly others. When you implement an AppleShare client, be sure to ask the developers whether it encrypts or hides the passwords in any way over the network. None of the AppleShare clients I found supported any third-party user authentication modules (UAMs).

- **Windows Networking**   Most UNIX-like operating systems support SAMBA, a free client and server package for Windows networking. You can find SAMBA at `http://www.samba.org`. Using the smbclient utility that is part of the Samba package, you can access Windows 95, 98, or NT volumes with the same access you'd have from any Windows client, with about the same level of authentication and security.

- **NetWare Servers**   The most common way to provide UNIX users with access to NetWare servers is to provide NFS support on the NetWare server, such as by installing NetWare 5 NFS Services. Once this is established, the UNIX user can implement the native NFS client to use the NetWare volumes. This also provides access to NetWare print servers from the UNIX system. Note that NFS is not completely secure and should not be depended on alone to provide secure access to files. See the section on UNIX servers in Chapter 8 for more information.

All of these clients exist for UNIX-like operating system users, but they may not provide the robust security you need for file access on your network.

Be sure to implement only clients that use secure authentication methods that don't depend on clear-text user IDs or passwords. If clients that meet those requirements aren't available and you can't implement a more robust form of third-party security on top of that, you may need to look for other solutions.

Other UNIX-Like Operating System Servers

In the UNIX world, there are as many ways to serve up information as there are variations of UNIX itself and, for each of those ways of serving the information, there are several client options to receive it.

For example, for something as simple as transferring files, you have numerous options:

- **FTP**   By default, this provides clear-text authentication and poor security, although there are ways to strengthen the security of FTP transmissions, such as making them Kerberos aware.

- **SCP**   Part of the SSH protocol. Very secure, using encrypted public key authentication.

- **SFTP**   Part of the SSH2 protocol. Also very secure, and provides more flexibility than SCP.

- **NFS**   Originally a Sun protocol. Very flexible, since it allows you to mount remote UNIX volumes as if they were local, but complex and difficult to secure.

NFS access doesn't ask who you are when you connect; instead, it depends on your local system to have already authenticated you. This can cause numerous security problems, made worse by the fact that NFS is complicated to secure successfully, even when the capability exists. However, its power and flexibility sometimes make it a good choice for your network, if you're careful.

- **Samba**   Remember, Samba is also a server, not just a client, and it can be useful as a file and printer server as well. In this case, you'll use the smbclient described above in the Windows networking section.

Generally, the client software you use for transferring data between UNIX-like systems depends on the server choices you make. However, very secure connections exist for all of the common methods of connecting, and the client side is not likely to be the source of your security vulnerabilities.

Overall Recommendations

- Run a port/security scanner on all computers, not just your servers. At the very least, this will allow you to keep track of which network services are listening on your network. At best, you'll be able to contact each user who appears on your scan to discuss the best ways to secure the workstation.

- Educate users not to enable unnecessary network services and to require strong authentication. Also, they should check with or notify your office before activating anything, so that you can determine the need and the security risks. (They may not follow this request, but if they do, it helps.)

- Provide centralized authentication so that, even if your users do enable a service, only authorized users can take advantage.

- Set up a strong firewall, packet filtering or NAT router, and other devices to protect your internal network from the outside, even if you don't think you need it.

- Consider the need or use for personal firewall software, such as ConSeal, AtGuard, or (for Mac OS) NetBarrier, installed on each workstation.

- If possible, make sure all client workstations are physically secure from unauthorized access. If that's not possible, install or enable end user authentication on each workstation, such as the Windows NT Workstation login process or the user authentication built in to Mac OS 9 and higher.

- Install antivirus and trojan horse scanners on all incoming email servers in your organization to prevent a user's workstation from becoming compromised through malicious email. Also, install onto each workstation one of the many antivirus packages available that can scan file downloads and all email received to prevent intrusion through these methods.

Summary

Client systems should use the most secure software available to connect to any servers on your network, encrypting user IDs, passwords, and the entire connection, if possible. This includes Web browsers (using SSL, for example, for internal Web connections to data on your network), email (using any number of encrypted email clients), and so on.

Also, client workstations are a major source of potential security holes because operating system manufacturers include so many connectivity options, such as Web servers, FTP servers, and file sharing. These services are useful, but they also provide risk. Your network security scans should include all systems, not simply your file and network servers, and your users must be educated and encouraged to disable all services on their systems that they don't need that may be listening for connections.

When You've Been Cracked

Regardless of all the warnings in this book and all the layers of protection you place on your network, crackers will attempt to break into your network—and possibly, one will succeed. Networking security is an ongoing process; it would be naïve to set up your network, firewalls, access control methods, and other security measures and then sit back and consider yourself safe forever. Doing so would be like putting a state-of-the-art lock on your front door and assuming that nobody could break into your house after that.

Even if you had the best lock on the market on your front door, you'd still need to keep an eye on the windows and check the lock occasionally to make sure it hadn't been tampered with. You might also follow the locksmith publications to make sure your lock was still the best and didn't have any weaknesses.

The same practices apply to networking security. This chapter discusses the practice of watching for *attempts* to crack security—which can show you where the weaknesses are—as well as for actual cracker break-ins, because if you catch the cracker quickly enough, you can sometimes prevent any damage.

Keeping your network secure consists mainly of the following practices:

- Identifying the warning signs of impending crack attempts
- Recording and receiving reports of crack attempts, whether successful or not
- Handling the warnings and crack attempts to prevent the break-in or damage from being done

Each of these practices is discussed in the sections that follow.

About Intrusion Detection Systems

Many firewalls and packet filters have optional utilities to identify and drop certain kinds of illegal activity, including some kinds of port scans (described later) and attacks. These attempts to gain entry to your network can be written to a log file or forwarded to another system, through SMTP management or `syslog` servers, for example. These log files can make you aware of the attempts (and there will be many) to find certain services running on your network or to determine whether any other holes in your protection exist. Log files, however, don't tell you the kind of traffic that has occurred, or whether it's malicious at all; they simply record activity.

However, a special class of software now available can monitor your network or a particular host computer on your network for suspicious activity and take a number of actions based on what it finds. These tools, called Intrusion Detection Systems (IDSs), are widely available commercially and can provide an important layer of protection to your network.

Two kinds of IDS are available, each of which is discussed here.

Host-Based IDS

Host-based IDS packages reside on the host they're set up to protect. They can perform a number of tasks to detect an attack on the host, most of which protect the integrity of the files on the system. They're good at file-security tasks such as detecting whether any critical or security-related files on the host are modified or whether a user has tried to achieve access to files beyond his security level.

Integrity checks are accomplished by scanning the host's files once and storing a cryptographic "signature" for each of those files as they are at that moment.

> **Note:** You must be certain that a system is not compromised at the moment that you install or update the signatures for the system's files. It would be very easy to install a host-based IDS after some of the security files are already compromised, in which case your sense of security would be false. The time to install a host-based IDS is immediately after it has been configured from an empty system and before it has been placed online, where crackers could begin making changes that you don't want.

Once the signatures are created, the IDS then checks the files against those signatures regularly and notifies you when one or more doesn't match. These signatures require careful, controlled updating as you make modifications, add system patches, and so on; but the signatures can be a valuable source of information if you ever suspect that a cracker has entered the system.

Some of the host-based IDS packages include

- AXENT Technologies' Intruder Alert at www.axent.com
- Tripwire Security Systems' Tripwire at www.tripwiresecurity.com
- Digital's POLYCENTER Security Intrusion Detector at www.digital.com
- Security Dynamics' Kane Security Monitor (Windows NT or Novell servers) at www.securitydynamics.com
- Network Associates' CyberCop Monitor (also provides network-based features) at www.nai.com
- ODS Networks' Computer Misuse Detection System (CMDS) at www.ods.com

Network-Based IDS

Network-based IDS packages are usually dedicated systems that monitor an entire network segment, often from outside the firewall but also from inside. These devices generally consist of a *monitor* (a device or software package that scans your network for suspicious packets) and some *agent* software that may reside on individual host computers, feeding information back to the monitor. There may also be a *management console* of some kind that connects securely (with authentication and encryption) to the monitor to receive reports and exchange configuration information.

For the most part, network-based IDS packages collect network packets coming into your network and analyze them, based on a number of factors, to determine whether they match any known attacks or suspicious activity.

Some of the network-based IDS packages include

- Cisco Systems NetRanger at `www.cisco.com`
- ISS RealSecure at `www.iss.net`
- Anzen Flight Jacket at `www.anzen.com`
- Computer Associates' SessionWall-3 at `www.abirnet.com`
- Security Dynamics' Kane Security Monitor at `www.securitydynamics.com`
- Network Associates' CyberCop Monitor (also provides host-based features) at `www.nai.com`

Many more IDS packages are available, but these are some of the better-known commercial packages. They also can be somewhat expensive, starting in the thousands rather than hundreds of dollars, although less expensive products are available.

How an IDS Fits into Your Network

The diagram in Figure 10.1 shows where an IDS might be installed on your network.

FIGURE 10.1

Each of the host-based IDS packages is running on a network server, whereas the network-based IDS appears on the network just inside the firewall.

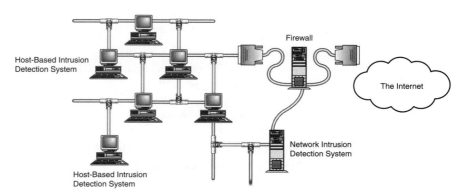

When an attack or other suspicious activity is found by either kind of IDS package, the IDS can perform any of several actions:

- Notify you by alert, email, pager, or other methods of the scan or attack.

- Log all available information about the connection, such as the source IP address, the date and time of the attempt, and other information that can help you identify the purpose of the packet.

- Reset the TCP connection in question, if the detector is in a position to do so. In theory, this action stops the attempted attack without affecting any other connection.

- Work with your firewall or router to block the packet and add the source address of the port scan to a list of "blacklisted" IP addresses (similar to what tcpwrappers on UNIX-like systems can do), so that any further traffic from that source will be denied. This often can be done automatically or, if you're concerned about possibly blocking legitimate traffic, manually when you respond to an alert.

- Execute a program of any kind that you specify. Doing so could be useful if you have a custom means of being notified of the scan or attack or if you want some special precaution (such as an orderly shutdown of some networking services) to occur.

Some IDS tools can even record the activity for later playback, showing the suspicious traffic as it happened.

IDS Advantages and Disadvantages

The presence of these intrusion detection systems on your network adds a level of protection that can be useful, especially if you have reason to believe you're more of a target than most (say, if you've seen numerous port scans in your firewall logs or if you have already been attacked once).

IDS systems—especially those products that can stop an attack once it's identified—are very powerful and potentially can save you from damage.

The disadvantages to using an IDS are as follows:

- **False positives**   In general, it's better for an IDS package to be too eager than not eager enough. But the result is the occasional false positive report that an intrusion has occurred when in fact nothing bad is happening. You need to decide whether the false positives are a problem. For example, if you have the network IDS package close down any suspicious connection, a false positive could cut off legitimate users of your system. If you're running a time-sensitive service (such as an e-commerce site), a false positive could be disastrous.

- **Performance slowdowns**   Although this is less of an issue as faster systems become available, analyzing network packets and system audit logs is a time-consuming and potentially processor-intensive activity. You may find that your network or host services are slowing down unacceptably, especially if you have a very busy network or server that generates a lot of data to analyze. Contact the manufacturer of the IDS to determine how much activity will be too much for their system, or install a demo version of the product to see what happens on a real network.

IDS Recommendations

Ultimately, if you can afford to sacrifice the money, processor speed, or network speed to implement an IDS package (or packages, because host-based and network-based systems can work together) on your network, do it. If your network is at risk, IDS packages can provide one more layer of warning when crackers strike.

About Port Scanning

Before a cracker can attempt to break into your network in any way, she needs to know one or more of the following things:

- What services do you have running?
- Which programs are providing those services (that is, which FTP server? Which Web server? Which CGI programs?)
- What kinds of products are protecting your network?

These questions can be answered by running a port scan of your network. Fortunately, a port scan can also give you advance warning of an attempted crack.

Port Scans and What They Mean

As discussed in Chapter 1, "Networking and Security Overview," a cracker could launch attacks on your network at random, trying to connect to various networking services to exploit their vulnerabilities, if any known vulnerabilities exist. However, this technique is extremely inefficient. A cracker can certainly try to target your Web server by trying to execute buffer overflow attacks, but if you don't have a Web server running on your network, the cracker has wasted valuable time when she could have been attempting to crack a network that actually has a Web server. The goal of a cracker is to identify targets as quickly as possible and begin the time-consuming work of identifying and exploiting the target's weaknesses.

For this reason of maximum efficiency, crackers employ utilities called *port scanners*. Port scanners check accessible hosts for open networking ports to see which services are listening for connections. For example, if you port scan a typical Windows 95 workstation, you might find that the workstation is listening on TCP or UDP ports 137 through 139 (used for NetBIOS, the Windows peer-to-peer file sharing protocol), among others. If the user is running personal Web sharing, port 80 will appear on the port scan as well.

Note: Your firewall, if properly configured, is blocking traffic on all ports except those for which you accept outside connections, such as port 80 for your Web servers or port 21 for your FTP servers. A port scan would then reveal the open ports to the cracker, rather than all services running on your network.

Another reason crackers scan for particular ports is to find trojan horses that may already be installed on the target machine. For example, the remote control trojan horse, Back Orifice, listens for connections by default on port 31337. Crackers (or aspiring crackers) will often scan whole ranges of TCP/IP host addresses sequentially, looking for ports that match known trojan horses that may be listening for a connection. Even if somebody else somehow tricked one of your users into installing a trojan horse, anybody who can scan for a port on which to connect will try to take advantage of it.

To scan your network, crackers use many of the same tools discussed earlier in this book, including nmap, SATAN, and so on. Of course, you'll follow the instructions we've already provided to scan your own network before the crackers do, looking for unnecessary or risky TCP or UDP ports. However, it may be useful to identify when someone is scanning for ports on your network, as a way of identifying when you're becoming a target.

Peter's Principle: Motivations Behind Port Scanning

There has been a lot of debate among security professionals about what port scanning actually means. Some compare it to walking up to a house and rattling the doorknob to see if the door is unlocked. It could be simply curiosity, with no breaking and entering intended.

However, others say that trying a doorknob to see if it's unlocked is, in fact, an attempt to break in, albeit a simple one. These people argue that scanning for active ports, just like rattling the doorknob, is a preliminary step to breaking in and should be caught, reported, and punished.

My feeling is that the motivation of the person scanning the ports (rattling the door) is irrelevant. As a network administrator, it's your job to make sure the door is locked, whether you think people will try to enter or not. Close off all unnecessary ports, and make sure all active ports are being listened to only by robust software that has no known security holes.

Repeated Connections or Attempts from the Same Network

If your network is anything like the ones I've managed, you'll see a sharp increase in the number of port scans during the evening hours in the U.S., with a couple of hours on either side of that to allow for time zone differences. That's because the evening hours are when aspiring crackers are away from their regular pastimes at jobs or school and have free time on their home computers to attempt to cause trouble.

This problem has increased as more households (most likely households with insufficient adult supervision) have become connected to the Internet.

For example, every evening while working on this section of the book, my firewall has reported numerous port scans and attempted connections on TCP port 31789. This port number is the default port used by a relatively new trojan horse called Hack'A'Tack. Hack'A'Tack is a program designed to provide undetected remote control of a computer, similar to Back Orifice or NetBus. As word of this trojan horse spreads, every would-be cracker out there is scanning for anything listening on this port.

That's not particularly risky, of course. Your firewall should be configured to deny incoming traffic on any ports other than those used by the services you want to allow and, because no legitimate service uses TCP port 31789, the incoming attempts were bound to fail.

It's more risky when you see repeated port scans on the ports you *do* allow. For example, if you see numerous port scans on TCP port 80 and you operate a Web server on your network, you might want to take that as a sign that a cracker is now aware that you run a Web server. You may want to check for updates and vulnerabilities for your server to be safe.

The bottom line is that you can use port scans as a warning and "harden" your network against the incursion attempts that may follow. Or, you can make sure you secure your network *as if* the port scans had already occurred and then either ignore the port scans that happen or, as a safer option, record them as useful background information in the event that an attack succeeds.

How You May Be Port Scanned

You may not be able to detect all port scans of hosts on your network. A typical port scan used to consist of opening a connection on a particular TCP port, which was easily detectable. However, crackers became more cautious and developed additional methods of scanning that are more difficult to detect, including

- **TCP SYN scanning** Remember that to open a TCP connection, a program sends a SYN packet, receives a SYN-ACK (acknowledge) in return, and then sends an ACK packet to complete the process. The connection is then open. For this kind of port scan, a port scanner sends a SYN packet to a particular port on a host computer. If the host responds with a SYN-ACK, the port is open, and the port scanner may or may not continue opening the connection. In some cases, this scan can go unnoticed by the firewall or packet filter as a connection, and thus it escapes logging.

- **TCP FIN scanning** An even harder port scan to detect is the TCP FIN scan. In this case, the port scanner sends a FIN (no more data from sender) packet to a port on the host computer. If the host computer is listening for a connection on that port, it sees the FIN packet and ignores it. If the port is not open, the host computer replies with a RST (reset the connection) packet, because no service is available. The port scanner records any port that received no response as an open service on the host computer. Because no connection was actually opened, the interaction may not be logged at all by the firewall or packet filter.

- **UDP scanning**   A UDP packet isn't generally acknowledged when it arrives at its destination, which makes it difficult to know whether a packet sent to a particular port on the host computer has arrived at all, much less whether there is an active service listening to that port. However, some host computers respond if the port scanner tries to connect to a closed port, and the port scanner can use the process of elimination to determine which ports are open and listening for connections. This method isn't foolproof, because a UDP packet that never reaches its destination will appear to be an open port on the host computer. However, this scanning method can yield useful information about possible connections to that host computer.

- **Slow-motion scanning**   This isn't a type of port scan, but rather a frequency. Many port-scan detectors watch for certain patterns before sounding the alarm, such as sequential scans or multiple ports being accessed by the same source IP address in rapid succession. One of the ways that crackers try to port scan without triggering your detectors is by varying the speed of the scans, such as waiting several minutes between scans, varying the port numbers scanned to avoid a sequence, or even changing their IP addresses (by setting up a new connection with their Internet provider, for example) to appear to be a new user. These methods, while more difficult to detect, can still trigger alarms on the more sophisticated intrusion detection systems.

There are other scans as well but, as they are invented, they can be detected. For example, with the UDP port scan, the host computer responds with a "host unreachable" packet. Your firewall or packet filter can be configured to log all outgoing "host unreachable" responses, and you can judge by the quantity, frequency, source, or a combination of these factors whether the responses were due to port scanning or simply an erroneous connection.

Generally speaking, a cracker can often mask the true source of a port scan, but not the fact that a port scan occurred.

What to Do when You've Been Port Scanned

Firewalls and packet filters usually have a setting that will keep track of unusual port activity. In addition, standalone Intrusion Detection System (IDS) packages can scan whole networks or specific host computers you suspect may be targets.

Your option, outside of blocking scans and other traffic from those sites, is to follow up through other channels to determine the purpose of the scan and act against the perpetrators. Follow the instructions later in this chapter for notifying the system administrator, abuse account, service provider, or even legal authorities of attempts to scan your network.

Finally, you can always do nothing to the perpetrators, who were ultimately not even connecting to a service on your network. They were simply satisfying their curiosity. Checking your network for vulnerabilities is not the same as exploiting those vulnerabilities.

About Activity Logs

Virtually all networking devices—firewalls, routers, remote access servers, Web servers, and so on—have facilities for keeping a record of all activity in a log of some kind. Often, this log takes the form of a locally saved file, such as the files saved by the syslog daemon on a UNIX-like operating system. It also may be stored on the firewall, router, or other server in a form you can read with administration software, Web browsers, or command lines.

In other cases, the log messages can be sent over the internal network to another system, to be collected there for you to read, analyze, and save.

Your firewall is the first source of information when your security is attacked or compromised, because 100 percent of your network traffic passes through the firewall first. The firewall can tell you which packets were received, where they appeared to be from, and where they were forwarded.

When it becomes clear that you have been attacked—say, a Denial of Service attack has stopped your e-commerce site, or somebody has replaced the home page on your Web server—you'll want to read the activity logs on the firewall and on the server that has been compromised. There can be numerous logs on the same host, such as in Windows NT, where you might have both the operating system's event log and the Web server application's log.

You might reasonably ask yourself why it's worthwhile to read the log files if most crackers hide their tracks by using one compromised network to attack another one. The reason is that the log file can provide a record of the cracker's preliminary work that can yield a source for the attack that might otherwise be hidden. For example, if you see a port scan from one network address for Sendmail (a UNIX-based mail server, some versions of which have known vulnerabilities), and then a Sendmail attack is launched shortly after from a different network address, you may be able to link the two to find the culprit's real source. Careful examination of the log files for all devices on your network can provide this kind of information. There are also packages you can use to analyze your log files for patterns, such as NetTracker (www.sane.com).

Activity Alerts

An alert is similar to an activity log, but the device in question (router, firewall, or server) notifies you *immediately* when something is wrong, rather than simply logging the event for future reference.

There are a number of ways to notify you of an error, a crash, suspicious activity, and so on, depending on where you are and how quickly you want to know about high-priority messages:

- **Built-in system messages**   Many operating systems, such as most versions of Windows and most UNIX-like systems, provide some kind of notification service for system messages to pop up on a user's screen. You can take advantage of this service to have security-related devices on your network send a message directly to your computer as necessary, so you can find out immediately about a situation while you are at your computer.

- **Email account**   Having higher-priority log messages sent to an email account allows you to retrieve them from wherever you are, onsite or offsite, as long as you have access to a computer and email connection. This option also lets you organize the alerts, because most modern email programs let you file incoming mail based on filter rules.

- **Alphanumeric pager**   Many alphanumeric pagers (and digital cell phones with paging capabilities) are accessible through special email accounts, so you can set up your servers to send the highest-priority log messages to your pager's email address. (For example, some AT&T cell phone accounts support alphanumeric pages sent to *phonenumber*@mobile.att.net, where *phonenumber* is the cell phone number.) For other systems, you may be able to purchase an add-on device that lets the server send the alphanumeric message directly to a pager, as Motorola's AirApparent software does. With this kind of immediate alert, you can be notified if a service crashes, if suspicious port-scanning activity occurs, if there are multiple failed login attempts to any account in a particular time period, or if some other potentially time-sensitive activity happens.

Once you are notified that suspicious activity is currently happening or that an attack is underway, you can act to prevent damage or to repair the damage quickly, before it interferes with your normal operations.

How to Handle the Intrusion

When you have identified an attempt to scan your network or when an actual attempt to crack a service occurs, take steps to make sure it never happens again. Also, ensure that no further activity from that source occurs.

> **Tip:** Many network security analysts recommend that you have an internal crisis management team that can be called into action the moment an attack or the threat of an attack is identified. By implementing a predefined game plan, this team can work quickly, efficiently, and without panic or alarm to contain a network security problem when it occurs.

You can take any or all of actions described here.

Notify Your Organization Without Using the Network

When you identify an attack, you want to notify your organization's management, any personnel who depend on the network services, and anyone who needs to know of the attack that the network has or may have been compromised.

Also, you should probably notify the necessary people off the network— without using email, network messaging, or other electronic format. Stick with paper, voice, and in-person meetings until the network is again secure.

Also, bear in mind that you may be taking legal action if you can identify the perpetrator of the attack. Take careful notes, maintain records and backup copies of all compromised systems, and keep everybody informed along the way. If you ever have to go into a courtroom because of the attack, make sure you have all of the information you'll need and that the level of detail is meticulous.

Close Up the Holes

The very first thing you should do upon finding suspicious activity on your network is to identify the target and make sure the security holes are closed.

Even if the firewall, router, or packet filter log doesn't clearly indicate where the attack came from, it should be clear where the cracker was heading, such as your Web server, FTP server, and so on. If necessary, you may need to take the targeted service off the network until you can close the holes, by installing manufacturer's updates for known security flaws, removing unnecessary services, and other actions required to make sure the cracker won't have any known vulnerabilities to exploit.

If your organization can function without network connectivity for a short time, consider pulling the plug on all networking until the problem is identified.

Notifying Abuse Accounts and System Administrators

The first step after fixing vulnerabilities on your own network is usually to report the scan or attack to the system administrator at the cracker's source, if you can identify that source. If your packet filter, firewall, port scan detector, or other device can determine the source of the packets coming in, you can use that information to trace the connection back, sometimes to a particular person.

> **Note:** You may also find that the attack or scan was launched from a site that was itself cracked. Crackers can hide their tracks by jumping from site to site, using one site to launch the attack on the next site. In cases like this, your only option may be to notify the system administrator that his or her site has been compromised and possibly to cooperate with that system administrator to locate the source of *that* attack. Unfortunately, not all sites along the way are keeping logs or using much network security at all, so the information you can get from those sites may be limited.

If you can determine the site of origin of the attack, you may want to send an email to root@*example*.com or abuse@*example*.com, where *example*.com is the domain name of the port scan's source. If email to these accounts doesn't work, you may be able to find out who's responsible for the remote domain by checking with any of the domain name registry services, such as http://www.networksolutions.com/.

You may also want to trace the route from your domain to the domain that is the source of the port scan. Notify the domain that provides service to the domain that was the source of the port scan, to see if they'll take any action to locate the perpetrator.

Making Backups of the Victims

As soon as you have identified the targets of the attack, but before you repair any of the damage, make complete backups of the systems in question. The damaged systems, when examined later, can provide valuable clues as to where the vulnerabilities were, where the attack came from, and ways to avoid an attack in the future.

> **Note:** This should *never* be your only backup of the system in question. One of the ways you can recover from an attack is to restore the system from a backup that is known to be secure and then close up the holes before putting it back online. However, you cannot restore from a backup you do not have. You should be backing up all networked systems *at least* nightly, and more often than that if they contain critical data that would be impossible to replace, such as customer transaction data.

Deceiving Crackers (Luring Them In)

One creative technique for dealing with crackers is to set up an apparently easy target to attract their attention. For example, you might set up a server on your network (at a low IP address, perhaps, to trigger those sequential port scans early) with weak Web, FTP, and other services that have many of the obvious networking security holes in them. This server would necessarily be isolated from the rest of your network, so that even if cracked, it would not provide a jumping-off point to reach the rest of your network.

Why set up this easy target? Essentially, to waste the cracker's time and efforts while gathering useful information. Here's how it works:

1. You set up the easy target, such as the UNIX-based Deception Toolkit (DTK) available at http://www.all.net/dtk. You can also use one of the utilities that pretend to be a dangerous trojan horse. NFR's Back Officer Friendly (www.nfr.net), for example, runs under Windows or UNIX and appears to a cracker to be Back Orifice but actually collects information and warns you. Network Associates (www.nai.com) provides a utility called CyberCop Sting, part of their CyberCopy Intrusion Detection package, that works similarly to lure crackers in to a safe target and collect information about them.

2. The cracker sees the easy target and attempts to attack it, stealing password files, changing security levels and access privileges, and so on.

3. The easy target provides the expected responses to the cracker's attempts and appears to yield useful information. In reality, it is logging every action the cracker takes, including each key pressed.

4. The cracker gives up and moves on to other hosts or other networks, by which time you are both forewarned of impending attacks and informed as to his sources and methods.

This technique not only wastes a great deal of the cracker's time that could have been spent attacking your important host computers. It provides you with the ammunition needed to block the cracker's attacks (by denying service to the cracker's IP address or network, for example). It also enables you to stop the cracker at the source by notifying the necessary authorities (legal or system administration).

As additional products become available, more and more cracking time will be wasted. Until then, you can determine whether your network would benefit by providing a seemingly easy target for potential crackers.

Summary

Run an intrusion detection system on your network or on sensitive hosts if you want to become aware immediately of the danger to your systems and block it automatically if possible.

The bottom line for port scans and cracking attempts is that, no matter how secure your network, somebody talented and determined may eventually get in. Port scans and early attempts may be all the warning you have, so you should at least know about them, regardless of the action you decide to take. Whether you follow up outside of your network on port scanners is a matter of your personal feelings, not networking security.

However, when information is taken or compromised or damage has been done to your network, you can and should take action against the perpetrators, while at the same time closing the holes through which your network was cracked. Legal action is reasonable when damage has been done but, even if you stop short of that, you can take steps to notify those along the way that a cracker has been active and should be stopped.

PART IV

Appendix

Keeping Track of
Security Developments

As mentioned throughout this book, keeping your network secure is an ongoing process. New versions of networking software, firewalls, routers, mail servers, and other vital elements on your network are being released every day. On top of that, security-related individuals, groups, and organizations (some on the side of good, some on the side of evil) are constantly trying to find security holes in the products on which your network is based.

Fortunately, the "good" security analysts are usually quick to notify both a product's manufacturer and the public when a security hole is found, so that all involved can be on guard and work to close the hole. The "evil" security people—the crackers and the not-quite-ethical hackers—are usually unable to remain silent (for a variety of reasons) when they discover a vulnerability, and word of their discoveries soon reaches the manufacturer, security organizations, and the public.

This appendix lists the organizations and locations on the Internet where you can go to keep track of security developments. Some are formal organizations whose self- or government-appointed job it is to keep the computer industry safe, while others are loosely formed security clubs, formed by those with a common interest in finding and publicizing security issues to help others, to tweak large corporations, and other reasons too complex to discuss here.

This is not by any means a complete or static list. Organizations come and go, and you will undoubtedly find one day that some links in this appendix no longer work. When this happens, note that most of the working sites contain links to other security-related sites, and you should be able to build a list of your own bookmarks to useful security sites.

Naturally, the governmental and academic sites will disappear or change locations the slowest, while the informal organizations may come and go with astonishing speed. Keep your list up to date, and check with them regularly.

It may help if you set aside a certain amount of time each day to read the security headlines; that five minutes may save your network from someone else who read the headlines first.

Governmental and Academic Organizations

Some governments have encouraged the formation of computer-related "emergency response teams," with the job of tracking risks to the computer industry (on which the government depends to operate) and notifying the government, and therefore the general public, when risks are discovered. Usually, they'll recommend ways to work around or fix the security problem, but often you'll need to go to the manufacturer of the affected product for a patch or upgrade.

> **Tip:** The advisories that come from these organizations are always carefully checked and extremely well researched, so you can usually trust the source. Note, however, that you shouldn't trust a report simply because it *claims* to come from or have the backing of one of these organizations. When in doubt about an email or newsgroup advisory, go directly to the site and see if the advisory is there. If not, what you saw may be a hoax.
>
> Also, many of these organizations make their PGP public keys available. You can use the public key, among other things, to verify the digital signature on an email or other posted advisory. Given that even a Web site may be cracked, a digital signature that you have previously downloaded can tell you if an advisory is genuine or not.
>
> Be suspicious, and verify any advisories you hear before taking any action.

CERT (Computer Emergency Response Team)

The primary CERT was founded by the United States Department of Defense in 1988, after the "worm" released by Robert Morris crippled roughly 10 percent of the computers then making up the Internet. This site contains recommendations for avoiding and responding to attacks, as well as advisories of new vulnerabilities and attacks that are identified.

Their site can be found at this address:

    http://www.cert.org/

Their advisories are posted at this address:

    http://www.cert.org/advisories/

Other countries have created CERT organizations as well, including the Australian CERT (AusCERT), found at this address:

    http://www.auscert.org.au/

AusCERT maintains an excellent list of computer incident response teams from around the world, organized by country or geographical region:

```
http://www.auscert.org.au/Information/Contact/irt.html
```

> **Note:** Many, if not all, of the CERT organizations are members of or affiliated with the Forum of Incident Response and Security Teams (FIRST), a coalition through which the various incident response teams communicate and work together. See `http://www.first.org/` for more details.

Other Computer Incident and Security Education Sites

In the United States, additional organizations have formed incident reporting and advisory groups, including

- **CIAC** (Computer Incident Advisory Capability, formed by the United States Department of Energy. See `http://ciac.llnl.gov/`) CIAC is a founding member of FIRST and is a component of CTSC (Computer Security Technology Center), a governmental group of organizations that help U.S. government agencies deal with network security issues.

- **COAST** (Computer Operations, Audit, and Security Technology, available at `http://www.cs.purdue.edu/coast/`) An excellent source of information, and now part of CERIAS (see below).

- **CERIAS** (Center for Education and Research in Information Assurance and Security) CERIAS, like COAST, is hosted by Purdue University. See `http://www.cerias.purdue.edu/` for details. CERIAS is the "world's foremost University center for multidisciplinary research and education in areas of information security," according to their Web site. It is a collection of experts sharing information and discussing how to keep thing secure.

- **SANS Institute** (System Administration, Networking, and Security, `http://www.sans.org/`) The SANS Institute is a cooperative research and education organization and provides a good source of educational, background, and current advisory information about security issues.

Manufacturers' Web Sites

A product manufacturer's Web site is set up to further the manufacturer's interests. As obvious as this may seem, it leads to varying degrees of responsible behavior when manufacturers become aware of security flaws in their products. You might assume that because a product manufacturer depends on its customers to survive, and any security flaw will hurt customers, then any security flaw would be quickly found, publicized, and fixed by the manufacturer.

However, in many cases over the years, manufacturers have proven reluctant to acknowledge any flaws in their products, security-related or otherwise. As recently as June 1999, independent security organizations (such as eEye) have had to publicize security flaws that manufacturers (such as Microsoft) have proven unwilling to recognize. In the face of publicity, most manufacturers proceed to admit to the flaws and issue patches or updates to fix them.

That said, the manufacturer's site is your best (and often your only) source for patches and updates. Even when you hear of a security flaw from other sites, you need to visit the manufacturer of the product affected (firewall, router, operating system, and so on) to see their response and the recommended method for dealing with the flaw.

The following list shows the security-related places to start at some of the more common computer networking product manufacturers in the industry:

- **Microsoft**   `http://www.microsoft.com/security/`
- **OpenBSD** (UNIX-like operating system)
  `http://www.openbsd.org/security.html`
- **Sun Microsystems**   `http://sunsolve.sun.com/security`
- **Silicon Graphics, Inc.**
  `http://www.sgi.com/Support/security/advisories.html`
- **Novell Inc.**   `http://www.novell.com/security`

For companies with more extensive and varied product lines, such as Apple Computer, Hewlett-Packard, Lucent, Nortel, Cisco Systems, Sonic Systems, and others, you may need to see the technical support pages for the specific product you're using.

Security and Hacker Groups

There are numerous security consulting groups and individuals out there who make it their policy to share their knowledge and discoveries with the rest of the world, perhaps as a courtesy, as a way of "giving something back" to the community, or as a way of generating consulting business. Whichever reasons prompt this practice, the security groups provide a great deal of useful information when you have questions or concerns, or you want to keep up with the latest discoveries and flaws.

Some of the best security consulting sites to visit include

- **Security-Focus.com** (`http://www.securityfocus.com`)   Security Focus is home to one of the best organized arrays of security information available, including the BugTraq mailing list and database (look under the "Forums" heading for details). BugTraq has long been a source of cutting-edge information about security vulnerabilities. Their policy is one of full disclosure, under the theory that we're safer with everyone knowing about a vulnerability than just the manufacturer and some crackers.

- **L0pht Heavy Industries** (http://www.l0pht.com)   Yes, that's a zero (0) in the name L0pht, not the letter "O," although either will work to load their Web site. L0pht provides many of the best security-related utilities available, including l0phtCrack for capturing and decoding passwords to determine their weak points.

- **eEye Digital Security Team** (http://www.eEye.com)   This firm provides security consulting and services but also runs an excellent Web site that has been the source of numerous security advisories about serious flaws in commercial products, such as Microsoft's Internet Information Server (IIS) and others. Even if you don't visit this site, their discoveries will be publicized elsewhere some time after they are released here.

- **NTBugTraq** (http://www.ntbugtraq.com/) and **NTSecurity** (http://ntsecurity.ntadvice.com/)   A Web site and mailing list for Windows NT–specific security, discussing known vulnerabilities and their fixes, where they are available, and other security-related news.

- **NTSecurity.net** (http://www.ntsecurity.net/)   Another Windows NT– and Windows 2000-related site that contains a great deal of cutting edge information and advisories about Microsoft's server operating systems and related topics.

In addition to these sites, hacker groups may be one of your best sources of information. Remember that hackers are simply those who enjoy delving deeply into the core of the systems they work with, and one of the areas they delve into most often is networking security. The hacker sites are the least formal sources of information, but often they will be the most up-to-date sources, if you can find what you're looking for.

Among other things, you may be able to find discussions of attacks and vulnerabilities that people are currently investigating, rather than those that have been discovered. This information could be useful in suggesting ways to harden your own network, but it could also be a complete waste of time.

Some of these less-formal sites include Rootshell (www.rootshell.com/), 2600 (www.2600.com), ATTRITION.ORG (www.attrition.org/), and HNN (www.hackernews.com/).

There are many other sites available, but any of these will give you an excellent start, as well as providing numerous links to other sites and information to stay current with security issues.

Newsgroups

The following Usenet newsgroups may also be of interest, although be aware that most of these groups are unmoderated, and the useful information is often buried by the kinds of discussions (off-topic posts, personality clashes, unsolicited commercial messages, and so on) that tend to fill up Usenet groups.

- alt.hackers
- alt.security

- `comp.os.netware.security`
- `comp.risks`
- `comp.security.*`, including `comp.security.announce`, `comp.security.misc`, `comp.security.firewalls`, `comp.security.ssh`, and `comp.security.unix`
- `misc.security`

Summary

The Internet, while a powerful and varied source of information, is also home to crushing quantities of garbage, hoaxes, and misinformation. Many of the sites mentioned here are carefully created to weed out the useless information and are more useful because of that.

For other situations, seek out moderated mailing lists and newsgroups, which tend to have less noise than unmoderated groups.

Above all, be cautious of any claims outside of the established official organizations. The newsgroups and hacking sites are useful for educational purposes, but what they say shouldn't be taken as the complete truth.

Index